# It's a Sin to Build a Nuclear Weapon

*The Collected Works on War and Christian Peacemaking of Richard McSorley, S.J.*

Edited by John Dear, S.J.

WIPF & STOCK · Eugene, Oregon

Wipf and Stock Publishers
199 W 8th Ave, Suite 3
Eugene, OR 97401

It's a Sin to Build a Nuclear Weapon
The Collected Works on War and Christian Peacemaking of Richard Sorley
By McSorley, Richard T., S. J. and Dear, John, SJ
Copyright©1991 by Catholic Worker
ISBN 13: 978-1-60899-058-0
Publication date 5/4/2010
Previously published by Fortkamp -- Catholic Worker, 1991

For our brother, Daniel Berrigan, S.J.

# ACKNOWLEDGEMENTS

Acknowledgement is made to the following for permission to reprint copyrighted material:

To Herald Press, Scottdale, PA, for permission to reprint the following sections from *New Testament Basis of Peacemaking*: "Does the New Testament Approve of War?" pp. 1-20; "The Just War Theory" pp. 54-77; "Answers to Objections to Pacifism" pp. 279-325.

To the *US Catholic* for permission to reprint "It's A Sin to Build a Nuclear Weapon" pp.103-108 and "The Rosary Can Be Disarming" pp. 271-275.

To the Center for Peace Studies, Georgetown University, for permission to use sections of *Kill? For Peace?* pp. 190-231.

Thanks to Grace Jefferson for typing assistance, to Paul Magno for editorial assistance, and to Sondra Scully O'Shea for both editorial and typing help.

# TABLE OF CONTENTS

## Part I: Gospel Peacemaking

Chapter 1. Does the New Testament Approve of War? (1982) ............ 3
Chapter 2. Shall I Take Life? (1982) ............................................. 17
Chapter 3. Peacemaking as an Act of Faith (1982) ....................... 21
Chapter 4. Serving God and the Bomb (1982) .............................. 24
Chapter 5. The Desire for Possessions Is Insatiable (1980) ............... 27
Chapter 6. Seeing Christ in All (1983) ......................................... 31
Chapter 7. Gospel Peacemaking and Evil (1983) ........................... 34
Chapter 8. The Problem of Evil (1982) ........................................ 38
Chapter 9. Obey God Rather Than Humans (1983) ....................... 41
Chapter 10. Religious Life: A Lifelong Commitment of Love (1983). 43
Chapter 11. Kill to Deter Killing? (1982) ....................................... 46

## Part II: The Violence That Is War

Chapter 1. The Just/Unjust-War Theory (1970) ............................. 51
Chapter 2. War Is Stupid and Immoral (1982) ............................... 69
Chapter 3. Did They Die in Vain? (1983) ..................................... 72
Chapter 4. Was the Grenada Invasion Moral? (1983) ..................... 76
Chapter 5. Tears in the Seamless Garment (1989) ......................... 85
Chapter 6. Is Deterrence Moral? (1986) ........................................ 88

## Part III: Nuclear Weapons, Nuclear Madness

Chapter 1. It's a Sin to Build a Nuclear Weapon (1976) .................. 93
Chapter 2. When Nuclear War Strikes (1983) ................................ 98
Chapter 3. The Auschwitz of Puget Sound (1982) ......................... 103
Chapter 4. Nuclear Patriotism (1985) ........................................... 106
Chapter 5. The Sin of Hiroshima (1988) ....................................... 109

| Chapter 6. | Is There Something I Am Doing That Supports Nuclear War? (1981) ..................................................................115 |
| Chapter 7. | Should We Abandon Deterrence? (1983).......................118 |
| Chapter 8. | Nuclear Crime and Punishment (1983) .........................121 |

## Part IV: Conscience, Civil Responsibility, Resistance

| Chapter 1. | The Draft (1982) ........................................................127 |
| Chapter 2. | Signing Your Life Away (1985)..................................137 |
| Chapter 3. | Only Doing My Job (1987).........................................145 |
| Chapter 4. | Responsible Citizenship and Nuclear Registration (1982)148 |
| Chapter 5. | Changing Soldiers into Objectors (1987) .......................151 |
| Chapter 6. | Inside the Bars: Peace and Harmony (1983)...................153 |
| Chapter 7. | Military Peacemakers? (1982)......................................158 |
| Chapter 8. | ROTC Militarizes Students (1981) ...............................162 |
| Chapter 9. | The University as Policeman (1982) ............................168 |
| Chapter 10. | Tell It to the Russians (1982).....................................171 |

## Part V: The Process of Peace

(From *Kill? For Peace?* 1982)

| Chapter 1. | Promoting Peace.......................................................177 |
| Chapter 2. | The War Process; The Peace Process............................182 |
| Chapter 3. | Action for Peace.......................................................188 |

## Part VI: Peacemakers

| Chapter 1. | A Sad Day in Atlanta: The Funeral of Martin Luther King, Jr. (1968)..............215 |
| Chapter 2. | The Berrigans Teach Truth (1980)................................223 |
| Chapter 3. | A Farewell to Dorothy Day (1980) ..............................227 |
| Chapter 4. | How a Mother Teaches Peace (1984)............................231 |
| Chapter 5. | The Poor, the Brave and the Archbishop Who Believed (1981)......................................................................235 |
| Chapter 6. | Four Bishops Stand up against Nuclear War (1982)........238 |
| Chapter 7. | Peacemaking As a Vocation ......................................243 |
| Chapter 8. | Horace McKenna: Servant of the Poor (1982) ...............245 |

Chapter 9. The Future of the Peace Movement.(1983)....................248
Chapter 10. The Rosary Can Be Disarming (1988)..........................252
Chapter 11. Peace Message at Medjugorje (1988)..........................257

# Part VII: Answers to Arguments Against Pacifism

(From *Kill? For Peace?* 1982 and *New Testament Basis for Peacemaking*, 1985)

Chapter 1.  Argument: The Lesser Evil ........................................263
Chapter 2.  Argument: People Are Sinful ....................................269
Chapter 3.  Argument: Personal, Not Group Morality...................271
Chapter 4.  Argument: Self-Defense.............................................273
Chapter 5.  Argument: Protecting Your Loved Ones .....................277
Chapter 6.  Argument: What About the Russians?........................281
Chapter 7.  Argument: Pacifism Is Not Practical..........................284
Chapter 8.  Argument: What Alternative Is There?.......................286
Chapter 9.  Argument: Unilateral Disarmament...........................289
Chapter 10. Argument: Saint Thomas Aquinas.............................292
Chapter 11. Argument: Obedience to Authority ...........................296
Chapter 12. Argument: Spiritual Values Need Defense..................298
Chapter 13. Argument: Vatican Council II Allows
            for a War of Self-Defense..........................301
Chapter 14. Argument: Conscientious Objectors Are Cowards.........304
Chapter 15. Argument: Deterrence Works.....................................306
Chapter 16. Argument: We Are Not All Children of God................310

# *FOREWORD*

International peace is the burning issue of our time for Christians. On the one hand, we have more clearly discerned that the Gospel calls us to be a people of peace, a people without malice or destructiveness in our hearts. On the other hand, we have become increasingly aware of the violence that eats away at our society and manifests itself in armaments whose destructiveness is almost unimaginable. As Father McSorley says in this book, "The taproot of violence in our society is our intent to use nuclear weapons."

Father McSorley puts flesh on the dry bones of the preceding paragraph. He begins with the Gospel imperative of peace, moves on to manifest the violence in our present national stance on war and weapons, appeals to our consciences and civic responsibility to change society, and gives us examples of modern-day peacemakers to inspire us to action.

I recommend this book to all who desire to appropriate more deeply into their lives the Gospel call to be the peacemakers who walk in the footsteps of the Prince of Peace.

Raymond Hunthausen<br>
Archbishop of Seattle<br>
November 25, 1990

# INTRODUCTION

Certainly, one of the more significant and challenging books of this century is *The Autobiography of Malcolm X*. After describing in vivid detail his painful and exciting life, after attacking the evils of racism and recounting his beautiful conversion to the truth that every human being is a child of God, a sister and brother of everyone else, Malcolm X offered a simple suggestion: "Let sincere white people dedicate themselves to the practice of nonviolence and teach other white people about nonviolence." That sentence was enough to stop me in my tracks. It sounded to me like a call, a vocation, like the Christian duty of every white person in America. It sounded to me like Christian discipleship.

Richard McSorley has been living that vocation as apostle of nonviolence for nearly all his life. In an age where racism and sexism and division have torn people apart, where 45 wars are currently being waged in the world, where 45,000 people die from starvation every day, where three-quarters of the world's population lives in poverty, where the use of 50,000 nuclear weapons threatens to destroy the planet, Richard McSorley has been a voice calling all to the wisdom of nonviolence. His message has been the ancient wisdom of the Scriptures: "Love your enemies; love one another; be compassionate; be nonviolent; let us disarm and live."

I first met Richard McSorley in 1976 when I was a student for one semester at Georgetown University. He was known all over Washington, D.C., for his passionate stands for peace. It was not until 1982 that I really came to know him, and saw up close his total dedication to peace-making; his single-mindedness. Everything in his life centers on the urgent mission to bring peace to the world. It was clear to me from the start: once Richard put his hand to the plow, he never looked back. (Luke 9: 62.) I thought to myself, such commitment and fidelity, as Jesus commanded, are what it means to be fit for the kingdom of God.

Richard McSorley was born into a large, devoutly Catholic, Philadelphia family on October 2, 1914. Seven of his fourteen brothers and sisters entered religious life. In 1932, he entered the Society of Jesus. Seven years later, after obtaining a graduate degree in philosophy, he was sent to Manila in the Philippines to teach at a Jesuit high school and seminary. With hundreds of others, he was captured and imprisoned by the Japanese on December 13, 1941, and held until February 23, 1945. He experienced starvation and lived under the threat of execution during those three years and three months in the prison camp. In 1945, US paratroopers captured the camp, took the Japanese by surprise and killed them. McSorley and the other prisoners were then released.

Upon returning to the United States, he continued theological studies and was ordained a priest at Woodstock College, Maryland, in 1946.

In 1948, he became pastor of St. James Church in St. Mary's City, Maryland, then part of the segregated South, where his experience with racism opened his eyes to the injustices of the world. He underwent a deep faith conversion towards the call to pursue justice for the poor and oppressed. "It really changed my life," he wrote later, "to come right out of the seminary where race relations had never been mentioned and to discover the church was racist in practice.... The white people came to communion first; the blacks waited outside. The blacks were on one side and the whites were on the other. I had never seen anything like that before.... I had never heard anything about racism in the seminary or in Catholic schools," he recalled.

McSorley soon realized that he had to take a stand against racism, so he started to preach about racism and the need to end racial discrimination and segregation in the church and in the world. His message was not well received by the white parishioners. On one occasion, he was warned of a plot to kill him, and he left town just before the posse arrived. Despite constant pressure from wealthy, white parishioners of southern Maryland to have him transferred, he stayed and spoke out against racism.

Eventually, in 1952, he was sent to the University of Scranton in Pennsylvania, where he taught philosophy until 1961. During that time, he also completed his studies for a doctorate in philosophy at Ottawa University in Canada. From 1961 until 1985, he taught theology at Georgetown University in Washington. In the early 1960s, he became the tutor to President Kennedy's children and to Robert Kennedy's children, spending many afternoons with them.

It was the influence of Martin Luther King, Jr., which caused him to change his life again, "When Martin Luther King, Jr., came on the national scene, I saw him as a great Christ figure, so I followed him and marched with him," he remembers. "King explained the meanings of the Gospels to me. He taught us that Jesus was serious about nonviolent love and justice and peacemaking, and King showed us how to live the Gospel as well." During the 1960s, McSorley became very active in the civil rights movement and marched in the South on many occasions, including at Selma. His experiences in the South, as well as his personal conversations with Dr. King, convinced him to speak out even more strongly in behalf of racial justice. The sight of Dr. King among the poor blacks of the South changed his faith.

As Dr. King and the Berrigan brothers began to speak out against the war in Vietnam, McSorley became more outspoken as well. In 1965, a student at Georgetown asked him to help organize an open discussion on the war. He agreed to help publicize the event, but was shocked to discover the controversy it stirred. The public support of the war at the time caused him to study the issue even more, and in a short time, he became convinced that the war was wrong, unjust, un-

Christian and evil. He started teaching a seminar on war and peace in the Georgetown theology department, and soon his classes were overflowing with young people eager to learn about peace. He began to work closely with conscientious objectors and to study the nuclear arms race. The example and words of Dr. King and an understanding of the nuclear nightmare led him to a deeper acceptance of Gospel nonviolence.

By the late 1960s, he organized regular anti-war demonstrations and spoke out against the presence of ROTC on campus. On one occasion, during the official, annual "War Day" celebration on campus, his students rented a helicopter and dropped anti-war leaflets on the campus.

From every corner of campus and city life, McSorley was criticized for his stand on the war. J. Edgar Hoover once called him "a disgrace," and asked his FBI aides if there "wasn't anything they had on him."

Throughout the 1970s and 1980s, McSorley continued to speak out for peace and justice. He became an early, active participant in Pax Christi USA, the national branch of the international Catholic peace movement. He worked with the International Peace Bureau in Geneva. For many years, he lived with the Community for Creative Nonviolence, and later, the St. Francis Catholic Worker community, both of which serve the homeless and hungry in Washington, D.C. And always he remained the prophetic voice within Georgetown University and in Washington, D.C. He founded the Center for Peace Studies on campus and influenced the lives of hundreds of students through his classes.

In the tradition of Gandhi and Dr. King, he has been arrested repeatedly for nonviolent civil disobedience on behalf of peace. After one demonstration during the height of the Vietnam war, he ended up in a jail cell with Dr. Benjamin Spock. During the 1980s, he was arrested at the South African Embassy for protesting against apartheid, at the Soviet consulate in New York City in the cause of nuclear disarmament, and at the US Capitol, with 241 others at the Peace Pentecost gathering of 1983, for protesting the MX missile.

Over the years, he has reflected on the lessons of peace that he has learned, writing hundreds of articles, giving hundreds of talks and retreats around the country, and authoring several books, including *New Testament Basis of Peacemaking, Peace Eyes,* and *Kill? For Peace?* His most famous article, "It's a Sin to Build a Nuclear Weapon," was reprinted in many journals and helped raise the consciousness of Christians throughout the country about the realities of the nuclear arms race. "Does God approve of our intent to use nuclear weapons?" he asked. "No. I don't believe so. Moreover, I do not believe God approves of even the possession of nuclear weapons." His insights laid the groundwork for the growing movement for peace within the church:

> *The taproot of violence in our society today is our intent to use nuclear weapons. Once we have agreed to that, all other evil is minor in comparison. Until we squarely face the questions of our consent to use nuclear weapons, any hope of large scale improvement of public morality is doomed to failure. Even the possession of weapons which cannot be morally used is wrong. They are a threat to peace and might even be the cause of nuclear war. The nuclear weapons of Communists may destroy our bodies. But the intent to use nuclear weapons destroys our souls.*

"I see my mission in life, as God has made it known to me, making the Catholic Church what it should be—a peace church," he told a student newspaper several years ago. "To be a Christian means to have respect for life in all its forms, and in today's nuclear age, for Christians must become active and uncompromising witnesses for peace and must firmly oppose all forms of war."

The message he preaches over and over focuses on nonviolent love and God's gift of peace to the human family. "What God wants is that all of us, all God's children, act like brothers and sisters to each other. The Hebrew Scriptures say, 'Thou shalt not kill' and the Christian Scriptures say 'Love your enemies.' If we believe that we are children of the same God and we believe that we are brothers and sisters to each other, we should act that way. The question always remains:

What does God want us to do? No matter what our faith, God wants us to love one another, to act as though we were brothers and sisters to one another. Building and possessing nuclear weapons and waging war are incompatible with that way of life."

In the Christian tradition of Dorothy Day, Thomas Merton, Martin Luther King, Jr., Daniel Berrigan, and Philip Berrigan, Richard McSorley has been a voice for peace in the war-torn world. He has said "No" to violence, war, and nuclear weapons, and "Yes" to life, love, truth, and nonviolence. Throughout the years, he has sought diligently to speak the words of Jesus, and to live these words. He has discovered that peace is at the heart of the gospel, and his discovery has helped us read the Gospel—and live it—through the eyes of peace.

In 1984, I began sorting through his many writings on peace and justice, selecting and editing some twenty-five or thirty articles which I thought best summed up his message of peace. Paul Magno continued the task in 1989, and thanks to Fortkamp Publishing, we now have this first anthology, a collection of those peacemaking years.

Since this is an anthology of newspaper and magazine pieces for the most part, the reader should expect both a traceable development of ideas (some dated, of course) and a repetition of arguments. Father McSorley's remarkable feat is his consistency over the long and turbulent last thirty years of peacemaking. I suggest that while the historian of ideas might want to read the book from page one through to the end, others might profit most from jumping, even dancing about in its pages. They are truly joyful pages from a peacemaker for our times.

Richard McSorley continues today to speak out this message of peace and justice with the same steadfast dedication he has shown all these many years.

For such a gift, the gift of a lifetime, for such a message and example, Malcolm X must surely be grateful. So must Martin Luther King, Jr., and Dorothy Day and all the saints and martyrs who pray in heaven for our conversion to nonviolent love.

And so are we.

May we all join Richard McSorley in learning the message of peace, speaking out for peace, and living that Word of Peace so that the Spirit of nonviolence may one day reign supreme in the world.

John Dear, S.J.<br>
*September, 1990*

# Part I:

# Gospel Peacemaking

*I say this to you who are listening: Love your enemies, do good to those who hate you, bless those who curse you, pray for those who treat you badly. To the man who slaps you on one cheek, present the other cheek too; to the man who takes your cloak from you, do not refuse your tunic. Give to everyone who asks you, and do not ask for your property back from the man who robs you. Treat others as you like them to treat you. If you love those who love you, what thanks can you expect? Even sinners love those who love them. And if you do good to those who do good to you, what thanks can you expect? For even sinners do that much. And if you lend to those from whom you hope to receive, what thanks can you expect? Even sinners lend to sinners to get back the same amount. Instead, love your enemies and do good, and lend without any hope of return. You will have a great reward, and you will be sons and daughters of the Most High, for God himself is kind to the ungrateful and the wicked.*

Luke 6: 27-35

*The duty of the Christian is to do the one task which God has imposed on us in the world today. That task is to work for the total abolition of war.*

Thomas Merton

*Chapter 1*

*Does The New Testament Approve of War?*

One way to get a focus on what the Gospel says about war and peace is to ask the question, "Does the New Testament approve of war—not just nuclear war, but any war?" To make sense of that question, I have to explain what I mean by "war" because the word is used in many different ways as, for example, war against poverty, war on drugs, etc. Here is a working definition of war: "War is intergroup lethal conflict." It is not just a shoot-out on the street between two people, but rather, group against group. If that definition of war doesn't clarify the concept sufficiently to distinguish war from everything else, then add these characteristics: much killing; a momentum of its own that leads both sides to savagery unplanned by either side; and a mobilization of group against group, spiritually and psychologically.

Now, using that definition, ask the question again about the Gospel. Does the New Testament approve of intergroup lethal conflict that has as its characteristics much killing, a momentum of its own that leads both sides to unplanned savagery, and a mobilization of group against group?

Once you ask the question that way, you have your answer: "No, the Gospel does not approve of war." The more clearly the definition is stated, the more obvious is the answer.

Why is this so? Why does the Gospel disapprove of war? Here are five principles of the Gospel, so basic to the Gospel, that they may be called "primary principles." They are: Love; God is our Father/Mother; the almost Infinite value of the human person; the relationship of agreement between means and end; and the imitation of Christ. These principles are so basic to the Gospel that if you denied any one of them, you would not have the Gospel. All of them oppose war.

**First Principle: Love**

Jesus summarized all of His teaching in the command "Love God and your neighbor!" He didn't leave what He meant by "neighbor" vague or unclear. He meant to include everybody, even outcasts. This is clear from the Parable of the Good Samaritan. In the United States today, neighbors include minority groups, blacks, Hispanics and Asians, and the anonymous poor.

Most mainline Christians would accept that. If I say, "I love the blacks, I love the whites, I love the poor, the children, the aged or the handicapped," people will say, "Good! God bless you!"

But if I go further and say, in view of Jesus' command, "Love your enemies," that "I love the Soviet Prime Minister. I love communists, and I want you, good Christian people, to love communists," they do not say, "God bless you!" Just the opposite! They will say, "Who let him in? Get the F.B.I.! Run him out of here! He doesn't represent my faith!" It is in response to this command, "Love your enemy," that most mainline Christians part company with Jesus.

They don't say, "Jesus, we are not walking with you any more." They are not that blunt. What they say goes something like this: "See that door there? Behind it are evil people: five, ten of them. They are communists, evil people. They are planning to kill you. They are atheists! I look at you and see you are good people. You are peace people! You are believers in God! You are good Christians! I am going to save you." They get out their guns and shoot the communists. They return and tell you,"I saved you!"

That is a simple, elemental way of putting the just/unjust-war theory, a theory that says, "I can kill some to save others."

When I say that to fellow priests, and ask their opinions, I get the reply, "Under certain circumstances, you can kill some to save others. That is so," they say, "provided certain conditions are fulfilled, namely, you save more than you kill and you do not kill the innocent. Under these and other like conditions, killing is allowed. You show love by risking yourself to save others."

I answer, "But the Gospel doesn't say we can kill to save others. Are you saying that in the act of killing communists, I am showing love to them? The Gospel says 'Love your enemy!' "

"No, you show love to those you save. I don't say you can love and kill the same person in the same act. That is where the two theories differ—the theory of Gospel nonviolence, and the Just-War theory."

But the command, "Love your enemy!" cannot be put aside lightly. It is not marginal or peripheral to our faith. It is central. When Jesus tells us, "Love your enemy," He is telling us to love others, all others, not just passively but actively. God loves us when we are sinners. God loves us no matter what we have done, no matter what we will do. God loves us as we are, without conditions. That is the way God wants us to love others, unconditionally.

In giving this command, Jesus is trying to make our dull intellects understand from faith what we already know from experience—that genuine love seeks no return. We instinctively recognize true love when we experience it. And we do experience it from God, from a parent, from a close friend. It may not be continuous, but we do experience it. We don't need anyone to tell us the difference between true love and false love that comes only with love's name but without love's spiritual and emotional force. If I say,"I will love you if you give me $50 a week, " you know that that is not love. If I say,

"I will love you as long as you appeal to me," that is not love because I am putting conditions.

We sometimes experience within ourselves a capacity to love and to be loved unconditionally. Ask anyone, anywhere, anytime, "Do you want to be loved?" and they will answer without hesitation certainly they want to be loved with a love that is perfect.

What does this mean and how is it applied to war? It means that my attitude towards my neighbor should not be determined by the damage done to me, or that might be done to me. It means I must respond in terms of the good of the person or the group involved. It is not a principle of do-nothing-under-attack, but rather, it is a principle that urges an active effort to express Divine Love, by seeking the good of the enemy.

Active love is the response Jesus wants us to have even towards our enemies. Our love is to be independent of the attitude of the other person. We are to love simply because God wants us to reveal ourselves by this love as true sons and daughters of our heavenly Father.

"For if you love those who love you, what reward have you? Do not even the tax collectors do the same? And if you salute only your brethren, what more are you doing than others? Do not even the Gentiles do the same?" (Matthew 5: 46-48.) In Jesus' teaching, all thought of reciprocity is excluded. We are not asked to love the Soviets because they love us, but because God loves us. When Jesus preached the Sermon on the Mount, He asked His followers to lead a certain way of life independently of what others might do. His words, "Blessed are you when men revile you and persecute you, and utter all kinds of evil against you falsely on my account." (Matthew 5: 11.) This makes it clear that there is no reciprocity.

Both the promise of persecution and the command to "Love your enemies" illustrate the universality of the love Christ commands. This rules out killing one person to protect others. I cannot exclude even one person from my love. Such a love would not be universal. The common argument used to defend war, "We kill these people to defend others," has no foundation in the Gospel. It violates the command of universal love. To comply with the law of universality, you have to argue that, in the act of killing, you are showing love to the person you are killing. That seems impossible to me—impossible and contradictory.

Some who defend war as compatible with Christian love argue that it is possible to kill and to destroy without feeling any hatred for the enemy.

One response to this is that the absence of hate is not what the Gospel asks. What it asks is positive, active love. Is it more virtuous to kill without hate, than to kill with hate? The blinding power of hate may make killing without hate less culpable before God than a cold-blooded murder. Nonetheless, it is culpable; it is not the Gospel.

A second response is that any use of force by a Christian is subject to conditions imposed by the Gospel. These conditions are:

1) Force can never be a substitute for the obligation to love.

2) Any use of force makes love more difficult.

3) Any use of force that is compatible with the Gospel must be preparatory to and directed towards love for the person to whom the force is used. An example would be: spanking a child with a few light taps that do no physical damage, but instruct the child about the danger of playing in the street.

4) If the use of force is such that it makes any appeal to love impossible, then a Christian can never resort to it—for instance, spanking a child abusively.

War does not fulfill these conditions. War kills. Death puts the person wholly beyond the reach of human love. The Gospel calls for personal love. Modern warfare with its long-distance, lethal technology is so impersonal that any kind of personal relationship with the enemy is next to impossible. War poisons personal relationships by lying, trickery, and distrust of the enemy, simply because he/she is an enemy. Even the training for war illustrates this. It is a training in depersonalization of both self and the enemy.

Training puts all in the same uniform; teaches all to march, to turn, to reverse, to count steps, to count numbers; to eat, sleep and to go when, where, and how you are ordered.

It is a training in taking orders, even though they are monstrous and stupid orders, until you get to a point where you see yourself as a cog in the military machine. At that point you obey orders without question, even orders to kill. All of your training aims at helping you to obey without thought, without question. You no longer think of yourself as responsible for what you do. You no longer think of the target you shoot at as a person. You think of a person as a target, an obstacle, an enemy, a demon. The training in depersonalization prepares you to kill.

War is contrary to the Gospel because war includes much killing. Killing leaves no room for the all-embracing love command.

Some who argue that the New Testament approves of war confuse police action with war. The two are not the same.

Police action may escalate to a point where it is similar to war, especially in time of war. Ordinarily, there are clear patterns of difference. While the police act within a limited area, their own country, the military move into other countries. While the police aim to arrest, the military aim to kill or destroy individuals, groups, and even whole areas. While police use small weapons, and mostly non-lethal weapons, the military use lethal weapons of mass destructive capacity. While police operate according to the laws of their country, the military operate in the jungle of international affairs.

Even if you believe that police action in general, for the sake of public order, is compatible with the Gospel, police action is so different from war that there is no contradiction in accepting one and rejecting the other. Where police action becomes lethal, it becomes more like war, and becomes subject to the same disapproval as war.

### Second Principle: God is Our Father-Mother

The New Testament teaches us that there is only one God, and that all of us are children of that one God. This is the basic theology of peace. It is taught by all the great religions of the world. It is so simple that a child can understand it.

The universalism expressed here seems at first glance to oppose the view that some personal response other than faith and obedience is required before one can be a child of God. But that opposition is not as great as it may seem at first. Even those who hold that faith and obedience are required to be a child of God would admit that we are all created by God, called by our creation to serve God and be with Him forever. We are all redeemed in the Blood of Christ. All of us are loved by God, and all of us are commanded to love each other, including our enemies. We are commanded not to kill each other. Furthermore, none of these beliefs is dependent on whether or not we or others are obedient believers. In this way, it is clear that there are many meanings of the term, "Children of God." We are children of God by creation, by universal redemption, by common destiny to be with God, by baptism and by response in faith and good works to God's call. Here I use the term in its broadest sense—our relation to God from creation. We are God's sons and daughters by creation and by the Creator's love for us.

If we are all children of the one God, it follows that whenever I kill a human being anywhere, I kill a brother or sister. And whenever I kill a human being anywhere, I offend the parent of that brother or sister. I offend God.

What does God think of us when we kill or plan to kill His children? What would you think of me if I said, "John, you are a fine man," or, "Mary, you are a good woman, but that brat of a son you have, I am going to kill him."

You might answer, "Look, I might not be the best of parents, but stop that talk. That is my child you are talking about."

God is better than any human parent. What does God think of us when we ask His help to kill His children?

This is the teaching underlying the command, "Love one another." It is why Jesus can summarize our relation to God and to each other in the love-command.

It is the basic theology that opposes war. This is the rock on which the Christian who opposes war can stand. I may not know all the intricacies of foreign policies or all the complexities of military strategies. What I do know is that there is only one God. We are all God's children. If foreign policy and military strategy cannot be reconciled with this belief, then I cannot accept them.

Jesus taught us to pray with the words "Our Father." Throughout His teaching He speaks of the Father's love for us. To deny that we are brothers and sisters to each other is a kind of implicit atheism. We deny God's existence as our common source of being.

There is quite a difference between believing that all humans are my brothers and sisters, and believing that some are and some are not. If I believe that some are not God's children, maybe I can kill them and please God; maybe I am better than they are because I am God's child and they are not. The bond between militarism and racism is evident here.

Prayer reflects belief. Prayer grows out of beliefs, and indicates what beliefs I hold. My prayer will be quite different when I believe we are all God's children, and when I do not.

For Christians who believe that Christ is our Brother, our relationship to each other as brother and sister is also an expression of our belief in and relation to Christ as our Brother and as God Incarnate. Through the Incarnation (God as person in human form), we are children of God because, if Jesus is our Brother, Jesus' Parent is our Parent too. Denial of our brotherhood/sisterhood is also an implicit denial of the Incarnation.

### Third Principle:
### The Almost Infinite Value of the Human Person

The redemption of each person in Christ's blood gives each one an almost infinite value. Christ's death is not only a measure of God's love for us, but also a measure of our value in God's eyes—the death through crucifixion of His Son Jesus, that is our value. It is the Christian belief that God so loved each one of us that, if I was the only person in the universe, He would have given His life for me alone.

The death of God on the cross is the cost of our salvation and the value of our individual worth. War denies all this with its depersonalization, its subordination of human life to the needs of the state, or to military necessity.

### Fourth Principle: Means and Ends Relationship

The Gospel teaches that there is an unbreakable, internal relationship of harmony between the means we use and the end we reach. The Gospel teaches us that the goal of life is participation in the divine life. The means? Feed the hungry, clothe the naked, visit the prisoner, take in the homeless, bear one another's burdens along the journey of life. All these activities are compatible and harmonious, and in agreement with the end—participation in divine love. This is all very familiar to us. In fact, even without faith, we recognize the internal harmony between means and ends in ordinary life. For example, I see a person driving around in a circle in a Washington parking lot. I ask, "Where are you going?"

"To Philadelphia!"

"But you will never get to Philadelphia riding around in circles."

"Yes, I will," he answers, continuing to drive in circles. I say he is out of his head. He cannot relate means and ends.

In every aspect of daily life we recognize the agreement of means and end. If I want to go upstairs, I raise my foot. If I wish to be healthy, I must eat. If a person cannot relate means to end, we consider that person insane. The story of a man who visited his friend in a mental hospital illustrates this. He found his friend constantly waving his right arm across and in front of himself.

"Why are you waving your arm, Bill?"

"To keep the elephants away."

"But there are no elephants around."

"Of course not, as long as I wave my arm," he replied.

To claim that war, even for a just cause, can be just, irrespective of the means employed, is possible only on the assumption that the end justifies the means. To hold that military necessity knows no law, or that the end justifies the means, is a betrayal of Christian principle. Jacques Maritain says, "Nothing is more terrible than to see evil, barbarous means employed by men claiming to act in the name of Christian order.... The character of the end is already predetermined in the means. A truth inscribed in the very nature of things is that Christianity will recreate itself by Christian means, or it will perish completely." This is quite opposite to the military method. There the means and end are contradictory. "Saving" is said to be done by killing and destroying. This is illustrated in the prayer at the christening of a nuclear submarine. "God bless this submarine! May it be an instrument of peace!" A submarine with nuclear weapons is seen as a means of peace.

Even the act of using the term "christening," in sending a warship under way, is a kind of blasphemy. Christening is for people, and is a sign of God's grace.

Armies try to achieve peace through war, order through chaos, security through violence, the rule of law through lawlessness, to preserve honor by dishonorable acts. In the end they claim they save by destroying. This was actually voiced by the US officer at Ben Tre, Vietnam, "We had to destroy the village in order to save it."

Mark Twain understood that a prayer for victory is also a prayer that God will help us kill, make widows and orphans, and make our enemies hungry and homeless.

In the words of Mark Twain when we pray to God for victory, we pray to take the bodies of our enemy's soldiers and tear them "to bloody shreds with our shells." We pray to God to "help us to lay waste their humble homes with a hurricane of fire."

We pray to God to "help us to turn them out roofless, with their little children to wander unfriended over the wastes of their desolated land."

When means and goal are separable and contradictory, the means tend to become the end as they do in Twain's *War Prayer*.

Gandhi said, "The creator has given us control (and that too very limited) over means; none over the end. Realization of the goal is in exact proportion to that of the control of the means. This is a proposition that admits of no exception."

While it may seem unusual to some readers to bring those who don't use the Bible as their holy book, such as Mark Twain and Gandhi, into a discussion of the New Testament, it may indeed help the discussion by giving Biblical argument more meaning. Also, it may indicate that, had Christians given a better example of following the New Testament instead of making war, worldly opinion shapers like Twain and Ghandi might have been Christians. On the evil of making war both of them are clear and forceful; they both agree with the New Testament in contrast to many Christians.

In Jesus' teaching, means and ends are always compatible. "You will know them by their fruits. Are grapes gathered from thorns, or figs from thistles?"

When the means are not only incompatible with the goal, but contradictory to it, both reasons separate it from the Gospel.

The fruits of war are horror, death, suffering, moral degradation, arson, rape, lying, murder, and more war. There are things worse than war, and war brings every one of them with it.

War denies the everyday, natural link between cause and effect. It teaches that there is a way of separating the effect from the cause. War denies the endless, changeless link of cause and effect. It says that a moral good (peace) can be obtained by an immoral means (killing).

It is not impossible to put means and ends together. We see an example of this in Mother Teresa of Calcutta. Interviewed on the BBC she was asked, "Mother Teresa, isn't it difficult for you to take care of the dying for twenty-five years? All those diseased, dying people?"

"No, not when you have faith."

"But, Mother Teresa, how do you keep faith going all those years?"

"When I hold the dying in my arms, I believe that I am holding Jesus."

There! You have complete identification of means and end. In loving my neighbor, I love God.

All of us know people who, in ordinary life, live their faith in God in harmony with their service to others.

Dorothy Day of the Catholic Worker says that there is no need of any special theology of peace. You just need to look at what the Gospel asks and what war does. The Gospel asks that we feed the hungry, give drink to the thirsty, clothe the naked, welcome the homeless, visit the prisoner, and perform works of mercy. War does all the opposite. It makes my neighbor hungry, thirsty, homeless, a prisoner, and sick. The Gospel asks us to take up our cross. War asks us to lay the cross of suffering on others.

Jesus refused to establish His Kingdom by means suggested by the devil, and contrary to His Father's plan. The devil asked Him to prove that He was the Messiah by changing stones to bread, and by falling down from the top of the Temple without being hurt. Both would be spectacular acts of power, far different from dying on the cross as a redemptive sacrifice. Jesus refused actions that were incompatible with

His Father's plan for the Messiah. The devil promised Him all the kingdoms of the earth if "bowing down, you will adore me." Jesus ordered Satan to "Be gone!" The means suggested by the devil were not compatible with His Father's plan, but contradictory to it.

Military means (killing and destroying) are a type of idolatry. It is worshiping a false god! the god of war—Mars. When we use military means, we trust in gods of metal, not in the loving God. We do not trust in God's way of love, of redemptive suffering. We think we will get the peace that only God can give, without God's help and even in contradiction to God's plan. In fact, we think we will get peace with Satan's help and advice. We yield to the temptation that Christ rejected. We will do it our way. We will put our talents, our resources, our youth, our treasures at the service of the god of war, not at the service of the God of love. The result that we get out of this is war.

**Fifth Principle: Imitation of Christ**

The Gospel teaches us that the best description of "holiness" is "imitation of Christ." Other descriptions like "doing God's will," "following the light," "being righteous," are all abstract compared to "imitation of Christ." Unlike an abstract definition, Christ's life reaches us on every level: intellectual, physical, emotional, and spiritual. His life is not just words or a book. It is a living example.

Jesus was born in a stable, not a palace. He lived in a poor home, just two rooms; in a poor town, with poor parents. In His public life as a wandering street preacher, He said He had no place to lay His head. He laid His head crowned with thorns on a cross, and He died a criminal, condemned by church and state.

We cannot seriously imagine Jesus pushing the button for a nuclear bomb, or registering for the draft, or wearing the uniform of any national state, or paying taxes for nuclear weapons, or working in a plant that manufactures weapons of death.

We, who know Jesus from faith, can be helped by the opinion of one who sees Jesus from outside the faith. During the Vietnam War a Catholic was appealing in court his claim to be a conscientious objector. At the beginning of the trial, the

Catholic lawyer said, "Your honor, I know you are a Jew. You may be surprised to find a Catholic claiming to be a conscientious objector, because the Catholic Church is not known as a peace church."

"Just a minute, Counselor," interrupted the Judge, "It is true. I am a Jew, but I understand that this Jesus, who you say founded your religion, was a Jew. He taught a doctrine of loving service to others. I have no trouble with people who say they are followers of this Jesus, and who refuse to take part in war. My trouble is with the big majority of those who call themselves followers of Jesus and accept war. Now you can go on with your case. You don't need to tell me about Jesus."

Any questions we might have about a text of Scripture— does it approve war or not?—should be resolved by comparing it with the example of Christ's life. For example, "Render unto Caesar the things that are Caesar's." Does this mean that we should kill when Caesar says "Kill"? Is it not clear from Jesus' life, and especially from His death, that even as Caesar killed Him, Jesus would not defend Himself? We need not imagine what Christ would do if asked to push the button that would send a nuclear weapon to kill millions. We have the example of His life. He was and is a pacifist, a peacemaker. He came to reconcile us to the Father. (Ephesians 2: 12-19.) Because of Him we are no longer Jew and Gentile. We are one people. He has broken the barriers that separated us, and has reconciled us to God and to each other. He has done this by the wood of the cross. (Ephesians 2: 16.)

Here we have the definition of peace. Peace is reconciliation between God, myself, and my neighbor. Peace is always three-sided: God, self, and neighbor. Peace can never leave God out. Nor can there be any peace with God and myself if I leave my neighbor out. Peace, like love, simultaneously includes God and neighbor.

For the Christian, Christ is the peacemaker, the reconciler. His method is the cross; accepting suffering with love, not inflicting it on others. The invitation of the Gospel to love is entirely contradictory with the use of military force. Jesus wins love through suffering service. The military achieve their goal by force, fear, and death. Christ's way of life, Christ's example, was not military. It was a way of pacifist peacemaking; a way of making peace through the cross, through redemptive love.

Jesus' whole life showed the pattern of using peaceful, non-coercive means to attain His end, the Kingdom of God on earth. He chose poor fishermen as His apostles, not the great and powerful. He called Himself the "good Shepherd," not a general. His spirit appeared in the form of a dove, not a hawk or an eagle. His way of bringing peace was not the sword, not physical force, but rather, the appeal of a lover suffering for the beloved, accompanied by divine powers that transformed suffering and death into joy and life. The military system of getting your way through death and destruction leaves no room for the Divine power that works through the paradox of saving life through losing your own, as exemplified in Christ's life and death.

His life is the "way" God teaches us to live. It is entirely opposed to the way of war. In three words He summarized all He taught and all He did, "Love your enemies."

*Chapter 2*

*Shall I Take Life?*

In its simplest form the argument is sometimes worded, "If a maniac was going to kill a baby, would you kill the maniac?" A "Yes " or "No" answer is expected. That leaves you with the choice of either killing the maniac or being responsible for the death of the baby. The hypothetical nature of the question and its many presuppositions are ignored. These need to be spelled out before an answer is given.

The question is hypothetical, conditional. There really is no maniac after a baby, but "If there was, what would you do?" One way of bringing out the hypothetical aspect of the question is to give a hypothetical answer, like, "I would drop a bullet-proof glass cage over the child," or "I would shoot an instant-sleep dart into the maniac." If asked where I got the glass cage or the dart, I would answer, "The same place you got the maniac and the baby."

Another way of showing that it is hypothetical is to point out that it is not related to life. I am 67 years old now and all my life I have never come across or even heard of such a maniac. Yet every year of my life I see the governments of the world forcing young men into armies to kill one another. And this is all supposed to be justified by reference to the imaginary maniac.

The presuppositions of the question are many. One is that I would have a gun and be ready to use it. Where would I get the gun? How would my mind be changed so I would agree to fire it?

A second presupposition is that I must save the child before the maniac kills it, because if I don't, it's all over. There is presupposition of an irreparable injustice after death, that everything has to be balanced off in this life and that I am in charge of doing it. This is quite contradictory to the Scriptures which put God in charge of everything. I am not asked to do a justice-balancing act. God has all eternity to do that. My job is to follow what God orders. Does God commission me to take the life of the maniac? Both Old and New Testaments reserve to God alone the right to take life. Nowhere does God delegate this right to people to use on their own authority.

A third presupposition is that the maniac is guilty or deserving to be killed. If he is really a maniac, he doesn't know what he is doing. He may be as innocent as the child. If he is innocent, why should I kill him? Does it make sense to kill an innocent maniac to save an innocent child? In either case I would be killing the innocent. If you say that the child is more valuable than the maniac, how do you know? The child might grow up to be a maniac or a criminal. The maniac might be cured or fulfill many purposes in God's providence.

A fourth presupposition is that the life of the child is more valuable than the life of the maniac. Yet both are of equal value in God's sight. Both are children of God.

The question is a concealed way of proposing and solving the problem of evil. Underlying the question is, "Why does God allow the maniac to exist, to threaten children?" "Why does God allow evil in the world?" The answer to this question is beyond human intelligence because it involves a full knowledge of what God is doing and why. That question is at the base of the problem presented. Any answer to the question presupposes some solution to the problem of evil. It also presupposes that if I decide on killing the child, I solve the problem independently of what God wants me to do.

The argument about taking the life of an innocent child is given as though it were isolated from all the rest of the world. An answer is asked just as though you were only dealing with this one issue. The truth is far different. The very reason this question is being asked is in some way related to war. And, although the jump from the individual to the group action is not valid because the difference is vast, that jump will be made. Once you agree that the saving of this innocent life by the other life is a good and moral act, then the jump is made that war is moral because all you are doing is standing in the way of the aggressor. So it is not simply saving the baby that is at issue here, but war itself.

The question about saving the baby is not isolated from the rest of human history. It has been used over the centuries not only for justifying war against an unjust aggressor, but any and every war. It has been used by Hitler and Genghis Khan and every murderer in history. They were merely saving innocent lives.

Before saying what I would do in this case, I think all the questions raised by these presuppositions need to be satisfactorily answered. Then the answer to the original question becomes clear. The answer is that, in the circumstances hypothetically set up, I am not given even hypothetical authorization by God to take life. In fact the question is phrased in such a way that it makes one think life is being saved.

The question should be "Shall I take life?" Then the moral issue becomes clear. The answer depends on whether I think God has commissioned me through these circumstances to take life. My answer is, "No, God has not commissioned me to take life."

# Chapter 3

## *Peacemaking As An Act of Faith*

One objection against pacifism (Gospel peacemaking) is that pacifism violates the theological principle that grace builds on nature. Reason tells us it is natural to defend ourselves. How, then, can grace ask us to lay aside our defense and die?

This is the way the objection is sometimes put. As worded, it identifies Gospel peacemaking with doing nothing. But Martin Luther King, Jr., and Jesus were peacemakers. They did so much nonviolent resistance to evil that they were put to death. They refused to use violent means to bring peace; but more important, they based their peacemaking on a faith that leads us to God and reaches beyond the grasp of reason.

Grace goes beyond reason and rests on faith. Gospel peacemaking does the same. Even though it reaches beyond reason or "nature," it does not contradict reason. For example, you might argue that because men and women have sexual capacity it is reasonable and natural that they have sexual relations. From this you might conclude that celibacy and marital chastity are contrary to reason and nature.

But if you bring the light of faith and our relationship to God into our relationships with one another, the picture changes. We reach beyond reason. We reach to God. Our vision is one of faith. This difference between reason alone and reason aided by faith is the difference between the just/unjust-war theory and Gospel peacemaking (pacifism).

The just/unjust-war theory is a self-defense theory. It is based on reason and philosophy, not faith. It was taught by Cicero before Christ came.

Gospel peacemaking is based on the faith that we are all children of the one God, brothers and sisters to one another.

St. John of the Cross wrote that neither reason nor sense are proportionate means for reaching participation in the divine life, but only faith. From this it follows that a theory like just/unjust war will never bring us to peace, provided we include our relationship to God as an essential constituent of peace.

It is interesting that most arguments against pacifism are that it is too simplistic, that it cannot be followed, that it is not realistic, and that it ignores the sinfulness of human nature. All these arguments leave out faith. They are arguments of reason alone, not based on faith in God or directly related to it.

It is sometimes objected that Gospel peacemaking is based on an absolutist moral principle. Though I think that is false, something is absolute about Gospel peacemaking. It is the certainty of faith. With reason alone you never get an absolute, but with faith you do. Reason does not even show us with absolute certainty that God exists, but faith does. Gospel peacemaking is built on an absolute of doctrine, not of moral principle. Those doctrinal absolutes are that there is only one God and that He calls us all to be His sons and daughters, and because of that we are brothers and sisters to one another. Because of that, when we kill another human, we kill a brother or sister. We then kill a child of God. In the killing we offend the Parent of that child. We offend God. We sin.

Suppose I said to you, "You are a pretty good guy. I like you, but your daughter is really a brat. I am going to kill her." What would you reply?

You might reply, "Now look, I may not be the best parent in the world but that's my daughter you are talking about. I am not going to stand for that stuff. Lay off my child."

What does God, the infinitely loving Father-Mother, think of us when we plan to kill God's children? Worse, what does God think when we ask God's help to kill? Every time we pray for victory we do that. Our prayer for victory is a prayer to "shred our enemy to bits, blast their hopes, blight their lives, turn them out homeless, prey to the icy winds of winter or the burning heat of summer to wander as exiles in their own lands," as Mark Twain says in his famous peace prayer.

Do we really think God is impressed by our philosophical balancing? Is God pleased to hear us say we have a good intention in killing, that we are choosing the lesser of two evils in killing, that we are protecting ourselves and others by killing?

Rather, God says, in the words of Jesus, "Whatsoever you do to the least of these my little ones, you do unto me."

God deals with us and we deal with God in the realm of faith, not reason. Our faith may be weak and dim, but only by faith do we reach God at all. Nothing shows this more clearly than the inability of human reason alone to prevent war or give us peace. Far easier to anchor the ocean liner with a thread of silk than to bind the pride and passion of humans with mere thread of reason. Faith which unites us with the power divine can lead us on to that peace in which we are simultaneously reconciled to our God and Parent and our human brothers and sisters.

*Chapter 4*

*Serving God and the Bomb*

"Nuclear weapons are illegal; a violation of international conventions that prohibit use of weapons of extreme cruelty, such as poison gas," said many of the lawyers at an international symposium in New York. The symposium, called to support the Second Session on Disarmament, brought together lawyers from many nations.

"Don't tell me that nuclear weapons are legal," said Burns Weston of Idaho University, speaking to the absent secretaries of the Reagan Administration. The symposium was supposed to debate the illegality and immorality of nuclear weapons.

There was a general agreement on illegality, even a call from the US Lawyers Committee on Nuclear Weapons to have more international conferences on the issue as a way of establishing legal precedents. When it came to immorality though, the lawyers didn't want God to be mentioned. "That would divide people," some said.

They didn't want church statements to be mentioned; not even the 1975 Kenya statement on the right to refuse to kill with nuclear bombs. Sean McBride, president of the International Peace Bureau, and a lawyer from Ireland, argued that the Kenya statement, written in 1974, represented a consensus of 500 different religious groups from all over the world. "No matter," said the vote of the assembly, "we don't want to get into the debate between churches on who speaks for God."

"The United Nations includes members who believe in just war. We don't want to offend them," said one delegate. "We want only morality, no God or church statements, just conscience and reason."

So, they ended up with a statement condemning the use and intention to use nuclear weapons as illegal, and offensive to reason and conscience. Why was God left out? Because of division over "who speaks for God?" The main aspect of this division is not orthodox differences between churches. It is that some religious groups identify God with war and killing and others don't. The Moral Majority sees God as served by piling up nuclear weapons for the US. Peace churches identify God with the love that refuses to kill. Mainline churches— Protestant, Catholic, and Jewish—are divided into majorities, who identify some kind of war and killing, even with nuclear bombs, as being approved by God, and minorities in each group, who disagree with the statement that killing is part of God's plan. This is the quagmire that the lawyers refused to enter. Their refusal deprives them and the rest of the human family of the support they should have from those who speak for God; it also illustrates the moral weakness of the churches in the face of the nuclear threat.

How can a church be both credible and silent on the nuclear danger? Worse, how can a church speak for God and support preparation to kill millions of people with nuclear weapons?

These questions underlie the refusal of the lawyers' convention to allow God or church into their final statement to the UN. They also illustrate the opportunity offered to the churches to unite on a life and death issue which transcends church differences and divides the human family.

Nothing does more to discredit God and church in the eyes of all than to identify God with war and the bomb. I know a Catholic lawyer who left the church and is very bitter because of some Catholics' approving of war and killing. What is a Catholic to think when he's experienced what war truly is, or has a psychotic brother who has been permanently scarred by war? What is a Catholic to think who may look to the Church founded on the principles of the Prince of Peace, to find books like *A Chaplain Looks at Vietnam* and *In Defense of Life*, both written by a former navy chaplain in the Catholic Church? What is a person to think as the nuclear cycle goes on—the manufacturing, the testing, the expenses paid out of our pockets, the threatening, etc., etc.—and his church remains silent? God and church are discredited.

We are serving God and the bomb. We put our security and trust in the bomb, yet we say we trust God. We give parts of our income to the bomb, and to God. We sign up our young men with the bomb, and pray for them to God.

This calls for a new application of the old message, "You cannot serve two masters." You cannot serve God and the bomb.

*Chapter 5*

*The Desire for Possessions Is Insatiable*

How often have you wished that you didn't bring so much baggage on a trip? The more you have, the harder the journey! You have to carry it, watch it, worry about it. It can get to the point where baggage endangers the journey!

For example: "My suitcase is missing. I left it outside my room to be carried down by the porter." A whole tour group can be kept waiting while a search begins for baggage.

"Would you like to buy a coat?" asks one of our group. "I don't like the color; it's too heavy. I'll never wear it, but my wife insisted I bring it. I hope somebody steals it!"

In Spain an elderly couple in our group paid $400 for a porcelain dish with two figures on it. For two weeks they carried it by hand lest it be broken in the regular baggage moves. Once, when we had to change hotels, they felt compelled to go with the baggage while the rest of us had the time free for other things.

Add to this bags that are too big to carry, bags too heavy causing the handles to break, lost bags, wrong bags, and you see what baggage does to a trip!

Barbara Hutton, the billionairess of Woolworth fame, always moaned that her life was ruined from her teens on by her Woolworth money. She saw her friends as fakes, her lovers as jewel thieves, seven husbands as diamond diggers. When she died, she was alone, with no friends or family, in a plush Hollywood hotel surrounded by beds of long-stemmed roses.

Not only for Barbara, but for all of us, life is a journey, and our possessions are our baggage. The more baggage, the more difficult and slow-moving the trip becomes. And we always run the danger of preferring the baggage to the trip.

The story is told that Mahatma Gandhi, en route from India to a conference in London, discovered that his staff aboard the ship had among them 13 trunks. He himself carried all his possessions in a small cloth arm-bag. He called his group together and said, "It is not proper for the representatives of the poor people of India to travel with so much baggage. So you can have your choice. You can go on to England without your baggage, or you can leave the ship with the trunks at the next port." No one left.

Like Gandhi, all the world's great moral leaders have praised freedom from possessions. Jesus was asked by a rich young man, "What must I do to attain eternal life?"

"Go sell what you have, give it to the poor, and come follow me," was the reply.

But the Scripture says the young man had "many possessions." He chose not to follow. That was one journey that was blocked by possessions. This tendency to collect baggage and possessions affects every level of life. I know a woman who pushes a supermarket cart through the streets by day collecting empty bottles, old food and clothes, and all kinds of odds and ends. All these items, which become her possessions, are piled high in plastic bags or tied to the sides of the metal cart. It is a wonder that she can move it. I tried to help her push it one snowy morning when the small wheels of the cart kept sticking in the snow of the street. At night she slept at a woman's shelter. She can't stay there during the day. There is no room for the pushcart in the shelter, so she laboriously unpacks her plastic bags and lugs them up the steps to the front door of the shelter. Then she takes the pushcart, half-loaded with empty bottles, and hides it behind a bush near the steps.

Why, I often wonder, does she burden herself with so much luggage and baggage? Yet her overloaded cart was all she had. How different is she from the home owner whose cellar, attic and closets are packed with things that may never be used? Doesn't she have a little more excuse for clutching a few possessions of little value than the homeowner whose house is cluttered with so much? Over the years the unused, even unknown possessions change a home into an attic.

The same process goes on in the nation.

We grow economically as a nation; we get more possessions. We decide that we need to guard them. Then we need an army, a navy, an air force, and a marine guard to protect these possessions. To get the army and the other military forces we have registration and soon, possibly, a draft. To pay for the army and the other military forces, and to pay for all their equipment, we tax the people.

As we grow, our enemies abound and threaten us more, or so we think. We increase the size of our military and the size and power of our nuclear weapons. This requires even more taxes again. As taxes and the size of the military increase, freedom decreases.

We are now loaded down with a peacetime standing military of 2,000,000 people with an arsenal of 30,000 nuclear warheads. We have spent a trillion dollars on our military since 1960. This is a million million. Whatever happened to it? With all that spending, you would think that we would have become secure. Yet we were never less secure in all our history. And we are planning to spend another trillion dollars of taxpayers' money in the next few years.

The poor woman with her overloaded pushcart almost seems very wise and sensible compared to what we are doing with our taxpayers' money. She has a heavy load to push. We have more. Can't we see that our military spending feeds our inflation? Don't we realize that our intent to use nuclear weapons threatens our own very lives and is a suicidal intent?

Of course we need food, clothing and shelter to live, but how many possessions do we need to live? How much do we need? How much more must we have especially when there are tens of millions of starving poor here and around the world?

St. Francis of Assisi used to say that all conflict is over possessions. Maybe he was right!

*Chapter 6*

*Seeing Christ in All*

I visited an 83-year-old priest, Father Horace McKenna, S.J., in the hospital a few days before his death. Summarizing half a century spent working with the poor, he said, "One of the most important truths I have learned is that Jesus Christ is present in every human person."

Not long afterwards, I attended a theology conference where "seeing Jesus in others" was criticized as a way of refusing to love them as they are themselves. "Loving others because of love for God" was called a heresy, a denial of individuality, a negation of the uniqueness of the person.

The priest who died, Father McKenna, had discovered Christ in the hungry man and woman, Christ homeless in the street people, Christ cold in the shivering poor. He had come to understand the blessing of St. Patrick: "Christ before me, Christ above me, Christ in the face of every one I meet!" He had discovered the meaning of Jesus' words "Whatever you do to the least of my little ones you do to me."

Was he refusing to love others as they were themselves? Not at all! Rather, he was getting to know them in their deepest, truest selves, as children of God, sisters and brothers of Christ. This is not some addition that belittles their individuality. It is their truest reality, their deepest self. We know from faith that we are children in God. God is in us. We are temples of the Holy Spirit. Reverence for God within us does not belittle us.

But we do not get to discover this merely by contemplating individuals and loving them for themselves as if they were unrelated to God. We get it by faith. We get to it with divine help. If we simply depend on our own experience of the goodness of others, we are extremely limited. We personally meet only a small fraction of the earth's billions.

Contemplating others as individuals with individual personal value has its merit, but it is no substitute for the faith through which we know in advance of meeting people that they are children of God.

Distance too makes it impossible to have the personal contact necessary for personal love. But faith that links us to God and to all humans overcomes distance.

Ideologies and government lies blind us to the good in others. We learn to hate them as enemies. Thus we learn to hate communists without ever seeing them, without knowing them. Only in the strength of faith can we believe that communists too are children of God, our brothers and sisters.

Even those we do meet may hate us. Their willingness to destroy us makes it impossible for us to see their individual good qualities. Faith strengthened by God can push aside all barriers and help us to love even those who make themselves our enemies.

No one close to God is far distant from us if we know our selves as children of God. If through faith we see ourselves primarily as children of God—not just as unique, interesting individuals—we may through faith come to believe and act as though communists and all others whom governments call our enemies are really our brothers and sisters.

*Chapter 7*

*Gospel Peacemaking and Evil*

In any discussion of the morality of nuclear weapons, I try to make clear the Gospel message, "Love your enemy," as the central teaching of Christ. After I had done this, on one occasion, someone asked, "What is your meaning of evil? You seem to say that everyone should love their enemy; but is there not evil in the world and a theology of evil? What is evil?"

Evil is the absence of, the privation of the harmony with the divine will which should be in the human will. It is a refusal to obey God.

The questioner was irritated at this: "You have proposed a simplistic theory with no muscle to it. And you refuse to give an answer about the theology of evil even though you talk about a theology of peace. What is your view of evil in the world? What is your theology of it? I demand an answer."

"Do you mean a theology of original sin?" I asked. "If you do, then Christian teaching says that through the sin of Adam and Eve, all of us come into the world with a tendency toward evil. This means our reason is weakened, our will is weakened and our appetites do not follow reason, but seek their own goods, seek their own immediate satisfaction without reference to reason, so that we are a kind of broken humanity. However, that is not all there is to Christian teaching.

"The gospel also teaches us that we have a Redeemer, that we have Christ who came and gave us both the example and the grace to follow that example, of following God's will. Although we were weakened by the sin of Adam, Christ is the second Adam, and he more than restored the harm to our nature by giving us the grace to know God's will and to follow it. God gives us not merely the grace of redemption, sanctifying grace, but the grace to resist evil. As St. Paul said, 'I can do all things in Him who strengthens me.'"

The questioner gave up his questioning, but seemed not to have been satisfied with my answer. In reflecting on this question afterwards and talking it over with others, I sensed that he had some idea of evil connected with communism that I had missed. Perhaps I should have asked him to say what he meant by evil, and then, understanding it better, continue to speak with him. What did he mean by a theology of peace that had a muscle to it? A theology of peace has divine wisdom in it when it says, "Love your enemies." Divine wisdom of course isn't muscle; it goes way beyond muscle. Maybe that's the point that needed to be clarified: there is no muscle in peace making. There is divine wisdom in it; there is divine strength in it; but that strength is not muscle.

The very use of the word "muscle" introduces the "macho" or military style of peacemaking: you overcome your enemy with physical force, subdue him, and call it peace. Divine wisdom, illustrated in Christ's teaching and life, goes in the opposite direction. Divine wisdom reconciles us to God by our accepting suffering voluntarily, our accepting even death as Christ did, voluntarily, as Christ accepted death on the cross.

We believe Christ is God, that what He did was done with the wisdom of God, yet it runs counter to the muscular wisdom of the world.

Or perhaps he meant that evil could be identified with a system, like, say, communism. That wouldn't explain very much, since communism only began in 1917 and not everything about it is wrong. Even if there is evil in communism, the peace message of the Gospel, "Love your enemy," is the way to confront that evil, not the muscular way of killing communists, of identifying the evil with living persons.

Maybe his question had a deeper meaning. Maybe he was asking why God allows nuclear weapons to exist; why does God allow evil? There is no fully satisfactory answer to this because it is a mystery. Whenever we deal with God at all seriously, we deal with the mysterious. Our minds are not capable of examining why God does things or why God allows things. We can find some explanation, some reason, but it is only superficial when it is given as an explanation of why God acts.

We can answer the question, for example, why God allows evil in this way. God wants us to love. In order to love, we must be free. In order for us to be free, it must be possible for us to do evil, for us to refuse to do what God wants. In order for us to love, it must be possible for us to refuse to love, because love has to be free. So God allows us to do evil in order that we may have the freedom to love. That's the best I can make of any answer, but there is still mystery.

An unanswered aspect of the question is: if God allows us to refuse to love, if God allows us to kill, then how can we say that God is in control of everything, including us? If He allows us to be free, how can He at the same time be in control of us? That is mysterious. We can clearly know that we are free, and we can clearly know that God exists and is in complete control of us and of all the universe, but how these two can be fully reconciled requires a knowledge of God that nobody less than God can possess. The mystery is something not contrary to reason, but beyond the explanations that reason can give.

Reason cannot explain how God creates, how there can be three persons in one God, how God can assume human nature and yet remain God. Yet we can know with the certainty of faith that God does create, and that God is a Trinity of persons, and that God became human without ceasing to be God. In a similar way, through faith, we know that God is good and loves us although God allows humans to be free and in that freedom to do evil.

*Chapter 8*

*The Problem of Evil*

Evil is involved in every decision to kill, whether it be abortion, the death penalty, or the possession of nuclear weapons. Nuclear weapons are a part of the evil in the world. The intent to use nuclear weapons is a part of the evil. Some bishops and others say that we must get rid of nuclear weapons, that we must not use them, not possess them, not make them, and not pay taxes on them. Then the bishops are called simplistic, naive, unrealistic, and further chastised for not offering an alternative for dealing with the dangers we face from other national powers.

Yet I think the critics of nuclear weapons are offering the alternative that the Gospel offers. The Gospel teaches that we must endure evil, but that we do not need to be a part of it or fuel it or feed it. The Gospel does not tell us how to rid the world of evil. It does not put any obligation on us to try to solve the problem of evil in the world. What the Gospel asks of us is not to be a part of evil.

Those who criticize the bishops for having no alternative to nuclear weapons are mistaken. The alternative to violence and to evil which the Gospel offers is the voluntary acceptance of violence against ourselves as we love others in truth and in justice. Christ gave us this example very clearly. Bishops opposed to nuclear weapons teach this alternative.

The critics often rejoin that this is all right for oneself, but it can't be imposed on others. That's true; the Gospel can't be imposed, only accepted. Yet the truth of the Gospel can be preached and made known.

The second mistake of the critics is their belief that nuclear weapons are an answer to the dangers we face. As Vatican II says, they are a trap in which humanity is caught. The more we use them as a method of dealing with danger, the further and deeper we put ourselves into the trap. It is a trap of nuclear destruction that comes closer to springing as more and more nations possess these weapons. About 40 nations are expected to have nuclear weapons within three or four years.

When we fail to follow the Gospel, we abandon our birthright and give up the only hopeful alternative to violence. Some say, "God has a sense of humor, but He doesn't go that far that He puts in us this primary instinct of survival and then asks us to cast it aside. God wants us to protect ourselves or he would not have given us a desire for survival. What about that?"

It's true that God has given us a desire for survival, physical survival, and more important, spiritual survival. St. Francis of Assisi said, "For those who die in God's grace, the second death has not terrors; they need not fear it." St. Francis also gave an explanation of how to deal with evil when he asked, "What is perfect happiness?" He answered, "Not acceptance by others. Not knowledge of all the secrets of nature." No! Perfect happiness consists in being able to rejoice in and endure suffering for following Jesus in His way of nonviolent love for all people. And we know that as we follow Jesus in His suffering for others, we shall follow Him in His glorious resurrection; survival is guaranteed.

I think of this when I think of my Jesuit brothers in prison in Ho Chi Minh City, Singapore, and Guatemala. If I could rescue them by killing their guards, how would I cure the evil in the governments that imprisoned them? Their jailers may be forced to do what they are doing. Killing those jailers will only bring more jailers and stronger prisons. The killing gives a bad example to the world around me and the next generation. Thus it spreads evil. The jailers must have a change of heart. Killing won't make them change.

The same sort of appeal to the heart is needed for those ready to use nuclear weapons. Our intent to use nuclear weapons has caused others to build more of them, and caused still other nations to want them. Our danger has been increased, although we sought protection when we started. This evil intent destroys our souls even before the weapons of our enemies destroy our bodies. Thus we kill ourselves spiritually by our intent to kill others physically.

The evil of nuclear weapons helps us to understand something about the reality of evil in this world. But this is no reason for being part of this evil, any more than we accept such an evil as theft by joining the thieves. Jesus endured evils of contempt, suffering and death. But He never became a promoter of them—just the opposite. By accepting suffering voluntarily, He transformed it into love. It is a love that was redemptive for us. He shows us how to overcome evil with good. I have not heard of another way; He does indeed bring Good News.

*Chapter 9*

## *Obey God Rather Than Humans*

The Supreme Court has ruled that abortion is legal. Most Catholics understand that abortion is also immoral. "Immoral" means it is against God's law. "Illegal" means that it is against human law. Where human law opposes the divine law, St. Paul tells us, "We must obey God rather than men and women."

The early disciples were flogged, imprisoned, and put to death because, guided by the Holy Spirit, they continued to preach about Christ after they were forbidden to do so. "You will be brought to trial before kings and rulers...to give witness before them on my account." (Matthew 10: 18.)

Many thousands of human beings died for their faith during the first three centuries after Christ. Some, like St. Maximillian, died because they refused to join the Roman army. Others died because they refused to give up their faith. "Blessed are you when they persecute you," Jesus tells us.

Today, Soviet bloc countries persecute those who openly profess their faith. In Central and South America and in the Philippines, priests, sisters, lay ministers, and their helpers are murdered because of their solidarity with the poor. Many of the murders are legal; none is moral.

At abortion clinics and at military bases people are arrested for blocking the gates to call attention to both abortion and the threat of nuclear death. Their acts are judged illegal. But are they immoral? Is it wrong to violate laws which protect the preparation for nuclear death and abortion?

Does the Apostle's word, "We must obey God rather than men and women," not apply here? Archbishop Hunthausen of Seattle believes it does. He is illegally withholding fifty percent of his income tax as a witness against the evil of paying taxes for nuclear weapons.

When we act illegally because we obey God, we follow the tradition of the early and modern martyrs. We follow Jesus Christ. He was put to death for claiming to be the Messiah. The Roman governor who condemned Him was acting legally. We all benefit from Jesus' refusal to obey men and women rather than His Parent. The Gospel invites us to imitate Him, "to obey God rather than men and women." Let us do so.

*Chapter 10*

*Religious Life:
A Lifelong Commitment of Love*

A mother of eight with five in grade schools told me that the Mercy Sisters were withdrawing from her parish school. "Why are there not more sisters?" she asked when I told her there were not enough.

Pope John Paul II asks the same question. He has appointed a committee headed by Archbishop John Quinn to find out why. I think that the reason will be found in our anti-family culture and in our misuse of technology. Both those aspects make a faith-based life more difficult.

Our culture puts self first, not God, not commitment to others, to children, to family. It is a culture that glorifies self-advancement, approves of divorce, artificial birth control, and abortion, and sneers at large families; a culture expressed in our slogans—"Do it yourself." "Keep on top of the pile." "Look out for number one." "Be the master of your fate." "Get ahead of the other one."

None of this is in accord with the Gospel that teaches us God is in total charge of the universe and that we are God's children, sisters and brothers to each other.

One obvious misuse of technology is television. It has become a habit-forming time-killer—a way of avoiding reflection, avoiding others, including God. The time that might be given to reflection and prayer is blotted out by the deadening grip of TV.

Radio extends this process so that even walking by the seashore or in the countryside, we can listen to portable radios instead of the sounds of nature.

Radio and television aren't bad in themselves, but they are very often misused to glorify murder, promiscuous sex, insolent, disobedient, know-it-all children, lying commercials begging us to buy what we don't need and can't use. They tell us of the importance of wealth, power, and pleasure.

Rarely do they show the value of putting God first in our lives or the merits of authentic, voluntary poverty, lifelong virginity chosen for the sake of the Kingdom of God and obedience to God's voice as expressed in nature, in the call of conscience and the inspired words of Scripture. The misuse of radio and television is only the tip of the technological mountain.

Military technology makes up its bases. The nuclear age, begun with the bombing of Hiroshima and followed by intercontinental missiles, has made it possible to destroy millions of people in half an hour. We accepted the nuclear bombing of Hiroshima and the situation bombings of Tokyo, Dresden, and Hamburg. We threaten to use nuclear bombs. That intent is the taproot of violence in our society. It corrupts our moral life and makes a life of faith in God difficult, if not impossible.

Once we have accepted that, other evils are small in comparison. Nerve gas, napalm, and advanced techniques of killing fetuses through abortion are lesser evils. We have learned to put our confidence for our future in "gods of metal," so faith in the living God is more difficult today than it was twenty-five years ago.

All of this is the opposite of what religious life requires—a lifelong commitment to love God and all others because they are God's children, in need of our love and of realizing God's love.

No doubt there are other reasons for the decrease of sisters—like the increased function of lay people and the failures of all of us in the Church to be all we should be. But I think these two causes—our anti-family culture and our misuse of technology—are basic.

Sisters develop better in a family life and in a culture that supports and helps faith-based living. All of us can do something towards making family life and our culture more directed toward God. Until we do, we are not likely to have more sisters.

## Chapter 11

## Kill to Deter Killing?

"People didn't elect me to fulfill their religious beliefs," a delegate of a state committee told me. The committee was considering a law to abolish the death penalty.

"Did your election as delegate mean that you relinquished your own religious beliefs?"

He didn't answer my question. He had already told me that he opposed the law. I asked him, "Why did you oppose the law?"

"Because the death penalty is a deterrent to crime."

"That is not what history shows. Pickpockets in England attended hangings to pick pockets. They found that when the attention of the crowd focused on the execution, there was a golden opportunity to pick pockets."

"I figure it deters some types of criminals."

"What type does it deter?"

"Serial murderers."

I doubted that was true, but I didn't argue about it. How would he know about events that motivate a serial killer? Their number is greater here where we have the death penalty than it is in the rest of the world where there is no death penalty.

"But my main objection to the death penalty is not its failure to deter. I insist my main objection is that by taking a life you usurp the authority of God. God alone gives life and he alone has the authority to take life. He does not delegate that authority to the state."

"The only thing I have to go on is common sense," he replied.

"You believe in God, don't you? [This man is a Catholic.] Your belief in God should guide you as well as your common sense. Is it common sense for the state to kill people to show that killing people is wrong? Our preparation for nuclear war and the millions of unborn killed by abortion ought to show us that common sense does not guide our killing. Common sense does not guide these programs of death. Neither does taking the lives of thousands in prison. It adds to our disrespect for human life. It adds to the insanity of nuclear war preparations and abortion.

"If you believe in what Jesus said, that we should love one another and our enemies, you have evidence stronger than common sense to abolish the death penalty. You surely do not argue we are showing love to the man or woman we are killing at the moment we are killing them. Neither is it true that you are protecting society by increasing general disrespect for life. By leading society away from the Gospel of love, you are not protecting it.

"And even if you were protecting society by killing some of its members, you would be doing it for immoral reasons. Evil means for a good purpose do not make a good moral act.

They make an immoral act. Formulating that immoral act into law helps make society immoral, not better."

After my discussion with the state delegate, I figured there was no possibility of any argument influencing him to change his mind. No doubt he considered it politically profitable to support the death penalty. He probably feels no moral responsibility at all to oppose killing people. He is part of our violent culture which approves of killing in war, in abortion, in self-defense, and in prison. We are proud of our wars, our military strength for the next war, even if it is a nuclear war, even if we all are killed in it. At least we will take our enemies along with us.

We feel that way, yet we don't see ourselves as a violent people. We think we are a peace loving, cultured people. We think this despite the fact that we have more people in prison proportional to our population than any other country in the world. We are one of the only two industrialized countries that have the death penalty in our laws. We have a higher abortion rate than any other country in the world. We wonder why we are not admired and loved by all the world.

What is worse, we think we are on God's side, doing God's work in all this killing and preparing to kill. I wonder how long God is going to patiently endure our trying to exercise God's authority over the lives of others.

With the death penalty we kill only the bodies of our prisoners, but at the same time we kill our own souls.

# Part II:

# The Violence That Is War

*The ultimate weakness of violence is that it is a descending spiral, begetting the very thing it seeks to destroy. Instead of diminishing evil, it multiplies it. Through violence you may murder the liar, but you cannot murder the lie, nor establish the truth. Through violence you murder the hater, but you do not murder hate. In fact, violence merely increases hate... Returning violence for violence multiplies violence, adding deeper darkness to a night already devoid of stars. Darkness cannot drive out darkness; only light can do that. Hate cannot drive out hate; only love can do that.*

Martin Luther King, Jr.

# Chapter 1

# The Just/Unjust-War Theory

With the accession of Constantine to power in the fourth century, the church as a whole gave up her anti-military leanings, abandoned all her pacifist scruples, and finally adopted the imperial point of view, says Cecil Cadeaux in *The Church in the First Centuries*. Even if the change was not that drastic, a new emphasis is evident among the leading Christian writers after the third century. Athanasius claimed it is praiseworthy to kill enemies in war. Augustine defended the position with detailed arguments.

The war question was settled, not on theological merits, but on a combination of circumstances, Cadeaux concludes. The joy of Constantine's deliverance was so great that it caught the church off guard. Christians had no part in Constantine's decision, so the problem of what was happening dawned on the Christian mind only in a fragmentary way, and slowly. A church that was drenched in the blood of hundreds of her martyrs had shown that she was strong and grew even stronger under persecution. Such a church could have opposed even Constantine if its mind had been set about war being absolutely and always opposed to the Gospel. But the mind of the Christian church was unclear by this time. Besides, church doctrine on peace or war had never been defined. The church had a clear aversion for bloodshed but had never formulated a clear theological definition of its attitudes. Now by default it began to shift into a practice of accepting war. The shift was hastened and strengthened by Augustine's formulation of the just/unjust-war theory.

The fourth-century theory is worth looking at, because it is the lever that separated Christian theory from practice, and it has helped to maintain that separation over the centuries. Apart from pacifism, it is the only other theory Christians have ever had that tried to relate Christian faith to war and peace.

Augustine formulated it like this: In general war is wrong; war is contrary to the Gospel of peace. But there may be conditions under which war may not be a violation of the Gospel, but may be an act of mercy and love. When these conditions are faithfully fulfilled during the entire war, then the war is not morally wrong.

### Conditions of the Just/Unjust-War Theory

The just/unjust-war theory maintains there are at least these five criteria by which war can be judged just:

1) Declaration of war must be made by a king.
2) War must be a last resort.
3) A good intention must guide the side declaring war.
4) The war must allow for protection of the innocent.
5) The proportion of good over evil must be kept.

The following is a general explanation of each condition of the theory.

*1) Declaration of war by a king:* There were no national states in Augustine's day. In today's world of nation states, the equivalent of a king would be the supreme political authority. In the US this would mean a declaration by Congress.

An undeclared war would be a misuse of authority and a threat to the innocent, inasmuch as they might be caught unawares. Use of nuclear missiles before declaring war would violate these conditions.

*2) War as a last resort:* Every other means of solving a conflict must be tried before war is declared. Every effort of reconciliation must be made such as arbitration and negotiation. Today that would certainly mean bringing the conflict to the United Nations for discussion and decision. In the Middle Ages, among Catholic kings, it would have included asking the pope to act as a mediator.

*3) Intention:* The intention of declaring war would have to be the restoration of justice: the king would be acting as vicar for the human family seeking to restore or preserve justice. The intention could never be a national state seeking its own benefit. The intention could not be land grabbing, economic control, or domination.

"Good intention" as used in this theory is not some vague, whimsical notion. As interpreted by its authors and supporters it means:

a) That you have a just cause. "Just cause" means these two features exist: moral guilt on one side and a sure, conscious knowledge of that guilt. How difficult this is becomes clear when you try to find an example in real life. There are no clear examples. For instance, imagine that nation A invades nation B in order to get land. In doing this, nation A is conscious what it is doing is morally wrong. There must be no doubt about this consciousness of wrongdoing. This must be clear before nation B would have a just cause for war against nation A.

b) No war can be just that includes a desire to harm, a lust for power, or for revenge. None of these are good intentions. Slogans like "Remember the Maine" or "Remember Pearl Harbor" are alien to the just/unjust-war theory.

c) In no war are both parties in the right. One side is always unjust. They can't both have the "good intention" required.

*4) Protection of the innocent:* The direct taking of innocent lives is never allowed. No cause is great enough to justify that. This condition limits direct killing in war to killing only the guilty. Conscripted soldiers are innocent, like civilians. Only volunteer soldiers are considered guilty in a just war.

Only "indirectly" killing is the way the innocent can be killed, so that their death is not intended but only a side effect of the necessary killing of the unjust enemy (for example, the destruction of a building full of enemy soldiers, in which there are also a few innocent non-combatants). How many innocents might be allowed to be killed as a side effect of killing the soldiers leads to the next principle.

*5) Proportionality:* This principle means that there has to be a balance between the evil done and the good hoped for—a balance favoring the good. For example, to destroy a building with one hundred enemy soldiers and two innocent children would be allowed. If conditions were reversed, and two soldiers were among ninety-eight innocent, there would be no justifiable position.

Even a superficial reflection upon these conditions raises doubts about how they could even be fulfilled. Yet these are the conditions that have to be fulfilled every day of a war to make a war "legitimate." As long as all of these conditions are completely fulfilled, war, according to this theory, is considered just. The defect of any one of these conditions, at any time in a war, would make it unjust, according to the theory.

The question of the difficulty of getting all these conditions together, operating throughout a war, and the opportunity for endless argument about whether certain conditions are fulfilled, indicate some of the weaknesses of the just/unjust-war theory.

## Weaknesses of the Just/Unjust-War Theory

Even before getting into particular weaknesses of the theory, it must be noted that there is a debate whether these five conditions constitute the just/unjust-war theory. Leroy Walters in *Five Classic Just War Theories* argues that there is no one "Just-war theory," but five different theories by five main supporters: St. Thomas Aquinas, Suarez, Vitoria, Grotius, Gentili. With Augustine there is a sixth.

Theorists differ on the number and content of conditions required. Some, like Aquinas, include proportion and care of the innocent under the heading "just cause." Others like Frabciscus Stratmann, O.P., who led the Catholic peace movement in Germany after World War I, refined the conditions and enlarged them into ten conditions.

Which theory is correct? Which should I follow? This kind of argument could go on forever and most likely will. What good is a theory whose very statement is not agreed on by those who support it? The war would be over before the argument was ended.

It reminds me of the seminarian who was trying to get a faculty member to go with a group to the White House to protest Nixon's forty-five day bombing of Cambodia. The faculty member kept delaying, asking for more time to think about it. Finally, the seminarian asked in disgust: "Will you come with us to demand that Nixon extend the bombing long enough for you to make up your mind?"

Aside from the debate as to which just-war theory to follow, the five criteria outlined about themselves have weaknesses.

1. Declaration of war by a king (or top political official) presents a special difficulty for us in the missile age. Missiles can travel between Moscow and Washington in twenty-four minutes. That doesn't allow Congress time to declare war or respond. Then, the response may be so massive that it will kill millions and create more killing than most wars in history. Even if Congress authorizes the president to use massive response, the condition of the just/unjust-war theory is not really fulfilled because it is doubtful that Congress has power to delegate the power to declare war to the President. Japan's attack on Pearl Harbor before a declaration of war violated this condition, as did Hitler's attack on Poland.

Of course, first-strike use of nuclear weapons, which Presidents Ford, Carter, and Reagan have accepted as US policy, would violate this condition. Even intent to use the first-strike capability is a violation. Development of first-strike weapons like the Trident submarine and the cruise missile is part of that intent. Those weapons are aimed at enemy silos (weapon sites). The highly maneuverable accuracy of those weapons would not be needed, if we were aiming to defend ourselves after being hit. The silos would presumably be empty before we fired if we had already been attacked.

2. Protection of the innocent is a condition which would certainly be violated by any use of nuclear weapons on cities. Such use would also come under the condemnation of Vatican II, which forbids the use of weapons of massive destruction on whole cities and their populations.

Since the use of nuclear weapons would very likely escalate to the point of killing whole populations, any use of nuclear weapons would probably violate this condition. Therefore nuclear weapons cannot be used at all. In matters of life and death, probability cannot be used for one side of an argument. Certainty is required. Likewise, the use of conventional weapons by a nuclear power risks nuclear war with its destruction of millions of innocent victims. Taking such a risk violates the "protection of the innocent" condition of the just/unjust-war theory.

3. Proportionality is a condition which undermines the theory in a nuclear age. In *Nuclear Disaster,* Tom Stonier estimates that if one twenty-megaton weapon were detonated in central New York City, seven million people would die from the blast and the resultant firestorm and radiation. President Kennedy estimated that any large-scale exchange between the US and another nuclear power would result in 80,000,000 American deaths, and almost double that in enemy lands.

In 1974-75, the annual report of the American Academy of Science said that a large-scale nuclear exchange between the US and the USSR would probably kill all human life on earth because the ozone layer would be damaged to such an extent that the lethal ultraviolet rays of the sun would cause blindness and finally destroy the food chain that sustains life. If this happened, it would lead to the extinction of the human species.

In a summary from his book, *Fate of the Earth,* printed in the *Congressional Record* (1982) by Senator Alan Cranston, Schell says: "There are some 60,000 nuclear warheads in the world. They are the nemesis of all human intentions, actions, and hopes—culminating in an absolute and eternal darkness in which no nation, nor society, nor ideology, nor civilization will remain; in which never again will a child be born; in which never again will human beings again appear on earth, and there will be no one to remember that they ever did."

On leaving office in 1980, President Carter said that in one minute of an exchange between the US and the USSR, more explosive power would be unleashed than all that was dropped on Europe and Japan by the Allies during World War II.

Carl Sagan, astronomer from Cornell, predicts that "nuclear winter" would follow an exchange of one-fifth of the world's nuclear arsenal. The dust sucked up into the stratosphere by the mushroom clouds would be enough to shut out the sun's sunlight so that the earth's temperature would go below freezing and cause deaths by starvation.

The Physicians for Social Responsibility say that only a very small percentage of those millions needing medical care during a nuclear exchange would receive it, because doctors would be dead, hospitals ruined, transportation destroyed, and medications ruined. They conclude that "preventive medicine" dictates that they speak out ahead of time and warn the public, according to their president, Dr. Helen Caldicott, not to expect any medical help during a nuclear war, for there won't be any.

The Council of the Federation of Concerned Scientists wrote an editorial in their F.A.S. *Public Interest Report* (Feb. 1981) which said that if the enormous stockpiles were ever used, the consequences in terms of human casualties and physical destruction would be virtually incomprehensible.

Because of the enormous destructive capacity of our weapons, both the US and the USSR would be destroyed as viable societies in a nuclear war. No one would win. This situation rules out the possibility of fulfilling the requirement of proportionality.

This condition by itself seems sufficient to invalidate the just/unjust-war theory in a nuclear age. As Pope John XXIII said, "No intelligent person could think of the use of nuclear weapons in a war to restore peace." *(Pacem in Terris)*

How is an ordinary person to know for sure when this condition has been fulfilled? To apply it one must know for certain how much killing, destroying, damaging of innocents and combatants is being done every day of the war. Where is the average soldier, or civilian, to get such reliable information during a time of war?

Consider Vietnam. In 1968 during the war the US Catholic Bishops asked in a public statement, "Have we already reached or passed the point where the principle of proportionality becomes divisive? How much more of our resources of men and women should be commited to this struggle? Has the conflict in Vietnam provoked inhuman dimensions of suffering? Would not an untimely withdrawal be equally disastrous?" Here the war has been under way for years and the bishops merely raise questions. They don't answer them. If they won't or can't, how is the ordinary individual supposed to?

We learned the truth about the Vietnam War from the Pentagon Papers—how much the US government deliberately deceived not only the public, but even Congress. Yet this theory presupposes that the soldier must know the truth about a war and make ethical judgments based on that knowledge.

4. The theory never worked in practice. From the time of its formation until the present, there is no record of any nation using it or of any war having been avoided by it. Even after a war was over no Conference of Bishops ever condemned any war on the basis of this theory—neither their own war, nor any war of any enemy nation.

5. The theory presupposes the very thing it is supposed to prove: that some killing is allowed on human authority.

6. Intention assumes that in a war one side will be just and the other unjust. This never happens. Instead, both sides claim they are right and kill each other—often in God's name.

7. The theory was formulated to show that some wars might be an exception to the law of the Gospel. Instead, it has become a theory used to justify every war that comes along. Instead of justifying an exceptional war, it is used to make all wars acceptable.

8. It allows each nation to judge its own cause. This violates the common-sense adage that no one is a good judge in his or her own case.

9. How could you ever know enough of the intent and actions of governments to make a sure judgment? Yet, according to traditional morality, you may not act, even on probability, where human life is concerned.

10. This complex theory nullifies the simple Gospel message of love, a message meant for all, and understandable by all. The theory is so complex that it is beyond the reach of the ordinary person.

11. The theory is unsuited to the age of total war and nuclear technology. The US Catholic Bishops' pastoral on peace (*God's Challenge and Our Response,* May 3, 1983) says that

use of nuclear weapons makes it impossible to protect the innocent or accomplish any good proportionate to the evil.

12. The theory is stretched to include almost anything. One advocate of the theory says that it allows torture of prisoners, and that non-combatants may be killed. Another advocate, Archbishop Phillip Hannan, argues at the final conference of the US Bishops' peace pastoral that you must allow a city's population to be killed if weapons are put into a city. Otherwise, you will lose the war. Any limitations make you less likely to win the war. So, in this way, advocates of the theory stretch the theory to allow killing without limit. For example, during the Vietnam War, if you decide not to bomb the dikes to flood the rice fields, gun emplacements will be put on the dikes. Obviously, you may bomb the dikes and starve the people anyway. This example shows how even the basic claim of the theory that it is a theory of limiting war, is shown to be false. It is twisted into a theory that allows war under the pretense of limiting it.

13. The writings and work of theologians such as Fuchs, McCormick, Schillibeekx, *et al.*, demonstrate that moral theology is historically conditioned and historically constituted. It is made up of concrete judgments made in the light of historical reality. All this is missing in the just/unjust-war theory as it is proposed.

When we look at the just/unjust-war theory in its historical context, we find that acceptance of the theory as a moral guide has led Western Christian civilization along a path of horror to the present time: the examples are wars of religion that set Christian against Christian, Christian against heretics, and the Christians against Moslems during the Crusades blessed by the popes.

In World War II, the just/unjust-war theory was preached by churchmen on both sides. Cardinal Mercier of France preached to parents, wives, and children of French soldiers that their loved ones were not only heroes, but martyrs for the faith. German Catholic bishops called on their people to support Hitler's war for folk and homeland. All of these evils throw historical light on what the just/unjust-war theory is, by showing what it does.

14. The theory is essentially a theory of limiting war. But there is abundant evidence that once nuclear war starts, it cannot be controlled or limited.

Any of these weaknesses would be serious. Taken together, they show that the theory is at least outdated, but probably never has been valid. Yet it is the only attempt at a moral justification of war by Christians. If it is rejected, the Christian is left with the Gospel, which rejects killing as immoral. Why? Because the theory is proposed as an "exception" to the Gospel of love. It does not deny that we are obliged to universal love. It states that the fulfillment of set conditions creates an "exception," i.e., a set of conditions so exceptional that when they are fulfilled the Gospel of love is not violated, but fulfilled. Once one is convinced that these circumstances are so exceptional that they can never exist, all that remains for Christians is the law of love.

## Benefit of Doubt

If you can't see in your own mind that all of the conditions required for a "just" war are fulfilled with regard to a particular war, you may be left in doubt. What do you do then? What most people do is accept the word of their government. "The government has the facts." "The government knows more than you do." These were the retorts I got during the Vietnam War, when I tried to show that the Vietnam War did not fulfill the conditions of the just/unjust-war theory.

My answer to this is that it was not enough for the government to know more. The government has to give the facts to me so fully that I can judge without doubt that the war fulfills all of the conditions of the just/unjust-war theory. Otherwise, according to the theory, I cannot go to war. In the matter of my taking life, hidden reasons are not enough; probability that the government has good reasons is not enough. The taking of human life is forbidden. It is not a neutral matter. It is forbidden. On other matters, authority may have the benefit of the doubt, but not where the taking of life is concerned. There, it must prove its case lucidly and fully before a believer in the just/unjust-war theory can accept any orders to kill. If there is any doubt, the practitioner of the just/unjust-war theory must refuse. Governments derive their authority from God. They never have authority to violate God's laws, nor may I give government the benefit of doubt when it orders me to violate divine law.

The just/unjust-war theory is essentially an effort to remove from war those characteristics that make it morally repulsive, e.g., murder, greed, desire for power, deceit, hatred. But when that is done, you no longer have war. That is why the just/unjust-war tradition is not, and never was, seriously followed by any nation. No nation accepts it as policy today; no nation ever did.

Jim Finn, author of *Politics, Protest and Peace,* and one of the most able exponents of the just/unjust-war tradition, ended an explanation of the theory with the story of Eisenhower getting into an elevator at the Pentagon and saying, "Take me to the eighth floor."

"I am sorry, Sir. There is no eighth floor. We don't go that high."

Eisenhower smiled and replied. "All right. Just take me as far as you can."

Then Jim concluded, "The just/unjust-war theory is like that elevator. It does not get you to peace. It is an unsuccessful effort to make rational, something which is essentially irrational: war. But it is good as far as it goes."

I disagree with that. It does more harm than good. It is used as a front for accepting all wars. Even when it is not used, it gives Christians the impression that they have some Christian basis for accepting war. It not only doesn't get you to peace, it does get you to war. Using the elevator analogy I say that if you are aiming at getting to peace, you should use an elevator that takes you there. The theory is a two-edged sword: It has both a "restraining" and "justification" or "apologetic" function. This second function predominates and outweighs the first. The bad outweighs the good.

Many Catholic moralists, influenced by Pope John XXIII and Vatican II, and by the new technology, have turned away from the just/unjust-war theory. Pope John XXIII saw any war as a denial of the unity of the human family. In his great encyclical *Peace On Earth*, he said, "There can be no doubt that relations between states, as between individuals, should be regulated not by the force of arms, but by the light of reason; by rule that is of truth, of justice, and one of the active and sincere cooperation." (par. 114)

Pope John XXIII had confidence in the human spirit's permanent capacity to open itself to truth. He saw the failure of Christians to trust in the truth of faith, and their willingness to resort to the use of force as a failure of faith. He declared that peace is to be found not in "equality of arms, but in mutual trust alone."

Pope John's theology called not for nuclear deterrence, but for a world-wide community. The Council participants were unable entirely to share John's vision, but his vision was put before them, and they responded in some measure.

In the *Constitution On the Church in the Modern World*, Vatican II presents a new perspective on war. At the beginning of the statement, it calls for "an evaluation of war with an entirely new attitude" because of the almost total slaughter, which threatens mankind from the new weapons.

Article 77 sets the frame of reference for the discussion with the subtitle, "The Human Family's Hour of Crisis." Chapter V, Part II, carries the title, "The Fostering of Peace and the Promoting of a Community of Nations." These two elements, the solidarity of the human family and the thermonuclear danger, make up the context for the entire discussion of war. They are essential parts of Pope John's vision.

The Council summarizes the attitude in these three elements: a condemnation of area destruction; an appeal to conscience that calls on men in the armed services not to obey blindly, but to weigh the morality of the orders they follow;

and the praise of nonviolence as a specific way of following the Gospel.

With regard to area destruction, the Council says:

"Any act of war, aimed indiscriminately at the destruction of entire cities or extensive areas along with their population, is a crime against God and man himself. It merits unequivocal and unhesitating condemnation." (par. 80)

In its entire text, this is the only time that the word "condemnation" is used. Because of the use of this word and the importance of the statement, this passage in a sense becomes the central declaration of the entire Council.

With this statement the Council moves the Church away from the acceptance of the just/unjust-war theory. There is no reference here to the weighing of conditions. What this statement says is that the moral limits of war are bypassed when thermonuclear destruction or area destruction is in question. The shift from the just/unjust framework back to the Gospel of peace of the first three Christian centuries has become a fact. Discussion of this statement in the Council proceedings by Bishop Taylor of Sweden makes the new position most emphatic. Bishop Taylor offered the following statement as an amendment:

> As total war is now a war against God's plan, against mankind itself, the actuation of the spirit of Christ is more imperative than ever. Christians should cultivate a deep awareness that violence is an actual expression of hatred, and should undertake a fuller exploration of the non-violent love, the teaching of Christ. (19)

The second element that the Council introduced in the new vision on war is conscience. The Council praised conscience with these words: "Actions which deliberately conflict with these same principles (natural law), as well as orders commanding such actions, are criminal, and blind obedience cannot excuse those who yield to them." (par. 79)

In Nuremberg the tribunal said that officers who followed orders are responsible for their actions. They cannot shift responsibility for immoral actions to those who ordered the actions. The United States accepted this idea in the treaty at London.

The final element in the new perspective on peace offered by the Council is a return to nonviolence. The Council said, "We cannot fail to praise those who renounce the use of violence in the vindication of their rights, and who resort to methods of defense which are otherwise available to the weaker parties too." (sec. 78)

These three elements of a new perspective toward peace are not part of a just/unjust-war theory. They clearly and positively point out the path toward peace. It is not a precise and specific path, but it does indicate the way. The new way initiates a return to the Gospel of love and peace. The Gospel depicts Christ as a lamb and not as a wolf, and the spirit of God as a dove and not an eagle. It brings back the Gospel story which speaks of Christ as a Prince of Peace, not a soldier at arms.

This is the spirit reflected by Vatican II. Instead of trying to show that, under certain conditions, some war might be just, it makes clear that certain acts of war are wrong. It points out the Christian mission of peace, and emphasizes that the Christian Gospel is opposed to all war.

Other Christian leaders reflect this trend away from all war. Karl Barth, the heroic Protestant pastor, who co-authored the "Barman Resolution" confronting Hitler's domination of the churches during World War II, asked (in 1959) that the mainline Christian churches confront their governments on the immorality of nuclear war, as the most urgent moral issue of our times. John Howar Yoder, John Ferguson, Ronald Sider, Richard Taylor, Jean Lassere, Millard C. Lind, G.H.C. Macregor, James Douglas, Edgar W. Orr, Gordon Zahn and A. Trocme are writers of today who call Christians to follow the Gospel of peace.

In an address at a meeting of the Dutch military chaplaincy, Cardinal Alfrink, primate of the Netherlands, took the position that a just war is no longer possible, holding that the existence of nuclear weapons excludes the existence of a just war, because the means that could be used to fight injustice, would cause much greater injustices.

Cardinal Lercaro of Bologna dismissed the idea of just war as something "left over from the cases and mental attitudes which no longer have anything to do with the facts."

The same idea is expressed by Bishop Giuseppe-Marafini, president of the Italian Bishops' Ecumenical Secretariat. At the August, 1969, meeting he declared, "For the church, any war is an inhuman, anti-evangelical, and an inadequate means for solving differences." He said the teaching of Pope John XXIII, Vatican II, and Pope Paul VI illustrates the change in the church's attitude toward war. It is a movement away from the acceptance of any war, toward a rediscovery of the Gospel message of peace. It is clear that the Council brought down the curtain on the just/unjust-war theory.

The theory was much talked about by theologians, but it had never received any formal theoretical approval from any council of the church. At Vatican Council II, some bishops tried to have the just/unjust-war theory acknowledged and accepted. This was never done. No formal reference to the theory was ever made, not even in a footnote.

## The Just Adultery Theory

Paralleling the just/unjust-war theory is the Just Adultery Theory. A look at it helps us see how differently Christians act towards murder and adultery. A Christian minister or priest who openly preaches the Just Adultery Theory would be run out of his church; not so with the just/unjust-war theory. Yet both theories equally violate commandments of God: "Thou shall not kill," and "Thou shall not commit adultery." Both set up conditions to get around the commandments. Conditions for just adultery are:

*1) Last Resort.* Every other means of getting along must be first tried: discussion, advice of a third party, reconciliation of differences, expressions of affection, anything short of adultery.

*2) Good Intention.* There must be no intent to harm one's spouse or any other person. Revenge for unfaithfulness of one's partner would not be considered a sufficient cause, nor would the need for more children, or a second home. The cause must be a genuine love and affection for the companion in adultery, needs that cannot be satisfied in any other way, and conversely, a genuine need of that love and affection on the part of the one initiating the adultery. The main point to be kept in mind is that the adultery must be in defense of love. There must be a pure intention. This condition entirely excludes aggressive adultery, which is sometimes called "rape."

*3) Protection of the Innocent.* The aggrieved partner must not be harmed. Every effort at secrecy must be made; no open flaunting or even informing the aggrieved partner would be consistent with this condition. If children are born of the adultery, both partners to the act must have the intention of caring for the children. The use of a contraceptive device, or the intent of having an abortion, violate this condition and make the adultery immoral.

*4) Proportion.* A favorable balance of good over evil must be reasonably hoped for. The foreseeable harm to absent partners, and to living children, must be weighed against the need of affection and love on the part of the adulterers. This need must honestly predominate over the cumulative harm.

The damage to family life, and the weakening of respect for the marriage bond, must be offset by the marked increase in human love, affection, and respect for the human person who is endangered by the social effects of adultery.

Provided these conditions are all fulfilled, adultery is not a violation of the Gospel, but an act of love and mercy.

Absurd? Perhaps, but less absurd than the just/unjust-war theory. Adultery is a personal act. It does not kill millions of people, or even one person. It does not have government support. It always allows for the possibility of repentance and reconciliation which are precluded by killing. On balance from the viewpoint of morality, the Just Adultery Theory has much more in its favor that the just/unjust-war theory. Why is it, then, that most Christians understand the weaknesses of the Just Adultery Theory, but are blind to the greater weaknesses of the just/unjust-war theory? Could it be that we consider morality to be limited to person and to personal conduct, and that what a group or a government does is beyond the limits of morality?

Or do we put the authority of a government above that of God? If a president, king, dictator, or general says an action is necessary for the defense of a country, do we say a Christian may do it, and not be guilty of sin? Since the president knows more about what is required for national security than anyone else, then each Christian can obey in good conscience. It follows that if the leaders says, "Rape," the Christian rapes. If the leader says "Kill," the Christian kills.

If, as a follower of Jesus, a person can intentionally kill another human because a president says it is okay, then surely he can rape another if a president, king, or dictator orders it.

Can we serve both God and government when the government orders what God forbids?

*Chapter 2*

*War Is Stupid and Immoral*

The war between Argentina and Britain over the Falkland Islands demonstrates the stupidity and immorality of war.

Stupid: Both sides said they are defending "their territory." The territory 8,000 miles distant was seized by Britain 150 years ago. Does that seizure entitle Britain to ownership?

Argentina seized the islands 300 miles off its coast and now pretends to be defending itself.

Immoral: Britain says that it must fight lest aggressors seem to be rewarded. President Reagan supports Britain on this. If it is wrong for Argentina to take the islands, how was it right for Britain 150 years ago? Is not supporting Britain supporting an age-old aggressor (150 years in this case)?

More basically, who gives Britain authority to kill Argentinians? Or who gives Argentinians authority to kill British people? If they claim God gives it, where is the evidence? Not in the Old or New Testaments. In both covenants the right to take life is reserved to God alone: not in the fourth-century just/unjust-war theory. One condition for fulfilling this theory is that war is a last resort. Every other means must have failed. Both Argentina and Britain violated this condition.

The just/unjust-war theory also requires that the good to be accomplished outweigh the evil done (killing, etc.) What good is to be expected from the war? The evils are clear: much killing; increased belief in war as a way of settling disputes (crazy in the nuclear age); increased bitterness in South America toward Britain and the United States; the possibility of the Soviet Union coming into it on the side of Argentina with a resulting spread of the war; maybe nuclear war; the buildup of a momentum of hate between nations; and the bypassing and weakening of the United Nations.

All of this and more to accomplish what? Outside of keeping two shaky governments in power, nothing good is likely to be accomplished. When the killing is over, negotiations will have to settle the same issues that were there before.

If Britain kills or captures all on the islands and occupies them, or if Britain fails, the war will not be over. There will have to be a negotiated settlement on the same issues that existed before the war. So, what did the war accomplish?

The whole mess shows how wars of the past continue their evil effects after 150 years. South Americans today resent the wars of colonization. Argentina, a place where 30,000 citizens have recently "disappeared" by government tyranny, now tries to solidify its hold on a restive population by appealing to their century-old hatred for colonies off their coast. The Thatcher government, beset with unpopular economic plans at home, seizes an opportunity to turn British minds from economic woes to former days of imperial wars when Britannia ruled the seas.

The populations in both countries, culturally addicted to war as a glorious solution to their woes, applaud the military gunfire. But will they continue to applaud as they begin to pay for the insanities of mutual killing? Certainly the side that loses won't applaud very much. In their way both sides may lose. We all may lose.

As we see this war build up, we should recall that nobody wins a nuclear war, and pray that this is not the beginning of one.

# Chapter 3

## *Did They Die in Vain?*

**W**hen the dead bodies of the US marines killed in Lebanon arrived at the US military base in Dover, Delaware, a ceremony was held. Marine Commandant General Kelly spoke to the relatives and other military officials as the caskets were lined up in the airplane hanger: "My prayer to God is that they have not died in vain."

After the general's speech, the mother of one of the dead marines came on the television and spoke through her grief. Her words were interrupted by her sobs: "I am proud of my son, and I know from his letters that he was proud to be a marine."

No matter what General Kelly thinks about the presence of the marines in Lebanon now that some of them are dead, he prays that their presence there was not in vain. More than that, he prays that these young men, whose lives are now over, did not live in vain; and since their time in the marines was the most public thing they did, he prays that that part of their lives was not in vain.

The parents of the dead marine, now that he is dead, want to be proud of him. No matter what they think of military life, or of America's involvement in Lebanon, they loved their son; they love the memory of their son now. They want that memory to be good. They want to be proud of their son; they recall that he was proud of being a marine. They would like to think that everything the marines did was good.

And so, the process of wishing something were good because it is already done and there is no way of undoing it goes on in a wider way to justify all the wars of all the world.

In every land, every general and every parent of a dead soldier would make the same prayer as General Kelly did and share the same pride as the parents of the dead marine. This is true even when they are on opposing sides of the same war. It is a rare general (and only a retired one) who will say that we should get our bloody hands out of another country, as we should have in Vietnam. It is a rare father or mother who would oppose the policy of the government in a war in which their son died. And that would only happen after the son had written home and said, "I am sick and tired of this war and I don't believe it's right," as some wrote from Vietnam.

What does God think of all this? The words of Scripture help give us God's opinion: "Vanity of vanities, and all is vanity except loving God and serving God alone."

All things pass away and all people pass away; all governments and empires pass away. The only thing that is permanent is God: the only thing that is not wasteful in our lives, that is not vanity, is serving God, fulfilling God's will, loving God.

To believe this requires faith, faith that there is a life beyond this one, and that the meaning of everything in this life is to be derived from how it affects us and others in the life to come, our life with God.

Put in this context, the prayer of General Kelly can extend to and cover all of life, not only war and military life, but every kind of life and everything in it.

How are our lives to be spent in loving God and serving God alone? Jesus gives us the answer when he tells us to love one another, and makes it clear that love is to extend to everyone, including our enemies. And it is very difficult to see how killing someone or preparing to kill them is an act of love for that person.

Christians have argued since the fourth century that they can show love by killing their enemies. They don't show love to their enemies, but they show love to those whom they protect. This point of view has its merit; it's better than attacking and killing everybody, but it's not the Gospel of Jesus Christ. The Gospel says clearly, "Love your enemies."

Despite this, Christians over the centuries have made war on each other and on others, and believed that they were serving God. And no doubt most of the soldiers who died in those wars believed, in good conscience, that they were serving God. And no doubt God accepts a good conscience, even if that conscience is erroneous, because a person has only one conscience. But in following a false conscience, by believing we are serving God and not acting in vain by killing and preparing to kill others, we lead the world further along the road to destruction, one which will ultimately lead to nuclear extinction. It would be far better for us to pray that God would forgive us our past acts of war and preparation for war, than trying to justify past wars. It would be far better for us to pray that we turn away from war entirely, than prepare for nuclear disaster.

The ages before us were not faced with extinction as we are. They always had some hopes that war could be won, that war was a way to peace. With the technology that we now have, we know that is not true. The deaths of our young marines, not to mention the deaths of the Lebanese, should be teaching us the stupidity and foolishness of war, instead of encouraging us to make more war.

Many of the young people who go into the military go because they are poor; because there are no jobs; because they need to pay for their education. Many of them go in because a relative or a priest tells them that's a good way to see the world. They don't go in to kill people. They don't go in to be killed.

Until mothers and fathers, priests and ministers, teachers and leaders say to these young people—"War is wrong. War is contrary to God's command that we love one another. Don't go."—until that is said, we are going to have more and more dead marines; more prayers and hopes that their lives were not spent in vain; more parents in tears.

Let us learn for once and for all that war in wrong, that we should not participate in it or support it and that we must pursue alternative, nonviolent means of defense.

*Chapter 4*

## Was the Grenada Invasion Immoral?

A US admiral once told me that he believed the Argentine invasion of the Falklands was immoral because it was "naked aggression." According to that norm, the Grenada invasion was immoral.

I asked him, "If naked aggression makes a war immoral, what is required to make it moral?"

He replied that England's seizure of the Falklands was clearly a "just war" because it was a response to "naked aggression."

If the admiral was right, then anyone who attacks the US in Grenada is waging a "just" war. Clearly we are aggressors, but maybe not "naked." We surround ourselves with token forces from five nearby, tiny nations to hide our "nakedness."

I asked the admiral if he counted "last resort" as one of the conditions for a just war.

"What does that mean?" he responded.

"It means that before military action, every other means must have been tried to settle differences. For example, England should have put the case before the UN before acting."

The admiral was not interested in that line of reasoning. He changed the subject.

President Reagan and Secretary Shultz talk much like the admiral. They do not address the moral issue. "We went in there to protect American citizens.... The president feared a hostage situation like Iran," stated Mr. Shultz.

None of these points alone would make a war moral. Over the centuries Christians have used only two ways of relating war to morals. One way is according to the teaching of Jesus: "Love your enemies.... What you do to the least of my little ones you do to me." This teaching, practiced by Christians of the first three centuries, finds all war immoral.

The just/unjust-war philosophy taken up by fourth-century Christians, and formulated by St. Augustine, is the only other way Christians have used to relate war to morals. It includes these four conditions: 1) The war must be chosen as a last resort. 2) The intention must be good. 3) The innocent must be protected. 4) The good accomplished must outweigh the evil. All these conditions would have to be fulfilled in the Grenada invasion to call it "moral."

These were not fulfilled. Could not US citizens have been "protected" by negotiations? This was not even tried. The chancellor of the St. George's Medical School of Grenada stated that they were not in danger and were free to leave.

By taking military action without negotiating first, we violated the condition of "last resort." That alone would be enough to pronounce the invasion "immoral"—even if all the other conditions were fulfilled.

It is doubtful that the "good" exceeds the evil. By invasion, we tell the world we settle disputes by violent force. In a nuclear age this is a disastrous dynamic. As the world's largest superpower, we overwhelmed a small island of 100,000 inhabitants. What evil can this do in a nuclear age? What good does it do? Does the good outweigh the evil?

In answering these questions, we must also weigh what our bypassing of the United Nations does to weaken that body, and thus weaken the prospects of peace in the world.

Was our intention good? Is President Reagan trying to get re-elected by winning a war as Margaret Thatcher did? Is he afraid of losing an election because of a hostage situation? Is he planning to use Grenada in order to attack Nicaragua? Is he trying to distract public attention from the deaths of 265 marines in Lebanon?

If the answer to any of these questions is "yes," or even "maybe," then the invasion into Grenada was immoral. This does not even include questioning the deaths of the nineteen Americans who were killed in the invasion and the deaths of many Grenadians.

My conclusion is that whether you judge the invasion according to the Gospel of Jesus or according to the just/ unjust-war theory, the invasion of Grenada was immoral.

Christians and all peace-loving people return to the attitude of Christians of the first two centuries, when they refused to kill and refuse to join the army on the basis that it would be opposed to the Gospel of Jesus Christ. What does the Gospel say about war?

Does the Christian faith, the Gospel of Jesus Christ, have a special way of meeting suffering, of meeting evil? Can war ever be the means to set wrongs right? Or does war so stultify the achieving of justice that a Christian can never condone it? This does not mean the repudiation of all force in dealing with humanity, or group dealing with group. Police action, for example, is not war.

The essential teachings of the Christian Gospel are not based on the interpretation of particular texts, such as when

Christ spoke to a centurion and did not condemn him. Anyone can choose a text like that and argue from it. One could just as easily argue that Christ spoke to a prostitute and did not condemn her. But this is all peripheral—individual texts are to be interpreted in the light of the central Gospel message about which there is no doubt.

The message is: *love,* love your neighbor; God is the Parent. Because God is the Parent, all men and women are brothers and sisters. The human person has an infinite value because he or she is God's child. If there is any doubt about the application of this, then Christ, the living Christ, the incarnate Christ, is the light and the way, and it is by His example that anything doubtful is to be interpreted.

Does war, does the killing of other human beings, the massive killing such as that which goes on in war, ever have the approval of the Gospel? The answer is clearly, "No." From the Gospel alone, the answer is clearly, "No." There are different schools of interpretation of the Gospel, but none of them denies that the Gospel is itself pacifist (leaving aside tradition for a moment). And in being essentially pacifistic, it clearly illustrates this point of view with the life and death of Jesus Himself. He had all power and did not use it to inflict suffering, but rather taught a way of salvation by accepting suffering. How, then, did Christians ever come to accept war?

They came to accept it through the set of circumstances which affected them in the fourth century. When Augustine observed the political situation, he saw a Christian church which had fought the Roman state and now was allied with it. Seeing a threat to the whole church from the barbarians, he urged Christians to join the army; but this position he limited and justified in a set of conditions he established, now known as the "Just-War Theory."

These conditions stated, approximately, that the Gospel does say "Thou shalt not kill" and "Love thy neighbor," but that under certain rigorous conditions, the killing that goes on in war is not always a violation of the Gospel, but rather is an exception.

The conditions are that war is waged only as a last resort; that war is waged under the authority of a ruler; that war is conducted in a just manner, so that there is no wanton killing; that the evil allowed is proportionate to the good which is being sought; that the innocent are protected; and, that the intention is good. All of these conditions must be present all the time in every war. And if this is true all the time, Augustine says, then war is not a violation of the Gospel but an act of mercy and an act of love in the reparation of justice.

What is wrong with this theory? In the nuclear age the theory is outmoded by technology. A common argument to show that the just-war theory is no good is simply to show that it has never worked. We have never yet had a war in history which has been condemned by society at large at the time as a violation of the just-war theory; nor has any such war been condemned retroactively. Not even the German bishops condemned the wars of Hitler on the basis of any kind of Christian theory. Cardinal Alfrink says that one of the weaknesses of the theory is that it allows each nation to decide for itself—each nation remains the judge in its own case.

The just-war theory also presupposes what was never really true: that one can be a just killer, or, to leave out the word "killer," that one side is just and the other side is unjust. The just-war theory supposes that some killing is allowable. This is illustrated in Paul Ramsey's book on the limits of nuclear war, which he subtitles, *How Shall War Be Conducted?* It omits the basic question: "Is any war just?" The just-war theory, by its very name, allows that some war is just. It also presupposes that the head of state is a Christian or a follower of the just-war theory. What good does this do when someone like Hitler is the head of state?

It impresses me, above all, that the just-war theory uses the arguments of Aristotle, Cicero, and Plato. Christ's love ethic and the example of his life have nothing to do with this use of philosophical argumentation. Christ might as well not have come if our arguments about the main moral problem of humanity today—survival in the nuclear age—are going to ignore Christ's example and his teaching.

The just-war theory assumes that the eighteen-year-old boy knows enough about the leaders of his country to make a sure judgment. In Vietnam a boy has to go out and kill people of another country. He certainly should not do this, even using the justifications of Augustine, unless he is certain that it is the right thing to do. Before you excuse the killing with the just-war theory—i.e., find the war to be an exception—you have to be *sure* of the facts. The theory results in both sides, the Germans and the Americans, for example, killing each other in the name of God.

The just-war theory presupposes that the army or the political leaders tell the truth about what they intend to do. The American soldiers who were ordered to bomb Dresden were lied to about their target. They were told it was a poison gas factory, or were given other, different briefings. Only one group of all the bombardiers was told the truth. Some of them might have had problems of conscience about bombing cities, so they were told lies.

A new perspective on war began with the Second Vatican Council. The Council saw some sort of spiritual revolution as necessary. At the beginning, the Council stated that an evaluation of war with an entirely new attitude was called for, because of the almost total slaughter which threatens humanity from the new weapons.

Article 77 of the *Constitution on the Church in the Modern World* sets the frame of the "Human Family's Hour of Crisis" (this is the subtitle) and chapter 5, part II, is titled "Fostering Peace and Promoting Community of Nations." These two elements—human society and thermonuclear danger—were the context of the entire discussion of war. The just-war theory is not even mentioned in any footnote, even though many Council participants suggested that there should be reference to it.

Such a context for the Council's statements came partly from Pope John, especially his *Peace On Earth* encyclical, where he states, "It is hardly possible to imagine that in the atomic era war can be used as an instrument of justice." Pope John spoke from the perspective, as he said, both of his own heart and from his position as father of the human family. The human family was the essence of the Johannine vision. To justify war in any form to Pope John would have been to deny this family communion. It would have demanded the division of humanity into just killers and unjust killers. He suggested the new perspective which the Council took up: the Gospel of nonviolence. He wrote: "Disagreements must not be settled by force, but in the only manner which is worthy of the dignity of humanity—an equitable reconciliation of differences." Italian bishops who met recently echoed these principles: "For the church, any war is an inhuman, anti-evangelical, and inadequate means of solving differences."

Pope John's faith in nonviolence is a faith in the human spirit's permanent capacity to open itself to truth. The failure of Christians to trust in the truth of their faith and to resort to the use of force, as the state does, is a statement of their failure in faith. Pope John declared that peace does not depend on "equality of arms but in mutual trust alone." Now, it is between fear and trust that you have these alternatives of war and peace.

Pope John said: "In every human being there is a need that is congenital to his nature and never becomes extinguished, a need for truth, compelling him to break through the web of error and open his mind to the knowledge of truth. And God will never fail to act on this interior being; a person who, at a given moment of his life, lacks the clarity of faith can, at a future date, be enlightened and believe in the truth."

This means that one should not kill even someone like Adolf Hitler. And in saying this, Pope John was in thorough agreement with Gandhi, who said, "Truth is God," a statement he preferred to the usual "God is truth." Truth *is* God. John said the power of truth is the power of God, not the power of the monarch. Thus the conclusion of both Gandhi and Pope John—nonviolence in every sector of life—is the same. Pope

John's theology called for no nuclear deterrents and a worldwide community of men and women. The Council proposed a new attitude: It condemned area destruction, appealed to conscience, and called on soldiers not to obey with blind obedience any orders which called for indiscriminate area destruction or city destruction. It praised nonviolence as a Gospel way of life.

To quote the Council: "Any act of war aimed indiscriminately at the destruction of entire cities or extensive areas along with their population is a crime against God and humanity. It merits unequivocal and unhesitating condemnation." In 103,000 words of Council statements, this is the only time *condemnation* is used. It makes this the central declaration of the entire Council. The implication for nuclear retaliation intent is very clear: The limits of any war are overwhelmed by the threat of thermonuclear destruction, which is declared immoral.

The shift from the just-war framework to the Gospel of peace is made. Bishop Taylor of Sweden, in the Council discussions, offered this amendment: "As total war is now a war against God's plan, against humanity itself, the actuation of the spirit of Christ is more imperative than ever. Christians should cultivate a deep awareness that violence is a natural expression of hatred and should undertake a fuller exploration of nonviolent love, the teaching of Christ."

Conscience is praised by the Council: "Actions which deliberately conflict with these principles (natural law), as well as orders commanding such actions, are criminal; and blind obedience cannot excuse those who yield to them." This was accepted by the United States in the Nuremberg trials, where officers were blamed for following orders which the victors judged to be immoral—"putting people to death." And nonviolence is praised by the Council: "We cannot fail to praise those who renounce the use of violence and the vindication of their rights to resort to methods of defense which are otherwise available to the weaker parties."

There was an Austrian peasant who, as a Christian, rather than yield to Hitler's demand that he join the army and fight for the Nazi cause, resisted and proclaimed in resisting both morally and with his life that suffering love is redemptive. He, Franz Jaegerstaetter, was executed. He said, "Christ himself, the most innocent of them all, endured the greatest suffering of all and that through his suffering and death and blood. Do we not want to suffer for him?"

War's central action, inflicting suffering and death, directly contradicts Christ's example and teaching that suffering and death are redemptive. The church has great reason for repentance for allowing itself to become involved, since Constantine's time, in an ethic that justifies something which conflicts with the essence of the Gospel.

The Constantinian church is now yielding to the Johannine church; the militant church is becoming the believing church of Christ crucified. Just war is fast becoming a relic for the Christian who recognizes that the nuclear age demands the fullness of the Gospel of Christ.

*Chapter 5*

*Tears in the Seamless Garment*

New York Governor Mario Cuomo is criticized by some Catholics for approving as governor laws that allow limited abortions, though he himself is personally opposed to abortion.

If the critics followed the same attitude toward war and the death penalty, their criticism would have more weight. They criticize Cuomo for separating personal and legal attitudes, but regarding war and the death penalty, they do just what Cuomo does.

They say, "I am personally opposed to killing others, but if the government kills in war or by implementing the death sentence, I approve. Even if I don't like it very much, I consent to pay taxes for it, and I vote for the politicians who approve of war and the death penalty."

How do they explain this inconsistency? "Abortion is murder of the innocent," they say. "It is always wrong to do it or approve laws that allow it. Politicians who approve such laws act immorally."

"How, then, can you approve of war and the death penalty?" I ask. "War and the death penalty kill the guilty, and unfortunately that is sometimes necessary," they reply.

But are not the innocent sometimes killed in war and under the death penalty? Is not the taking of human lives in war and by capital punishment the same as taking the lives of the unborn? Does God forbid the taking of life only in abortion and not on the battlefield and in the gas chamber?

To say that abortion violates the sacredness of life is certainly a valid argument. To go further and criticize those who personally oppose abortion but approve laws allowing abortion is a valid and consistent criticism. But to abandon respect for life when the state legalizes it in war and death penalties is to do exactly what you criticize in others. God does not say, "It is wrong to kill the innocent by abortion but right to kill whomever the state says, 'KILL!' " God says, "Thou shalt not kill. Love your enemy."

God makes no distinction between innocent and guilty, friend and enemy. We are commanded not to kill anybody. We are commanded to love everybody. When God asks us on judgment day why we killed people in war or approved of those who killed people, it won't help us much to say, "I killed people because the state told me they were guilty." God might very well ask, "Do you think that obedience to the state takes precedence over obedience to me? Does the state have the authority to command what I forbid? Why was it so clear to you that abortion was wrong when you approved of killing in war and the death penalty? If the state has the right to make laws that approve of war and the death penalty, why can't the same state make laws approving abortion?"

As I see it, the only way opponents of abortion can give a consistent answer to these questions is to say neither the state nor anyone else has the right to take life. That authority is God's alone and there is no evidence that God delegates that authority to any state or doctor. Laws that allow the taking of human life are an attempted usurpation of divine authority. They approve of what God forbids. They violate the divine laws. "Love your enemies. Thou shalt not kill." Abortion is not the only way to violate those laws!

## Chapter 6

## Is Deterrence Moral?

John is an officer in a nuclear silo. His job is to help fire a US missile on order. He wonders if this is right. He knows that the firing of the missile will be the beginning of nuclear war in which he, himself, would probably die, together with millions of people in the US and the USSR. He knows that we intend to use our weapons to devastate the USSR, if it attacks us. He knows that the Soviets have the power to retaliate and destroy us. John understands that he is part of this intent and its possible execution. He asks his confessor if this intent to use nuclear weapons is moral. Is it wrong for him to continue with his work in the silo? What should the confessor answer?

Definition: Nuclear deterrence is the credible threat to retaliate with nuclear weapons when attacked and to devastate the attacker. Vatican II says that the destruction of whole areas and their people is immoral. The US Catholic bishops say that nuclear war cannot be limited once it starts. (May 3, 1983, Pastoral Letter)

Principles: The morality of a human act is determined by three elements: The end, the means, and the circumstances must be good, or, if neutral, converted to good by the good means and end. All three elements are necessary for a good human act. The defect of any one of these three essential elements renders the act immoral.

It is never allowed to do evil that good may come of it. A good end does not justify the use of an evil means. I may not intend to kill or actually kill a person to prevent his probable attack on my life. What it is wrong to do, is wrong to intend to do. I may not threaten to kill, or actually kill, millions of people in order to prevent them from killing me.

Solution: Clearly the United States has an intent to use nuclear weapons in retaliation on the Soviet Union, if we are attacked. Our intent to retaliate is the heart of our deterrence policy.

The very preparation of the weapons, their positioning, targeting, and readiness are all evidence of our intent. If that is not enough to make our intent clear, each year the secretary of defense reaffirms our intent in the annual military posture statement of Congress.

Our purpose in intending to retaliate is to deter the Soviet Union from attacking us. A good end. Does this end justify our intending to use or actually using nuclear weapons to devastate the USSR? No. The good purpose does not justify the evil means.

The principle of double effect does not apply here. That principle requires that one act simultaneously brings about two effects, one good, one bad, in which our intent goes only to the good. Here the intent and results are two separate acts separated by many years. Since 1950 we have intended to use nuclear weapons, if attacked. Retaliation, if it occurs, will be a separate act. Deterrence is not one act with two effects—one good, preserving peace; and one evil, intending to use nuclear weapons on people. It is not a double effect from one act. We have already intended to use nuclear weapons for four decades.

Conclusion: John may not work at the silo and thus be a part of the intent to fire nuclear missiles. Nor may he fire the weapon, even if ordered to do so. With deference to better opinion, this is what I would answer John.

# Part III:
# Nuclear Weapons, Nuclear Madness

*Chapter 1*

*It's a Sin to Build a Nuclear Weapon*

Does God approve of our intent to use nuclear weapons?

No, I don't believe so. Moreover, I do not believe God approves of even the possession of nuclear weapons.

The danger of world suicide through nuclear war "compels us to undertake an evaluation of war with an entirely new attitude," Vatican II said. Einstein put it this way: "When we released the energy from the atom, everything changed except our way of thinking. Because of that we drift towards unparalleled disaster." Something of what Einstein meant is this: We still look upon war as a conflict between two armies. The armies try to break through each other's front line to reach the civilian population. When they do, the suffering is so great that the war is ended. However, war with nuclear weapons will reach the civilian immediately. Nuclear missiles take only twenty-four minutes to travel between Moscow and Washington. Both the speed and total penetrability are so different from war in the past that the word "war" should not be used. Something like "mutual suicide," "Doomsday," or "Apocalypse" would be more accurate.

What can a nuclear weapon do? In his book, *Nuclear Disaster*, Dr. Tom Stonier of Manhattan College describes what would happen if a 20-megaton nuclear weapon was detonated in the center of New York City.

The first result would be death: Ten times as many deaths as all the battle deaths that occurred in all the wars of US history—from the Revolution up to and including the 55,000 battle deaths in the Vietnam War. Seven million people would die from blast, firestorm, and radiation. The blast would cover a radius of ten miles. It would dig a crater 650 feet deep and a mile and a half across, even if it was dropped in solid rock. All living things, even in the subways, would die. Trucks and automobiles would be hurled about like giant Molotov cocktails spewing gasoline and fire. Most of the victims would be killed by falling buildings.

As the shock front moved out to its ten-mile radius, the huge vacuum at its center would begin to draw the winds back at speeds up to 125 miles per hour. A house or tree caught in this double pressure would be blasted from both sides.

Above the blast a ball of fire would form. This fireball, four miles wide, would swiftly rise to a height of about 20,000 feet. At its center the heat would be eight times hotter than the sun, its heat so intense that the unexposed human body forty miles away would receive second-degree burns; 250 miles away, as far as Washington, D.C., many people would suffer severe eye damage.

Within a thirty-nine mile radius a sea of fire would roll and boil fanned by the winds of the shock wave. Asphalt, which we do not generally consider combustible, would pass its combustion point of 800 degrees and burn.

From the huge cavern dug by the blast, vaporized material pulled up into the air by the fireball would form a radioactive cloud of death. This cloud would blow with the wind over Connecticut towards Hyannisport and out to the ocean. The cigar-shaped cloud would grow until it covered an area of 4800 square miles. At the center the radiation intensity would be measured at about 2300 roentgen units. One roentgen unit is severe enough to damage a primate cell. Four hundred roentgen units are fifty percent lethal. The lethal capacity of this radiation would decrease as it got farther from New York. What would a person need for protection from radiation? A shelter enclosed on all sides by two feet of concrete or three feet of earth with its own oxygen, food, and water supply for at least ninety-six hours, perhaps twelve days. At the end of ten months there would still be a dosage of 100 roentgen units over most of the area.

This is not imaginary. It is carefully deduced from scales made through US testing and through measurements from the Hiroshima and Nagasaki bombings.

How many bombs do we really need? If it were not sinful to make a nuclear weapon, how many could we get by with? Between 200 and 400 megatons delivered on an enemy would be enough to destroy the possible enemy as a viable society. Former Secretary of Defense Robert McNamara once argued this before Congress. No one has contested his figures. Delivery of twenty to 400 megatons would destroy seventy-five percent of the industrial capacity of the Soviet Union or any other collection of enemies.

The Soviet Union has roughly 200 cities with a population over 100,000. A bomb or two delivered on these cities would destroy them. McNamara's argument was that we won't need any more than 200 to 400 weapons delivered on target. He was trying to show the Congress and the country that beyond that amount we are not dealing with deterrence but overkill.

How many nuclear weapons do we have in our stockpile today? We have over 30,000 nuclear weapons—8,000 large (strategic) weapons and 22,000 smaller (tactical) weapons. We are making one new nuclear weapon every eight hours. We have enough weapons in our arsenal to deliver over 615,000 Hiroshima bombs. We can destroy every Soviet city of 100,000 or more forty-five times over. The Soviet Union can destroy every American city of 100,000 or more thirteen times over.

Can the use of these weapons be reconciled with the Gospel? Can even their existence be reconciled with the command "Love your enemies"? The United States policy is that we will retaliate with massive nuclear destruction if we are attacked. This is the very heart of our nuclear-deterrence policy. This is what we mean by deterrence. Is there any way that the Christian conscience can accept this policy of nuclear deterrence?

There are only two ways in which Christians have tried to reconcile war with the Gospel. One is the way practiced by the Christians in the first three centuries. During the first three centuries Christians considered joining the army incompatible with the following of Christ. The other is the just/unjust-war theory of St. Augustine of the fourth century. This theory holds among other conditions that in any war there be a proportionality between the evil done and the good to be hoped for, and that there be no direct killing of the innocent. Have we in the nuclear-war age reached the point where we finally must say that war is incompatible with the Christian conscience? Can we imagine Jesus pushing the button that would release nuclear weapons on millions of people? Vatican II says that military personnel who refuse orders of this kind are worthy of the highest commendation. Vatican II calls the arms race a trap in which humanity is caught. Vatican II points out that the massive outlay of money for the weapons of death ensures the hunger and deprivation of the masses of poor of the world. Vatican II condemns the use of weapons that destroy whole areas with all their people. Nuclear weapons will do all these things.

Can we go along with the intent to use nuclear weapons? What it is wrong to do, it is wrong to intend to do. If it is wrong for me to kill you, it is wrong for me to plan to do it. If I get my gun and go to your house to retaliate for a wrong done me, then find there are police guarding your house, I have already committed murder in my heart. I have intended it.

Likewise, if I intend to use nuclear weapons in massive retaliation, I have already committed massive murder in my heart.

The taproot of violence in our society today is our intent to use nuclear weapons. Once we have agreed to that, all other evil is minor by comparison. Until we squarely face the question of our consent to use nuclear weapons, any hope of large-scale improvement of public morality is doomed to failure. Even the possession of weapons which cannot be morally used is wrong. They are a threat to peace and might even be the cause of nuclear war. Human history shows that every weapon possessed is finally used. Since use of nuclear weapons is sinful, and possession leads to use, possession itself is sinful. Just as possession of alcohol is wrong for an alcoholic, and possession of drugs is wrong for a drug addict, so possession of morally unusable weapons is wrong for a government addicted to using weapons. The nuclear weapons of communists may destroy our bodies. But our intent to use nuclear weapons destroys our souls. Our possession of them is a proximate occasion of sin.

Technology in the nuclear age teaches us what we should have learned from our faith. As John Kennedy said at the United Nations in 1962: "Because of the nuclear sword of Damocles that hangs over us, we must cooperate together on this planet, or perish together in its flames through the weapons of our own hands."

*Chapter 2*

*When Nuclear War Strikes*

The immorality of building nuclear weapons is even confirmed by medical opinion. Your friendly doctor won't be able to help you when nuclear war strikes. That's the grim message of thousands of doctors who call themselves Physicians for Social Responsibility. In many conferences around the country and in international conferences abroad, they describe nuclear war and its after-effects. With scientific facts and passion they proclaim that nuclear war would be so devastating and that medical help would be practically non-existent.

Concluded Dr. Howard Hiatt, dean of Harvard's School of Public Health, "The conditions are not unthinkable. Rather, they are infrequently thought about. Not to make the effort to eliminate nuclear arms would be an insupportable betrayal of ourselves and our culture."

These doctors have committed themselves to an effort to arouse opposition to nuclear weapons.

Here is what the doctors say nuclear war would bring—total destruction of major American cities. In a major city such as Boston, well over two million people would be killed. To draw up plans for civil defense and post-nuclear-attack medical services is madness. Previous bombing experience from even conventional bombing at Dresden shows that bomb shelters become ovens and pressure cookers.

Physicians for Social Responsibility ask all physicians to join in an appeal for reduction of US-Soviet tension, a ban on the use of nuclear weapons, and gradual nuclear disarmament.

Yale psychiatrist Robert Jay Lifton talked of the numbing effect that the nuclear bomb has already had on our minds. According to him, the bomb has already worked a terrible deformation in the human brain. "We live with a terrible danger that we don't even acknowledge."

I think it has also deformed our moral senses. The bomb cannot be related in any way to what we profess to believe as Christians. We can't love our enemies with nuclear arms. We can't fulfil the Gospel command, "Love your enemies."

During the first three centuries, Christians took this command seriously. During those years Christians considered joining the army incompatible with the following of Christ.

The Pentagon likes to minimize the grim realities. The military "experts" pretend that most Americans will survive a nuclear war. Most Americans stand by passively and let them play this dangerous game. It's a little like a playground situation, where a rough gang has gotten out of control, and its wild play is beginning to alarm a few of the people standing by. In this case the wild play is so serious none of us can really imagine what it might mean. We have to alert all the people standing around and passing by if we hope to stop the nuclear threat.

Nothing else will matter a bit if this genie gets out of the silo. Using our weapons is not worth the retaliation we would suffer.

For two thousand years the Gospel has been telling us that we must love one another, and we've ignored this basic message for the most part. Now, technology tells us we can't use the weapons we have invented. Our consciences tell us the same thing. Our common sense and all the sages through history tell us the same, but the military and the politicians who support them disagree.

This anxiety over nuclear war is no imaginary thing, and it cannot be lightly dismissed. A twenty-megaton bomb has more destructive power than a mountain of TNT four times the height of the Empire State Building. Its blast would make a hole in solid rock deep enough to contain a twenty-story building; and the hole would be a half-mile wide. The detonation would set a huge pressure wave in motion that would roar out from the explosion center as a shock front backed by winds moving at over 1000 miles per hour.

A vast vacuum would be created behind this pressure front, and winds from the surrounding area would rush in as the pressure diminished. Structures not toppled by the shock front might be toppled by the winds sucked in by the vacuum from the opposite direction.

Casualties would come from falling buildings and flying objects. People would be killed by being blown against walls and hard surfaces, and by being crushed by incredible pressures.

Trucks would be lifted and thrown like grotesque Molotov cocktails to spew gasoline, oil, and automotive shrapnel onto and into everything in their path. In an instant, most underground gasoline and oil tanks would rupture and explode within the blast area.

Ten miles from the blast center, basement shelters would be buried. All living things in the subway systems would die. The blast would destroy hospitals, rupture water mains, and paralyze transportation. The winds from the blast would fan the fury of the fires.

After the first incandescent flash across the sky, a fireball as hot as the sun and many times brighter would begin to rise from the earth. It would be four and a half miles across. Like a hot-air balloon, it would rise to a height of twenty miles, emitting visible and invisible radiation and scorching the countryside. Clothing on people twenty miles away would burst into flame; paper would pass its combustion point at thirty-seven miles.

A sea of fire would roll and burn in a radius that would stretch thirty-seven miles from the center. The eyes of people three hundred miles away from the blast would suffer retinal damage if they looked at the fire wall. Rabbits at that distance from the US Pacific tests of smaller bombs had their eyes burned by the flash of the bomb.

Radiation effects are something that we don't know from past wars, except for the victims of Hiroshima and Nagasaki, and the US soldiers who witnessed the US tests and are now dying at a premature age from cancer and leukemia. After the blast of a nuclear bomb the deadly radioactive cloud would follow; 450 roentgens of these deadly rays would kill immediately; lower doses would bring disease and death at a slower rate.

The deadly radioactive fallout or the deadly rays from a twenty-megaton ground burst would cover an area of about 4800 square miles. If a bomb fell on New York City, this would include Connecticut and Cape Cod. The deadly cloud would not blow away quickly, but remain lethal for at least twelve days and possibly for as long as two months.

The only adequate protection would be three feet of dirt or two feet of concrete, but such protection would become merely a death trap.

Any survivors who were distant enough from the bomb would receive radioactive deposits within their bones. From there the deadly rays would continue to cause damage. All responsible scientists admit that the fallout from a large megaton

101

bomb would leave us with an appalling number of deformities which would continue for many generations. Besides causing all the death, a nuclear war would leave us with millions of cripples, idiots, and invalids.

The results of nuclear disaster are so ghastly that they are difficult to imagine and visualize. Hoping for the best, we shy away from such a terrible vision. There's a film called "War Games" made by British television that gives some idea of it. People change their thinking about nuclear war when they see it. It shows the impact of three one-megaton bombs lobbed into Britain in a simulated nuclear exchange with East Germany. Seeing the effects of bombs on people helps remove nuclear danger from the never-never world of nightmares. It helps us experience what these bombs do. Twenty-four project engineers in the Pentagon saw the film through the efforts of a friend of mine. After seeing it, they said, "This ought to be part of our regular education. We don't think of the effects on humans of what we are doing. We just deal with the physics of the action." They petitioned the Pentagon education director to make it part of their regular training. He refused. That refusal seems to me more evidence that the film helps one feel what the bombs will do to people.

*Chapter 3*

## The Auschwitz of Puget Sound

Navy Secretary John Lehman objects to Archbishop Raymond Hunthausen calling the Trident submarine base the "Auschwitz of Puget Sound." He thinks there is something "deeply immoral" in a religious leader speaking out about the preparation for nuclear war. He considers such talk to be "political."

Hitler likewise considered many bishops who opposed his military program to be intruding into politics. Hitler threatened to revoke the church's tax exemption unless that was stopped. In that way, most religious opposition was silenced. Voices that might have spoken early enough and loudly enough to stop Hitler were not heard. Had they spoken out, perhaps today we could be proud to say that the bishop, in whose diocese Auschwitz was located, had publicly condemned the mass murder going on there. We could be even prouder if that bishop's warning voice had caught world attention and helped lessen the killing.

Far from wanting bishops to be silent about Hitler's killings, some complain that the pope did not speak out loudly enough. They argue that the pope, as a moral leader, should have openly spoken out in condemnation of Hitler.

If we soon have a nuclear war (as many believe we will), the unlucky survivors may remember the prophetic voice of Archbishop Hunthausen calling the Trident base the "Auschwitz of Puget Sound." After the Trident has gone into action and incinerated hundreds of Soviet cities and their people, and after the returning Soviet weapons have turned the Trident base and hundreds of American cities into heaps of radioactive ash, Archbishop Hunthausen's comparison to Auschwitz may seem like an understatement.

It is no secret that the Trident is as big as two football fields put together, that it travels under water at forty miles per hour, that it carries 192 nuclear warheads that can be shot from underwater to targets 6,000 miles distant. It is no secret that the Trident's nuclear bombs are five times the size of the Hiroshima bomb. It is no secret that we already have enough bombs in our arsenal to destroy every Soviet city of over 100,000 people forty-five times over. It is no secret that we cannot defend ourselves against Soviet missiles. Surely the secretary of the Navy knows all this!

At the Trident base, we prepare for a nuclear war that no one wins.

Vatican Council II forbids Catholics to be a part of nuclear war, and by implication, to intend one or plan one. Most American Catholics don't seem to realize this, so Secretary Lehman may have done much to get the discussion going by broadcasting the Archbishop's "Auschwitz of Puget Sound" statement.

Open discussion on the issue of nuclear war and the preparation for nuclear war is badly needed. No nuclear war, nor any preparations for it, can be morally justified. No version of the just/unjust-war theory will fit it or give any more basis to it. Is it too much to expect the secretary of the Navy would be interested in convoking an important discussion about this?

*Chapter 4*

*Nuclear Patriotism*

"I am no less the good servant of the king by being the good servant of my God," said Thomas More when asked about obedience to God and to the king. Camus phrased his response similarly: "I wish I could love justice and love my country also." Both statements make clear that patriotism has limits. What both say is that love for country is not shown by leaving God out.

Our nuclear age shows further limits of patriotism. To do anything that might reduce America to a radioactive ash heap can hardly be patriotic. If the arms race moves us in that direction, it is not patriotic. For patriotism to be a virtue, it must be an aspect of love, as are all virtues. To be an aspect of love, it must be related to people, not just the land on which they live. Thus patriotism is a virtue that leads us to serve God by serving the needs or the common good of all the people.

How did we get from that lofty definition to the perversion that patriotism is simply readiness to kill on government orders? First, we limited our vision of common good only to those within our borders. Then we made our proof of patriotism our readiness to kill. Thus we have ended up with a strange sort of virtue: one that does not require that we love a single person, only that we be ready to kill on order. Love is out. God is out.

Even before the nuclear age, this changed patriotism from a virtue to a vice. In the nuclear age it is also a formula for world suicide.

The central assumption of this "vicious" patriotism is that the state has the right to take life. Yet Scripture tells us that only God, the author of all life, has the right to take life. God does this through old age, sickness, flood, drought, storms, and other acts of nature. But God does not delegate this power to humans. When we do kill on government orders, we may be called "virtuous." We may even get a medal for killing. But what does God think of it?

Before the nuclear age it was easier to delude ourselves into the belief that by killing those our government designates as "enemies" we defend our country. Now there is no defense. If we use our nuclear weapons, we die. No one wins a nuclear war. Those who survive the first few hours will envy the dead. Physicians, scientists, even most government and military officials tell us this. Is it not about time to revise our definition of patriotism to get love, and God, and all of God's children back into it?

"Patriotism" derives from the Latin word, *patria*, which means "fatherland." In the age of instant worldwide communication, supersonic jets, and bombs that can reach around the world in less than half an hour, can we not see that we are one human family, that our "land" is the round ball of Earth, that nationalism is a relic of the dead past?

*How then should we practice "patriotism" in the nuclear age? Freeze the arms race!* Work for worldwide disarmament! Refuse to be a part of the death machine in any way. Do not make the weapons of death or pay for them. Follow conscience, which tells us that all life is sacred, all people are God's children. Recognize that in every aspect of life, business, transportation, communications, or commerce, we are one international, interdependent world.

Our fatherland *(patria)* is this globe. We can travel it, enjoy it, live on it; or we can destroy it and die.

The twin technologies of missiles and nuclear bombs have given us that destructive power and have made nation-states obsolete. Nations can no longer defend themselves. Technology has destroyed them. Just as the long-range cannon ended the city-states, so has nuclear-missile technology ended the nation-state. Patriotism built on the nation-state ended with the inventions of missiles and nuclear bombs. We can understand this, even if we have no faith in God.

Once more the weapons of war have changed political structures. We refuse to recognize it, but there are signs that things are changing.

Almost a million young men have refused to register for war. Few people are enthusiastic about either side, as Britain and Argentina kill each other (over the Falkland Islands) before a watching world. In our international world, neither war nor registration for it makes much sense. Rather we are beginning to realize that they endanger us all.

*Chapter 5*

*The Sin of Hiroshima*

Today as we reflect on the forty-third anniversary of the bombing of Hiroshima, there is much to think about. We are forty-three years into the nuclear age. We can thank God that no nuclear bombs have been dropped during those forty-three years. We can pray and labor to see to it that no nuclear bombs be dropped during the next forty-three years.

As a help to accomplish that I suggest that we reflect on the following three points. First: The bombing of Hiroshima was no accident; second: If we use nuclear weapons in the future, it will be no accident; third: The only way we can be sure that we will not use nuclear weapons in the future is to change our attitudes towards each other.

## Hiroshima Was No Accident

The preparation for Hiroshima began with a letter from Albert Einstein asking President Roosevelt to take up the task of making a bomb through the release of energy from the atom. Later Einstein said, " If I had known that Hitler would never get the bomb, I would never have lifted a finger to get it." Roosevelt replied by starting the Manhattan Project that worked for two years in deepest secrecy and spent over two billion dollars. The genius Robert Oppenheimer was brought in to manage the project and begin the Los Alamos laboratories. Oppenheimer was able to organize the help of our best scientists. Our most talented physicists joined in the secret work.

The first testing of the bomb, called TRINITY, was done with the full knowledge that the chain reaction might ignite the hydrogen in the atmosphere and destroy the world. The risk was taken in secrecy without consulting the endangered world.

After the test, in July 1945, the US government knew it would work. Germany was already out of the war when we started planning to use it against Japanese cities. Thirty-eight scientists led by Einstein and Oppenheimer appealed to our government not to use it on cities. They suggested an offshore island of Japan or a drop in Tokyo Bay. But our government, intent on stopping the Soviet Union's march in eastern Europe and Manchuria, decided to drop it on a Japanese city as a warning to the Soviets that we were not afraid to use it on people.

The plane and the crew had been segregated from others and carefully prepared in great secrecy on Tinian Island. Five Japanese cities had been spared ordinary American bombing and reserved as possible targets for the atomic bomb. In early August we had full control of the air and could bomb at will. In the predawn darkness of August 6, 1945, Father George

Zabelka, a Catholic chaplain, prayed for God's blessing for the crew and for the success of their mission.

As they roared off into the dark sky, the crew knew that a pending request that the people of Hiroshima would receive a warning of disaster had been turned down. Approaching Hiroshima they heard the Hiroshima radio come back on the air at eight o'clock A.M. after the air-raid signal had been canceled, because the approach of one high-flying plane looked like it was on reconnaissance, not a bombing mission.

There were no clouds in the sky. Below them in the morning sunlight, a city of 250,000 people went to market and prepared for another day of work. Because the young men were away at war, the population was mostly women, children and old men.

The pilot and crew knew there was danger for themselves. Would the bomb destroy them, too? After releasing the bomb they would have only fifty-seven seconds to escape. Would the air pressure be so great that they would be killed?

The bomb bay doors were opened, the bombsight focused on the center of the city to do the maximum damage. The bomb was set to explode 1200 feet above the city. The last seconds were tense, silence broken by the command of the bombardier, "Bombs away!" A small bomb, two feet wide and ten feet long, floated down in the morning sunlight. Above it, the plane turned sharply to escape. Below it, people went to market.

At precisely 8:12 A.M. the bomb exploded 1200 feet above the earth. A Japanese mother standing at the back door of her home saw the flash of light as she watched her small child playing in the garden a few feet from her. She ran for her child. Too late. In blinding heat her house came crashing down upon her. Pinned beneath the wreckage she heard her child screaming a few feet beyond her reach.

Above her, the Enola Gay bounced and struggled to stay up as the air pressure from the bomb hit it. Surviving the blast, the pilot returned to fly over the city. "It looked like the bottom of a barrel of tar on fire," he said later.

What moments before had been a populated city beginning a new day was now a burning mass of rubble in which people lay buried or trapped or burning.

Eleven seconds after the blast leveled almost all the buildings, a fire ball of superstellar heat formed over the city, a million times hotter than the surface of the sun. Its heat scorched and set on fire everything combustible for a radius of two miles. Then it rose quickly to a height of 22,000 feet, sucking up behind it vaporized debris of human bodies and buildings and earth. Meeting the cold air of the stratosphere, the fireball flattened out into a mushroom cloud of radioactive dust that began to blanket the city and the countryside.

In the doomed city people on fire threw themselves into the river to die with thousands of their companions. Those pinned down in the rubble watched as the fires grew bigger and nearer. Unheeded cries for help pierced the air.

200,000 people died from the immediate effects of the blast, the firestorm and the fallout. Another 200,000 have died during the last forty-three years from radiation and the effects of the bomb.

**Future War Will Be No Accident**

Now, forty-three years later, you would think we would have repented for the sin of Hiroshima and turned away from it. Sad to say, we have never repented. As a result it will be no accident if we have a nuclear war. We still say the bombing was necessary to save American lives. Now we add to that lie, and more nuclear bombs are necessary to protect more American lives. We continue building bigger and better bombs, many of them thousands of times more powerful than the Hiroshima bomb. We have developed missiles to carry them around the world. From Washington to Moscow we need only twenty-four minutes to deliver a bomb.

We have bombs underwater, underground, in planes, bombs that hug the ground and bombs that ride the stratosphere. Not content with that, we are now planning to put bombs in space. We produce four of these bombs every day.

We say we are doing this to protect American lives, but what is the result? We are less secure today than ever in our history. Before the bomb exploded at Hiroshima we were the strongest nation on earth, protected by two oceans; the strongest Air Force, Navy, and Army in the world. Today we are only twenty-four minutes away from complete destruction, even extinction.

We have the equivalent of about one million Hiroshima bombs in our arsenals and we say we intend to use them. This is no secret and no accident. We want the Soviets to know that we are ready to use them. We all pay for them with our taxes, work for them in our factories, vote for them in our elections. Today we need to remember Hiroshima lest we *become* Hiroshima.

## Change of Attitude Needed

Our decision to drop the bomb on Hiroshima has brought us to our present state of vulnerability, and our non-repentance for Hiroshima has poisoned our moral life. The decision has led to what we have today. Our intent to use nuclear bombs on people is the taproot of violence in our society. Unless and until we repent, there is no hope of any broad-scale improvement in public morality. While we have held to this intent for the past forty-three years, we have seen abortions increase to half a million a year, the death penalty restored and death rows crowded. We have stirred up war in every corner of the globe, allied ourselves with tyrants, refused to support the suffering black people in South Africa, and watched our culture become saturated with drugs, sex, and violence.

How far removed is this from the change of heart that Hiroshima should have brought and can still bring? No one has explained the change needed better than Jesus of Nazareth. Whether we are Jews or Buddhists, Moslems or Christians,

Jesus' teaching of love for each other gives light and hope in a world filled with fear and darkness.

*Chapter 6*

## Is There Something I Am Doing That Supports Nuclear War?

"The nuclear arms race can sum up in a few final moments the violence of thousands of years...a demonic reversal of the Creator's power of giving life. I am convinced that a way out of this deepening crisis can be discovered by our deepening in faith and prayer so that we learn not to rely on missiles for our security, but on the loving care of the One who gives and sustains life. We need to read the Gospel again with open hearts and learn what it is to have faith." So says Archbishop Raymond Hunthausen of Seattle.

How does this lead him to advocate war-tax resistance? If our security is in a "loving, caring God," he says, then we must dismantle our weapons of nuclear terror.

How do we accomplish this? Should we go with hammers into the General Electric nuclear weapons plant in Norristown, Pennsylvania, as the Plowshares Eight did? That is a good and dramatic way. It requires the generous willingness to accept a prison sentence. Refusal to pay taxes for the portable cremation furnaces carried by our nuclear missiles is another way suggested by the archbishop. I suggest this also.

When people ask me, "What can I do to prevent nuclear war?" I try to get them to turn the question around and ask themselves, "Is there something I am doing that supports nuclear war? Can I begin with stopping that support?"

The most obvious way we support the coming of nuclear war is by paying taxes that go to the military. About $25 billion will be spent this year on nuclear weapons. Our taxes fund them. Our government plans to use them. Are we not responsible for what our government does in our name and with our money?

Suppose you told me you needed money for a gun to kill your enemy. Suppose I give you the money and you do the killing. Am I not responsible for the murder with you? Any court would say yes.

Likewise, if I give my government money to use in my behalf to develop and use nuclear weapons, am I not responsible? "But we don't want to go to jail," you say. Do you know that no one in the United States has ever gone to jail for refusing to pay war taxes when the refusal was clearly stated on grounds of conscience? The government is very worried about this issue. People don't want such large chunks taken out of their paycheck, especially for something they don't believe in. Give people the example of a good moral person in prison for refusing to pay a percentage of his or her taxes, and many might decide to refuse. Tens of thousands of Americans, like Dorothy Day and Ammon Hennacy of the Catholic Worker, have refused to pay war taxes. None of these has gone to jail.

If the government agents can find that you've falsified your income tax, that is another matter. They will jail you for that, but not for conscientious tax resistance. So even though what Archbishop Hunthausen recommends seems heroic, it really isn't. It is a big step. It makes prison a legal possibility, but very improbable. Nuclear war, turning our cities into radioactive ash heaps, is much more probable. If even ten percent of us refused to pay war taxes, we might stop nuclear war. The government would have to cut ten percent of war spending, and the political effect would be immense.

Archbishop Hunthausen asks us to reflect on the words of Christ: "The word of God is like a seed that a farmer sowed in a field." Our hearts and minds are the field in which the word of God grows. The word of God is "Love! Love your enemies! Forgive!" If we let these words as seeds grow in our hearts, we may be able to begin to trust God's way of love and reject the military way. With God's word growing inside us, we may turn communist enemies into friends and bring about the hope for peace. Unless our hope is in God, where is it? In ourselves? In our nuclear weapons? Even our generals see no hope of peace in more and more weapons. Can we in good conscience continue to pay war taxes?

*Chapter 7*

*Should We Abandon Deterrence?*

"Deterrence has worked for over forty years. What alternative do you offer if we give it up?" That is an argument often used, but it presumes much that is not true. Is it true, for instance, that any major power has been stopped from anything it would otherwise have done because of the nuclear threat? The Cuban missile crisis, for example, was resolved by other means than deterrence.

Two fallacies presumed true by the question, are: 1) Deterrence is a response to, rather than a cause of, our hostile world climate; and 2) we have no other choice, even if we wanted to use one. Our acceptance of these similar fallacies blocks us from a serious look at what deterrence is and what it does.

After forty years of deterrence, we are closer to nuclear war than we were when it started, and we are rushing towards it at a faster rate than before. Deterrence has cost the world so much in money that two-thirds of the world is undernourished and half of the world is hungry, while the industrial nations annually spend 600 billion dollars on arms, much of it for deterrence.

This hunger breeds hatred and a cry for justice that must be heard, or the hungry will not remain peaceful. Thus, from an economic point of view, deterrence works against the peace it claims to promote.

Morally, deterrence includes within itself the taproot of the violence in our society, our intent to use nuclear weapons on people. This has corrupted the fiber of our moral life to such an extent that, in the US alone, we have one and a quarter million abortions each year; violence and killing are staple entertainment on our television screens; our prison population has doubled, and our military budget has more than tripled. All of this is linked to our acceptance of deterrence which has at its heart our intent to use nuclear bombs on people.

When I said this to a US colonel, he replied, "But we aren't using them. We haven't done anything wrong yet."

"You told me you were a Catholic," I said. "Then you should know that what it is wrong to do, it is wrong to intend to do."

His response was, "Well, you can't win every ball game," and he changed the subject.

The fallacy that there is no other alternative seems to say that it is morally right to have deterrence, since you can't do anything else. Deterrence thus not only becomes an accepted military strategy but also seemingly morally acceptable. Its acceptance redefines peace as "deferred war." This cuts peace off from its Biblical roots and makes a mockery of the Gospel call to reconciliation.

If people of faith accept the "only option" myth, they either put their faith aside, or refuse to apply it to the issue of nuclear war: an issue of survival that deeply affects our economy, our moral life, and the continued existence of humankind.

There are in fact multiple options. We could begin to take seriously the Gospel command, "Love one another." We could negotiate mutual reductions. We could take unilateral initiatives. (George Kennan suggests we could cut our stockpile in half without any danger to our national security.) We could unilaterally put aside all our nuclear weapons; this is less dangerous than continuing to build more. We could freeze building, deploying new weapons on our side alone or on both sides together. (The Soviet Union has stated it is willing to do this; so has the US House of Representatives.) We could lay the matter before the United Nations to decide.

We might not like any of these options; but they are options, and they all are better than the nuclear extinction that faces us if we continue the policy of deterrence that fuels the nuclear-arms race.

## Chapter 8

## Nuclear Crime and Punishment

The murderer in Dostoyevsky's *Crime and Punishment* argues that he should have known what would happen when he took up the axe. (Similarly, today, we should know what will happen now that we have taken up nuclear weapons.)

> " 'Who is that man who sprang out of the earth?' " [asks Dostoyevsky's murderer when someone accused him of murder.] " 'Where was he? What did he see? He has seen it all. That is clear. Where was he then and from where did he see it? Why has he only now sprung out of the earth and how could he see it? Is it possible?—An infinitesimal line, and you can build it into a

pyramid of evidence. A fly flew by and saw it. Is it possible?' He felt with sudden loathing how weak, how physically weak, he had become. 'I ought to have known it,' he thought, with a bitter smile. 'How dared I, knowing myself, knowing how I should be, take up an axe and shed blood! I ought to have known beforehand.... Ah, but I did know,' he whispered in despair."

If the nuclear bombs start falling on us, we may not have time for all the ruminations that went on in the mind of Dostoyevsky's murderer. But we will have time for the last part of it: *"I did know."* Even President Reagan, who is planning to build more than 17,000 nuclear weapons and to move them closer together in Europe, knows. He has said on several occasions: "No one wins a nuclear war. It must never be fought."

We could, if we wanted to, answer the earlier questions of the murderer. We could do so if we could overcome the psychic numbness in which we hide from our danger. If we are not killed in seconds by the blast, the firestorm, or the electromagnetic pulse, we may have time to ask, "Is there no protection from the bombs? Did no one know that our bombs could not save us? Is it only now we find out? Now, that it's too late?"

"How is it possible that this could happen to us?" we may end up asking. "Did we not spend billions of dollars on defense? Why is it only now we realize the danger?" We will feel a sudden loathing of ourselves. "How weak, how vulnerable we have become," we will say. "We ought to have known it," we will think with bitterness. "We could have negotiated if we had truly wanted to. How dared we, knowing the danger, the violence involved, build more bombs and prepare for nuclear war? We ought to have known that every weapon made is finally used!"

"Ah, but we did know," we will say in despair. "We hid the danger from ourselves," like a friend who laughed when I told him we might have a nuclear war before he got his building program done in 1987. "You have been saying that for years," he replied, still laughing. "I hope you can laugh in 1987," I thought as he continued laughing.

I can't believe he doesn't think about it. He is not in exactly the same position as Dostoyevsky's murderer. He is not alone preparing for nuclear murder. We are all part of it, inasmuch as we are part of the country that is preparing for nuclear war. We pay taxes that support it. We know that preparations are going on. We have at least some resources at our command, and we don't use them to stop it.

My friend is kind, but he has smothered his conscience, as Dostoyevsky's murderer did. "If I kill the old woman, I will rid the world of a witch who preys on the poor. A hundred thousand good deeds could be done with that old woman's money.... Dozens of families saved from destitution, from ruin, from vice.... Kill her; take her money, and with the help of the money, devote oneself to the service of humanity.... Would not one tiny crime be wiped out by thousands of good deeds?" asks the murderer.

We say, "We will have peace by preparing for nuclear war, by building more bombs. Russia will be scared.

"Russia will become so poor she can't keep up with us."

"We will have more bombs than Russia. We will save the world by threatening to destroy it!"

Dostoyevsky's murderer did not want to kill anyone. He just wanted to pay the rent and to settle his debts. So he took an axe and hid himself in the room where the old woman lived. As she closed the door behind her, he sank the axe into her skull.

We do not want to kill anyone, or so we may think. We just want to stop the Russians. We just want to stop Russia, or anybody else, from stopping us. So we build more and more nuclear weapons and prepare to use them.

Before the violence, the firestorms, and the radiation finally kill and destroy us, we will have time to realize with the murderer that we knew. We really knew.

# Part IV:

# Conscience, Civil Responsibility, Resistance

*The hottest places in hell are reserved for those who in a moment of moral crisis seek to maintain their neutrality.*

Dante

*Our problems stem from our acceptance of this filthy rotten system.*

Dorothy Day

*Chapter 1*

*The Draft*

One point at which the theory of peace enters into the practical, political life of today is in the refusal to go to war because of conscience. A sign of the change is Vatican II's statement: "It seems right that laws make humane provisions for the case of those who for reasons of conscience refuse to bear arms."

In the United States this was followed by the American Bishops' 1968 declaration and their call for the Selective Service System to open itself to the conscience of those who object to particular wars. This marks the first time that the Catholic Church has gone on record officially in favor of conscientious objection to war, either on the international level or on the US national scene. For that reason, it is worth taking a closer look at the history of the Selective Service System in the USA. A close look at the draft shows that it is both unconstitutional and immoral.

General Hershey was the head of the Selective Service during the Vietnam War, and he looked on the System as being as American as apple pie. During the war, he said on television that the registrant for Selective Service had no rights except the right to be conscripted.

I was present at a group interview with General Hershey where a young man asked whether it was true that the first peacetime conscription law passed in the United States was in 1948. He and his assistant, Colonel Omer, replied by talking about conscription in the colonial army, citing vague stories of two hundred years ago. These two men refused to admit even under repeated and earnest questioning that the first peacetime conscription truly was in 1948.

But the history of the US shows that we came as immigrants escaping the wars of Europe. When we wrote our Constitution, we had a strong determination that we could not accept the quartering of armies among our people or the conscription laws from which we had escaped. The Constitution says nothing that can justify conscription. It is doubtful, from the Constitution, whether the federal government has the right to raise an army. This was the view expressed in all the discussions of Congress from 1790, when George Washington first suggested conscription, until the Civil War. A typical example of the expressions of senators and congressmen was given by Congressman Daniel Webster:

> Where is it written in the Constitution, in what article or section is it contained that you may take children from their parents and parents from their children, and compel them to fight the battle of any war in which the folly or wickedness of the government may engage itself...?
>
> Who will show me any Constitutional injunction which makes it the duty of the American people to surrender everything

valuable in life, and even life itself, whenever the purposes of an ambitious and mischievous government may require it...?

A free government with an uncontrolled power of military conscription is the most ridiculous and abominable contradiction and nonsense that ever entered into the head of man.

Congress said "no" to the requests for a conscription law up to the time of the Civil War, when the first limited draft was adopted by the federal government. It was promptly declared unconstitutional by the Supreme Court of Pennsylvania. This decision was overturned, and the right to conscript during war has been upheld by the Supreme Court in many cases. After 1948 the draft was used during peacetime.

During both World Wars, the military made efforts to obtain universal military conscription, which would consolidate the power they gained during war. During World War I, conscription met with significant congressional opposition. In the April 1917 debate, Rep. George Huddleston from Alabama said, "Conscription is state slavery. It is involuntary servitude, not for crime."

Congressman Carl Hayden from Arizona said, "Much as I like to disbelieve it, yet I am convinced that most of the propaganda in favor of selective service is founded not so much upon a desire to win the war as it is to accustom the people to this method of raising armies and thereby to establish it as a permanent system in this country."

A Selective Service Law was adopted and signed by Woodrow Wilson on May 18, 1917. This was a wartime law authorizing the draft of all male citizens between their twenty-first and thirty-first birthdays. Ministers, divinity students, and certain public officials were exempted.

During the war, in 1918, the military tried to impose universal military training that would not be subject to periodic congressional review. This failed when the issue was brought to a vote in the Senate in 1918. Another effort made after the war was again opposed, and a system of volunteer recruitment was adopted with the National Defense Act of 1920. General

Douglas MacArthur endorsed this act and said, "Tradition and public sentiment have always precluded conscription as the basis of a peacetime defense policy."

As the threat of World War II faced America, the military pushed for selective service legislation in September of 1940. Opposition was very strong in Congress. Representative Jerry Voorhis of California said:

> I believe that what we are asked to vote on in this bill...is the adoption of compulsory selective military service and training as a permanent policy for the United States of America and to do it under the impulsion of an "emergency." It is going to be difficult ever to repeal such a measure once you get it established, for you will have made your whole military establishment one of the greatest economic factors in your whole country. You will have vested the greatest power in the Executive and the Army that the Congress has ever granted in all American history.

Senator James Frazier of Tennessee argued, "pass this [conscription bill] and we will have forged the first link in the chain which will drag down America to the same militaristic level of Communistic Russia, Fascist Italy and Nazi Germany."

The 1940 Act was adopted for one year only. It was the first peacetime conscription for the United States. It was expanded in 1941 by a one-vote margin in the US House of Representatives: 203 to 202.

During 1944 the military again maneuvered to impose universal military training as a permanent pattern on American society. The military saw their influence lessening and tried to keep the draft. But Selective Service legislation was not renewed immediately after World War II. A strong coalition of peace and libertarian groups helped defeat it, and the draft law expired on March 31, 1947. After the Czechoslovakian coup, a crisis thought by some to have been exaggerated by the army into a false war scare, conscription was reinstated upon appeal of President Truman in 1948. The new draft law was amended in 1967 and 1969.

In 1975 the draft stopped, largely because of dissatisfaction with the Vietnam War. Local draft boards were disbanded, but the Selective Service System remained. To reinstate the draft the president had to go to Congress to get authorization for conscription.

In all the debates on peacetime conscription, two main arguments were used against it: the undemocratic and compulsory nature of a system which amounted to servitude, and the power it gave to the president to engage in overseas military adventures without consulting Congress. Without conscription already in force, it would have been impossible for President Johnson to build up the Vietnam War forces to 50,000 men. He would have had to go to Congress for approval of the draft before he acted.

During the Vietnam War General Hershey administered the draft in a high-handed manner. According to the law he was limited to direction through memorandum to local boards and letters to the legislative representatives or state directors; although none of the directives had the force of law, they were followed by most of the local boards. Since they were not the law, there was no requirement for any record of them. Until 1969 no copy could be obtained. The vagueness and confusion that resulted in many cases made it extremely difficult for young men who sought judicial remedy from the injustices that arose from the boards' own actions and interpretations.

For instance, if a registrant felt unjustly classified—perhaps denied conscientious-objector status—he had to commit a felony by refusing induction before he could bring a case to court.

In other situations where injustice is threatened or damage is imminent, an injunction can be sought to block that damage. If I work in a federal agency, and my agency has refused to allow me to make a speech to a certain group, I may go to the courts and obtain an injunction restraining the head of my agency from blocking my speech. With the Selective Service

Board I must violate the orders and get arrested before I can get the courts to adjudge the merits of my case.

Until the Seeger decision of the Supreme Court in 1965, applicants for conscientious-objector status had a special advantage if they belonged to a "peace church" like the Society of Friends. The Seeger decision ruled out a "belief in a Supreme Being" and left only the requirement of "religious training and belief." The Welsh decision of June 15, 1970, gave a broad meaning to the word *religious*. "Religious" was interpreted to mean "deeply and sincerely held beliefs which are purely ethical or moral in source and content." Because his beliefs function as a religion in his life, an individual is as much entitled to "religious conscientious-objector status" as is someone who derives his conscientious opposition to war from "traditional religious convictions."

The Welsh decision was essentially a reinstatement of the Seeger decision. The local boards responded to the changes so slowly that it was 1970 before items reflecting it appeared on the forms to be filled out by applicants for conscientious-objector status. Local boards still retained discretionary power to decide each case. There were no national standards whose proven fulfillment entitled any citizen to exemption. The standards dealt merely with eligibility to apply for exemption: they gave no right to exemption.

Another provision of doubtful constitutional validity was that the law allowed a local board to deny the registrant presence of counsel or of a witness when he made his personal appearance. This procedure was a denial of due process in that it involved a juridical judgment that might mean life or death for the registrant.

There was no draft between 1975 and 1980, but the Selective Service System was still there to reinstate it. In 1980 President Carter asked for compulsory registration even though there was no need for it. By executive order he could have reinstated registration because the Selective Service law was still the law of the land. He needed only to go to Congress to begin the actual draft.

He took this step because he was searching for some example of military muscle-flexing in an election year. It was a response to Russian military adventure in Afghanistan. His opponent said he was opposed to registration; but after he won the election, Reagan kept the process in force. Now the Justice Department has slowly started prosecuting non-registrants.

The Selective Service System is now preparing a draft that will make it much more difficult to be a conscientious objector. Formerly the C.O. applied for C.O. status when he registered. This will no longer be allowed. When the draft is set in motion, those to be drafted will be picked by lottery. The potential draftee will be sent a letter notifying him that he must report to the military in ten days from the date the letter is mailed. Within those ten days he must apply for and get any desired deferment or conscientious-objector status. Delay in receiving the mail will shorten the opportunity to act.

Because of this short period of time, young people hoping to have conscientious-objector status are being advised to make a public record of their intent by a letter recorded with their church or some support organization. They are also advised to write up their reasons for seeking conscientious objection so they will be ready when the time comes. Pax Christi, USA, 6000 N. Mango Street, Chicago, Illinois, is one of the recording agencies.

Selective Service is also trying to make alternative service, the usual requirement for C.O.'s, more difficult. It will be administered by the military. Alternative service persons will be required to work at jobs designated by the Selective Service, not by local agencies working in cooperation with Selective Service, for example, peace churches. Alternative service people may even be required to do war-support work.

Peace groups are strongly opposed to these plans. The National Interreligious Service Board for Conscientious Objectors has made this plain to the head of Selective Service.

By registering, a young man signals to our government and to the rest of the world that he is ready to be part of a nuclear war whenever the government decides on it. In registering, the registrant says, "Here is my name and number. Call me if you want some killing done, even in this nuclear age."

Refusal to register gives the opposite signal. "If you are insane enough to start a nuclear war, or a conventional war that might turn nuclear, count me out. I won't help."

The million young men who have already said "No" are doing more for world peace than those who register. They are making our government and other governments realize that preparations for nuclear war do not have the support of the people.

Our government is so impressed by the large numbers refusing to register that it has been very slow to begin prosecutions. The government fears that prosecutions would result in an even larger number refusing to register. Prosecution makes registration a much greater subject for debate and concern. It calls attention to former President Reagan's failure to keep his campaign promise of no draft. It may further lessen the popularity of an administration that is weighed down with the burden of trying to cope with the deficits and mismanagement of the Reagan era.

In the past, during the Vietnam War, operation of the Selective Service System was termed unfair by many political leaders. Local draft boards were administered by white males who averaged about fifty-eight years in age, former members of the American Legion, and largely opposed to the idea of conscientious objection.

In the past the draft divided the country, exploiting the poor and diverting the talents of all young men from constructing an alternative future that might be moral and sane. The Vietnam War forced an estimated 85,000 young men into political exile and imprisonment, or desertion. Two-hundred thousand violations of the Selective Service Law were reported to the Justice Department, unknown tens of thousands did not register; 8,000 were convicted of violations.

A draft destroys our values because it departs from the American tradition which has always regarded conscription as alien to the American way of life; it undermines the ideal of voluntary service given to one's community and nation; it violates conscience. The recent history of having a draft causes us to forget that we had only eleven years of draft, during the time from the Civil War and the two World Wars. We forget that many immigrants came here to avoid the demands of the standing armies of Europe. For those who were born since 1945, the age of nuclear weapons, and the age of the peacetime draft that started in 1948, there's nothing to forget. This is a big change in America, a change that was pictured as the destruction of the Republic in the days when the draft was being argued.

The draft militarized our nation. It has added greatly to the influence of the military establishment in our country by giving it power to control involuntary servitude. Under the pretense of producing a citizen army, it simply gives more status to our professional army. Through military indoctrination and brainwashing and training in the use of weapons, conscription contributes substantially to the spread of violence in the US today and in the future.

Should the draft be reinstated, it will weaken democratic control over foreign policy and provide manpower for military intervention overseas without approval by Congress and the people.

Our draft laws have never allowed sufficient space for the intensely important workings of young people's consciences. It requires young men to go to kill in wars they do not believe in or to go to prison. There is no right to claim conscientious-objector status; there has only been a right to make an appeal. Local boards were allowed broad discretionary powers on granting C.O. status that weren't guided by national standards. Appeals were denied in the Vietnam War to those opposed only to a particular war and not to all wars. Young men who were opposed to nuclear war were treated the same way. Such practices were immoral because they violated conscience. Because the draft laws have been immoral, many argue that it is immoral to register under such a law.

Vatican II said that no one is free to evade his personal responsibilities by allowing the government to make his moral decisions. This statement supports those who, on moral grounds, oppose the Selective Service System.

The Vatican II statement has been supported by many in the Roman Catholic Church, and among other religious leaders, faiths, believers, and humanists. It has pointed the direction for many who are trying to build, in today's difficult nuclear world, a sane, moral society based on the vision of God's kingdom on earth. I invite others to join in building this vision.

*Chapter 2*

*Signing Your Life Away*

Registering for the draft may seem harmless enough. It appears to be another government form to fill out with little meaning beyond signatures and statistics on a piece of paper. The draft itself seems unlikely and unreal. Not really anything to worry about; and possibly much to worry about if you don't follow the law.

But consider. A draft could be voted by Congress at any time, should the mood of war take over the country. For instance, suppose the Russians had decided to resist our invasion of Grenada. Such an event might have brought about a mood of war that reinstituted the draft. The registrant would then have been required to report to the military within ten days. All other plans of career, family, vacation, personal development would have to be put aside to satisfy whatever the military dictates.

What would be involved in being in today's military? It sounds like a good deal for some. Those at college under ROTC get everything paid for plus a living and spending allowance. Those in military medical school get an officer's pay, while all their expensive medical-school bills are paid for. Those at West Point have no college expenses and an income of $500 a month. But what happens when an order comes?

There is no choice—you must obey it. You are part of a huge machine where everybody obeys orders. All those you associate with every day will be in the same situation. You will all have to obey orders, no matter what they are.

Some of your fellow workers can expect the order to kill, to kill everybody and everything; and as with a boomerang, the effect of modern nuclear weapons will be to kill those who fire them.

Once in the military, how swiftly your life will change!

You may be in a different country, performing missions that are the choice of the military. You may see and hear first hand what killing in war is really like. Your individuality will be submerged as you conform to the role of becoming an efficient military robot. If you decide you don't like the situation, you will have a very difficult time getting out of it.

How beneficial for you, then, to take time now to decide whether or not you wish to sign your life into the control of the military. It is your life, the one that you are responsible for to God. You may not want to say goodbye to all your life has been and might become.

But what about patriotism? Isn't it unpatriotic to refuse to serve your country even in the military if that is what is asked? Like many US citizens, you may appreciate much about this country despite its faults. You appreciate freedom, and the struggles for justice that have gone on here. You love the rich land with bountiful harvests, vigorous people, diversity and opportunity. You love the beauty of the vast country, and the ingenuity that has made so much available to so many with communication, transportation, and economic opportunity. You want to share responsibility for this marvelous land, and you wonder if the opportunities that the military provide for service may be the best place to fulfill your obligations.

The famous American writer, Mark Twain, had the same love for our country, but felt that if one has a difference with what a part of the government does or wants done, in no way does that person express lack of patriotism when he chooses to differ with actions of the government. That person is a thinking, spiritual being who is using his or her own mind and conscience, and has no need to be an unquestioning pawn to another group of people. As Twain noted:

> "Our country, right or wrong!" An empty phrase, a silly phrase.... Have you not perceived that the phrase is an insult to the nation?
> 
> For in a republic, who *is* the government for the moment in the saddle? Why, the government is merely a servant.... Its function is to obey orders, not originate them. Who then, is "the country"? Is it the newspaper? Is it the pulpit? ...Why, these are mere parts of the country, not the whole of it; they have not the command, they have only their little share in the command. They are but one in the thousand; it is in the thousand that the command is lodged; *they* must determine what is right and what is wrong, and which course is patriotic and which isn't.... Each must decide what is right and what is wrong and which course is patriotic and which isn't. You cannot shirk this and be a man. To decide it is against your convictions is to be an unqualified and inexcusable traitor, both to yourself, and to your country, let men label you as they may. If you alone of all the nation shall decide one way, and that way be the right way according to your convictions of right, you have done your duty by yourself and for your country—hold your head up! You have nothing to be ashamed of.
>
> *(from "A Glance At History" by Mark Twain)*

Mark Twain thought of each one of us as a "country" ruling himself or herself as a large body of land and people. Being patriotic to him meant supporting our family, our neighbors, ourselves and our land. *Patria* is Latin for fatherland.

What does patriotism mean in the nuclear age? Has it changed its meaning in the last forty-five years? In a nuclear age, is it patriotic to spread the probability of nuclear war by signaling willingness to be a part of a military institution that endorses and perpetuates the idea of nuclear war? It is an institution that yearly asks for more money to create the weapons of nuclear destruction and devises new methods to make these weapons arrive more quickly and accurately at their targeted destinations. Is this really what you want your life to be part of? When you consider before yourself and your God what you have done with your life, do you want this to be your answer: "I have been a small part of a very large death machine"?

To do anything that contributes to making and reducing the US to a radioactive ash heap can hardly be called patriotic. If you consider the arms race and find that it moves us in that direction, then it is not patriotic.

What is true patriotism in this situation? Perhaps in a nuclear age it has become taking a conscientious stance against using nuclear war as a means of resolving conflict. Since we saw in World War II that there is no major dividing line between the use of nuclear weapons in the case of an all-out war, it is necessary to consider whether this shouldn't include all wars.

Perhaps we are at a time when the honors should go to those who restrain themselves from involvement in such madness, to the conscientious objectors, who realize that for reasons of conscience and a belief in God, they cannot participate in such a system and uphold institutions which unquestioningly crave such tools of destruction.

For it is because of love of God and of country that these conscientious objectors cannot support what they realize is not good for the moral health of the country, nor for the physical well-being of the land and the people. I think these are the people who are displaying responsible citizenship.

There are many ways to serve country that have nothing to do with serving in the military, ways that preserve important beliefs in the value of all human life. Our cities are full of poverty, sickness, hunger, illiteracy, and helplessness.

As we look at our beautiful land, we see that we have strayed far from being good stewards of God's creation. We pollute the air and streams, slaughter wildlife, and create noisome dumps for the waste products of our overconsumption. We are all a part of a horrible plan, the determination to use nuclear weapons in order to "deter" enemy attack. Nuclear war would bring a halt to the four and a half billion years of evolution that are the miraculous result of God's plan of evolution.

In this situation America needs patriots, patriots with a new vision that fits the needs of a country and a planet that are so threatened. America needs young people who will challenge these desperate situations, and bring about the change that will bring a new direction to foreign policy abroad and a new direction to social policy at home. It is important that the young care when a nuclear facility is built near their families and homes, that they try to stop factories from polluting our waters and other valuable resources. America needs new patriots who will lobby and labor to channel our monies to better health care, nutritious food for everyone, good education, a sound roof over everyone's head, and jobs for all who need them. Such new patriots will provide *real* service to our country.

When we consider these vital human needs in our country, then patriotism judged only on the basis of whether one will cooperate with the military and go along with commands for killing on orders is an old and somewhat warped idea. To register with an institution capable of, and seemingly committed to, a program that ensures willingness for mass killing, may in fact be the most unpatriotic thing a person can do today.

Remember that "country" cannot ever define whether you are being patriotic or not. As Mark Twain so eloquently said,

"Each must for himself and by himself decide what is right and what is wrong, and which course is patriotic and which isn't.... If you alone of all the nation shall decide one way, and that way be the right way according to your convictions of right, you have done your duty by yourself and for your country—hold up your head! You have nothing to be ashamed of."

In denying compliance with a misguided government, the non-registrant is in good company. In the 1940s a young Catholic farmer in Austria refused, for reasons of conscience, to be part of Hitler's gang of murderers. His name was Franz Jaegerstaetter and he lived in the small village of St. Radegunde. He was a devout Catholic who served as sacristan in the town church. He was impressed that the priest did more than talk about his anti-Nazi beliefs, and refused to give Holy Communion to members of the Nazi party.

When the draft came to Austria, Franz refused to register for military service. The German officers accused him of being afraid, and wondered who he was afraid of.

Franz answered, "The Judgment of God." He explained that we must carry our cross and that we will be judged by God for all our actions: "We cannot turn the responsibility of our actions over to others."

The officers were impressed by his convictions and wanted to help him. "We can get you in the Medical Corps, where you won't have to kill," they said. But Franz remained committed to his conscience. "I cannot in any way support Hitler's war, not even in the Medical Corps."

His case was brought to trial. He was asked, "Do you know of any bishop who has called on Catholics to refuse military service? Do you know that there are many Catholics, including priests, in the army? Are you better than they?"

Franz replied, "I don't reproach them. Perhaps they have not been given the grace. I follow my conscience."

Franz was put in prison. His wife pleaded with him to relent. "Franz, they will kill you!"

He was steadfast: "Fear not those who can kill the body. Rather, fear him who can cast both body and soul into hell. I cannot swear allegiance to a government engaged in an unjust war. Both the bishop and the priests have told me, 'No one sins when he follows his conscience.'"

Franz' refusal brought a sentence of death. He was beheaded in Tekel Prison in Berlin, August 6, 1943. As he was laid face down on the platform of the guillotine with his hands cuffed behind his back, he prayed the psalm, "Though I walk through the valley of the shadow of death, You are with me."

Franz Jaegerstaetter did not die forgotten. His story was told to the 2500 bishops who gathered at Vatican Council II. It was an important influence in their decision to declare that "all governments should make provision in law for those whose conscience will not permit them to bear arms."

Hitler seems such an aberration, such a madman, that we may think that this example does not apply to today's world. The gas ovens at Auschwitz and Dachau were bad, but is the nuclear inferno that will be created if one Trident submarine releases its weapons any better? What is so much better about our nuclear death machine than the German torture chambers? If released, our nuclear arsenal will create conditions that will turn the entire northern hemisphere of this planet into a type of torture chamber.

We cannot even *fathom* the point in history that we now face. Humanity may cease to exist. We may self-inflict the extinction of the human race as well as that of all other living creatures—and yet we allow our country to continue on course.

Is the situation bad enough for us to consider breaking the *law*?

Consider what the law allows. All of the nuclear buildup, the financing, building, testing, and deployment is perfectly legal. What about using the weapons? Also, perfectly legal.

To refuse to go along with this, we break the law of the government. But what is the government's relation to our divine right to make this crucial decision on our own? The military has set itself up as a dictating god, commanding us to do as it sees fit, regardless of the sanctity of our own consciences and the words of the living God.

As Christians we should, if necessary, be solitary witnesses, refusing to let a military god control our lives and change our morals. Jesus, the Prince of Peace, calls us to embrace His way of peace and to follow His solitary witness.

What did Jesus Christ ask of His followers? Jesus' foremost message was love. One cannot deny this and remain His follower. This means love for one's neighbor should be as strong as love and thoughtfulness for oneself. This love should radiate out and permeate the whole society in which the Christian lives.

Jesus gave a formula for expressing this love: Forgive one another as He forgave us, feed the hungry, clothe the naked, give drink to the thirsty, visit the imprisoned, care for the sick, and give aid to those who ask.

Jesus wanted His disciples to be lights to the world, vessels holding the uniqueness of God's unending love. Jesus wanted His disciples to show perfect love—sacrificial and selfless love. He wanted them to do good to everyone, even to those who hated them. When people cursed them, He wanted them to return a blessing. Jesus wanted His disciples to love their enemies, proving they were children of God by revealing God's love.

*Chapter 3*

*Only Doing My Job*

General Turnage, the former head of Selective Service, met with me and some peace church representatives recently. He said he wanted to open a dialogue with us and that he wanted to be fair in administering the program for conscientious objectors.

I told him that I was grateful that he planned to be fair, but I told him that, in this nuclear age, he was ordering young men to register for probable nuclear war. I told him that Vatican II forbids Catholics to be a part of nuclear war or to prepare for it.

"I and other Catholic priests and bishops may advise young men not to register," I said, "because it is contrary to conscience to be part of a nuclear war no one can win. Nor is it right to register for any war that may become nuclear. There is no way one could obey the Gospel command, 'Love your enemy,' by using nuclear weapons on them, or by intending to use nuclear weapons. Nor could the Gospel command 'Love your enemies' be obeyed by killing one's enemies in any war less than nuclear."

I think I was respectful to General Turnage. I told him, "You have a more difficult job than any of your predecessors. You are the first director of the Selective Service asked to recruit for a nuclear army." Afterwards one of our group thanked me for my candid presentation.

The general answered that he disagreed with me, and that he was only doing his job. I did not press him or ask: "With what do you disagree? Do you think nuclear war is winnable? Do you think we can love people by killing them?" I doubt he disagreed on those points. He just put them aside under the heading, "I have a job to do."

He told us how Ed Meese, then President Reagan's White House assistant, had phoned him and asked him to take the job. He told us he had freely consented to take it. It occurred to me that he could just as freely have phoned Ed Meese and said, "I resign." He wasn't forced to take the job.

According to the Nuremberg principles, "Each person is responsible for his or her crimes even if they are done 'under orders.' " He should resign if he saw that he was doing wrong. We put Germans to death for disobeying that principle. We accepted the Nuremberg principles as the law of the United States when the Senate ratified the Treaty of London. General Turnage could honestly say, "American law forbids me from being a part of organizing for nuclear war. I must resign as head of the Selective Service because I believe nuclear war is wrong."

He told us he was a Lutheran, so he also could have appealed to his obedience to the Gospel command to "Love your enemy." Instead, he said, "I'm only doing my job."

His argument is as old as that of the Roman soldiers who put Jesus to death. They were "only doing their job." Similarly, the soldiers under Hitler's regime who shot US soldiers were only doing their job.

I don't doubt his good conscience. He told us that he had spent twenty-nine years in the military. He cited all kinds of bad examples in the history of Christian wars and Christians participating in wars. At one point he said, "Suppose the country we were fighting was pagan and we were defending Christians, what would God think of that?" I told him that I believed that God would think we were killing God's children. Apparently the general did not think that pagans are God's children.

It is clear that a general with a conscience which allows him to organize killing for a nuclear war is contributing to the likelihood of that war. That should illuminate the point of the young person who refuses to register, saying, "My conscience will not permit me to register for a nuclear war." Such a choice by a young person helps make nuclear war less probable. It follows that if enough of us, and every one of us who has a conscience, say "No," and support all who say "No," we will be taking an important step away from nuclear catastrophe.

*Chapter 4*

*Responsible Citizenship
and Nuclear Registration*

"Responsible citizenship requires that we register for war. Why object to registration when there is no draft?" That's what many say. They leave out of their vision the reality of our nuclear age. The release of energy from the atom has changed everything about our lives except our way of thinking. Thus we drift towards unspeakable disaster. They don't seem to realize this. The old way of thinking was, "Registration and draft add to our military security." *Nuclear* registration has changed that. It adds nothing to our security. We were never less secure than we are today. Registration may in fact be increasing the danger of nuclear destruction. In view of this, is it "responsible citizenship" to register in the nuclear age? This is the question.

One hour of nuclear war will reduce the United States to a radioactive ash heap. Military men, scientists, and medical doctors all give evidence to support this. Is it "patriotic" or "responsible" to spread the probability of this happening by signaling my "willingness to be a part of it." That is what registration does!

What about the morality of registration? According to the Second Vatican Council, it is forbidden to take part in a nuclear war. Is not registration for such a war being a part of it?

It may be the *only* part we can play. Delivery time for a nuclear weapon between Moscow and Washington is twenty-four minutes. The weapons have to travel at 17,000 miles per hour to stay up. We are naked to Soviet attack. We have no defense. A seven billion-dollar missile defense system (antiballistic-missile system) was decommissioned one day after it was completed because we knew it wouldn't work.

Nor is there any foreseeable defense. Nuclear technology has made national states no longer able to defend themselves. The speed and destructive capacity, the total penetrability of nuclear missiles have changed the very nature of war. National defense is now a massive lie. We have no defense.

If the Soviets shoot 100 nuclear warheads at us and we shoot 100 at them, our weapons pass each other in flight. We both get hit. Both sides lose! No one wins! We destroy their cities. They destroy ours. All this can take place in half an hour. One hour's nuclear exchange between the US and the USSR could destroy both as viable societies.

Would the USSR do this? Would not the USSR be "deterred" by our ability to retaliate and destroy them? After all, they have suffered from wars and want to survive. True. But if they get to the point where they see us as crazy enough to attack even though we would die as a result, they might do it. Enthusiastic registration by all our young men might give them the signal. Why? Because it is a kind of insane registration. Why? Because there is no draft. We never have had registration without a draft before. There is no good reason for it now except to give a signal to the Russians that we are ready for nuclear war. And what a crazy signal it is! A paper signal! A signal Ronald Reagan said he objects to; a signal that Dr. Rostker, former head of Selective Service, said was useless! A signal that will save only seven days of mobilization time, according to Rostker; a signal which ignores the insanity and speed of nuclear weapons.

No longer can draft and mobilization save us—much less mere registration. The 927,000 or more who have refused to register are a hopeful sign. They weaken the signal we send to the USSR. They say that many of us are opposed to nuclear weapons. Their refusal helps preserve peace and lessen the danger of nuclear disaster.

*Chapter 5*

*Changing Soldiers into Objectors*

Nathan Hale's claim, "I regret that I have but one life to give for my country," stands in stark contrast to the declaration of Bishop Michael Kenny of Juneau, Alaska: "I will not kill for my country."

The line is often incorrectly drawn between soldier and conscientious objector. The actual difference is not about willingness to fight, but about willingness to kill. The soldier is ready to kill on order; the conscientious objector refuses to kill.

During the Vietnam War, a soldier wrote home: "I object to the Vietnam War, not because I am afraid to die, but because I don't want to meet God while killing others in an unjust war."

The objector sees the fighting in war as killing forbidden by God. The soldier sees war as "protecting" others. The objector's focus is on the means used—killing. The soldier's focus is on the goal sought—protection or defense. Because of the different focuses, they come to contradictory conclusions; war is wrong; war is right.

It follows then that the way to change a soldier into an objector is to change his vision of what he is doing.

How can this be done? One way is to tell him, as Casper Weinberger does, that we plan to wage a protracted nuclear war with twenty million American deaths, followed by years of radioactive fallout all over the world. Explain to the soldier that nuclear bombs can annihilate but not protect. Explain to the soldier that if we ever use our weapons, we are finished. Explain that deterrence between Soviet and US governments will not deter as more nations get nuclear bombs. Explain that our plans for increased nuclear weapons add more to our danger than to our protection. Explain that "a nuclear war cannot be won, must never be fought" (according to Ronald Reagan), that there is no defense against nuclear bombs.

The objector sees all humans as children of God. He sees killing as contrary to God's law: "Love one another; love your enemies." He sees it as impossible to both kill and love the same person in the same act.

Like the soldier, the objector is ready to give his life to protect, but he is not willing to disobey God. He believes that if God does not protect us, then our efforts are in vain.

In our nuclear age, there are more objectors than ever before, including Catholic bishops. They are objecting because more people are coming to realize that nuclear war protects no one, and because it is obvious that we cannot love each other with nuclear arms, that we cannot serve God and kill God's children.

In the nuclear age, a soldier might consider himself as helping to protect by objecting to war altogether. In the nuclear age, conscience should make objectors of all people to all wars.

*Chapter 6*

*Inside the Bars: Peace and Harmony*

On the steps of the US Capitol we listened to Delegate Walter Faunteroy, who said, "Your 'No MX' cry is music to my ears. The black community and the poor suffer as we spend trillions for weapons of death." We were almost 1,000 from all over the US. We came to pray in the Capitol, on the day after Pentecost, at the invitation of religions-based peace groups: Sojourners, Fellowship of Reconciliation, and Clergy and Laity Concerned. After speeches and songs on the steps, 242 of us walked into the rotunda. Under the dome we prayed the Lord's Prayer. As we sang hymns, the press filmed us.

We had informed the police ahead of time what we would do. They soon ordered the press to leave and announced, "The rotunda is now closed. If you stay, you will be violating the law."

We stayed. We read statements from the Society of Friends, Presbyterians, Lutherans, Catholics, Episcopalians, and many other religious groups, all denouncing the arms race as immoral. I said, "On May 3 in Chicago the Catholic Bishops issued a pastoral letter. In it they said 'No' to the nuclear war, 'No' to the arms race. I am here today to make that 'No' visible to the Congress." The crowd applauded.

The police began to escort us one by one to desks set up inside the rotunda. There, we were photographed with the arresting officers, handcuffed, and escorted to buses. Cheers from the crowd outside encouraged us as we drove off to the lockup in the basement of the courthouse; a place too small for half our number.

Forty-eight other people and I were locked in a cell 17'x31'. Iron benches along the walls could seat about thirty. The others stood or sat or lay on the concrete floor all night.

Separated only by bars another seventy-five, all men, were in an even more crowded lockup. No beds, four benches, a bare cement floor with a stall commode in a semi-private corner—not bad compared to some jails! It was somewhat clean and the police were friendly. They supplied us with a pitcher of water and refilled it occasionally. The women were in similar cells not far away.

Almost one-third of the group were experiencing jail for the first time. Our time in jail was ecumenical, though most of us were Catholics. About half were priests, ministers, or women religious. Three or four Dominicans wore their habits. "Get to know your clergy, go to jail with them," one wit suggested.

We had talent inside the bars—good singing, harmonizers, too. "Gimme that Old Time Religion," sung in harmony, made the roof rattle and the police in the hall kept time, tapping on their desk. "It was good enough for Gandhi, it's good enough for me." The context gave it new meaning. Without changing key or beat, the song leader began, "Do Lord, Oh Do Lord, Oh Do Remember Me." We beat time with claps and despite the crowded space a few dozen jumped up and danced. As they were swinging their partners in square-dance fashion, one policeman said, "I ought to go home and get my guitar."

The police called out for a man over seventy, "Your son is on the phone and wants to come and bail you out. What shall I tell him?"

"Tell him I am okay. I will stay."

The police were as helpful as they could be. They thought we would be in holding cells only a few hours. But no judge could be persuaded to sit for the arraignment until the next morning.

The next day, we appeared in groups of ten before judges in two courtrooms. Both told us how they believed in our sincerity but added, "You are not in court because of your beliefs but only because you violated the law against demonstrations." He fined us each $50 or five days in jail.

When my turn came to speak, I said that both the law and our beliefs were the causes, and our belief was the major cause. The judge interrupted me and told me I should have better sense after my seminary training. I continued, "Our action is both legal and moral. The US law recognizes the principle that greater human necessity prevails over lesser laws. The necessity of warning the US of the nuclear danger takes precedence over demonstration location laws. At Nuremberg the US rightly found Germans guilty because they had failed to speak out against Hitler. Now the US government sentences us for speaking out against a greater danger than Hitler, nuclear incineration." A German woman prisoner had said this earlier in tears. I repeated it and continued, "The US Catholic Bishops have said 'No' to nuclear war...."

"They didn't tell you to come into the rotunda," interrupted the judge again.

"They told us to work strenuously against the arms race, to stop it."

The judge cut me off despite his praise for our freedom to speak. Other powerful statements were made. One woman said, "My three-year-old child began to cry as I left her to enter the rotunda. I almost went back to her, but I thought of the cries of all the children of the world if the nuclear bombs fall. I believed I should think of them too. So I am here to prevent the cries of the world's children."

Deane Mowrer, who is blind and elderly and a member of the New York Catholic Worker Community, explained: "The enormity of what our government is doing requires that we cry out in public. The danger is so great I feel obliged to be here." When asked if she would pay the $50 fine she answered, "I live in voluntary poverty so I cannot pay. If I had the money, I could not in conscience pay. I go to jail to protect others." She was sentenced to five days in jail.

One woman said, "I can pay, but I want to do penance for what our country is doing, so I will go to jail." She summed up her position: "Guilty under this law, but not under God's law."

A Sister of Mercy stated: "When we see what our government did in Vietnam and in El Salvador, we have good reason to doubt the judgments of this government. I did it as a fulfillment of a promise to Salvadoran refugees that I would do all I could to stop the funding of killing in El Salvador."

A law professor testified, "The application of this law is done in violation of the Constitution of the United States."

Another woman explained, "My civil disobedience is obedience to a higher law."

Still another Christian said, "I have written thousands of letters and lobbied for years, yet the arms race grows worse. And so I have to break the law."

On my return to the Jesuit Community at Georgetown University, I was asked, "Why did you do it?"

"To stop the arms race."

"Do you think you will stop the arms race by prayer?"

"Yes, if we have faith. And even if our faith is weak, our willingness to suffer makes known the truth that the nuclear arms race endangers us all."

"But doesn't the pope want priests to stay out of politics?"

Is praying in the rotunda political? Or is it religious? Can true religion ever be separated from politics? I think our action indicates our answer. Our faith has to have real implications and real consequences in today's world.

## Chapter 7

## *Military Peacemakers?*

A nurse at Walter Reed Hospital's psychiatric ward was trying to console a disturbed Vietnam soldier. He said, "The trouble with me is that I've been seven years in Vietnam, teaching people to kill. My job as a sergeant was to get them to scream, 'Kill! Kill! Kill!' and to mean it, as they stabbed dummies with their bayonets. I was the best one in the whole group at doing it. Now they tell me they don't need me anymore." The nurse tried to use her advanced training in psychiatric nursing to help him. "Maybe it was a mistake from the beginning to train to kill. Perhaps it wasn't good for you or for the marines or for the country to teach killing."

The marine began to scream at her, "Who the ---- do you think you are? You're wearing those captain's bars on your shoulders, and you're telling me now the same as the others. First they tell you to kill, and now they tell me not to kill. You're a ------- hypocrite."

The nurse left him, went to her own room, locked the door, lay down on her bed, and cried. The screams had brought back a flood of doubts and memories. She had been very upset by the military when she was in Korea for a year. The US Army venereal disease rate was about 90%, compared to the Korean rate of about 50%. She had wondered why. Was the army she belonged to part of the reason? She felt the Korean government, despite the millions of dollars given to it by the US, was stealing the US blind. She had questioned the role she was playing as a part of it all. She remembered the young nurse she had taught at Walter Reed, who had left the nursing corps on the claim of conscientious objection. The young woman had written a letter in the nurses' journal explaining why she could not in conscience give her nursing skills to support war. Here was a soldier who brought the whole question up again.

She could see clearly the hypocrisy of saying "maybe you shouldn't kill" while continuing to wear the military insignia of a captain.

Something similar applies to the priest who is also a military officer. It is difficult for him to advise the military on what to do. Father George Zabelka, the chaplain to the men who dropped the bombs on Tokyo, Hiroshima, and Nagasaki, remembers how hard it was for him. A pilot, whose flaming napalm bombs had burned to death a four-year-old child on the street in Tokyo, asked if it was right to be bombing civilians. The chaplain wasn't upset at the time. He just said that the bombing was necessary. That's what his superiors told him.

Years later, he looks back and believes that, by his silence, he failed as a man, as a priest, as a chaplain, and as a Christian.

In the Nagasaki bombing, three entire convents full of religious women were vaporized. Were they guilty people? They were doing their regular works of mercy until the atomic bomb hit them.

Father Zabelka recalls, "I was silent. I was told it was necessary."

Can a Catholic chaplain speak to the soldiers about the immorality of the use of nuclear weapons or the bombing of civilians? Yes. But it is more difficult while he wears a military uniform, and is subject to military discipline. He is very likely to lose his job if he speaks against military policy.

Some of this difficulty is reflected in the letter that Cardinal Cooke sent to the military chaplains in December, 1981. He wrote in response to questions from chaplains who asked whether or not, in view of the condemnation of nuclear war by Vatican II, and the statement by the US Catholic Bishops that, "As it is wrong to use nuclear weapons, so is it wrong to intend to use them," Catholics could handle nuclear weapons at all.

These questions are not asked in a vacuum. They don't come from the imagination. They come from chaplains, who are actually advising the men who handle the weapons; the men who have problems of conscience about their work because of what they hear from bishops and priests.

It is not an academic question. It is something from everyday life. The pressure is on the chaplains and their cardinal to agree with US military policy and say, "Oh yes, it's all right. The government says it is necessary." What kind of argument is that?

What about a Catholic who wants to follow what Christ wants, what Christ teaches? The Church has never taught that war is good. The Church has never taught that killing is what God wants, or that war is necessary to be a follower of Christ. He taught us how to die, not how to kill.

It is true that Catholics have not practiced this Gospel teaching as they should. The crusades are the most extreme example. But love of enemy has always been taught as the

Gospel ideal. The danger of nuclear disaster now helps us to see better than ever the importance of practicing what we preach about the immorality of nuclear deterrence. How can the chaplains object to nuclear deterrence policy, when they are part of the military?

Is it not legitimate and moral for a military person to ask, "Can I be part of nuclear deterrence, part of preparation for nuclear war?" But the chaplain, who is an officer, will appear to be a hypocrite if he disagrees with policy, and yet is an officer. So he will feel pressured to find some way of agreeing with national policy. Cardinal Cooke's letter to the chaplains illustrates this. Army regulation (65-202) makes the same point, "The chaplain's duties are those which normally pertain to his profession as a clergyman...modified by the mission and distinctive conditions and circumstances of the Department of the Army." A short reflection brings the realization that this is a very strong condition, which includes an assortment of circumstances. In back of it all is this simple message: moral teaching better not conflict with Army policy.

The military uses the Church to help bring acceptance of its methods, but seeks to restrict the Church in its moral teaching.

*Chapter 8*

*ROTC Militarizes Students*

ROTC (Reserve Officers Training Corps) is only a small part of the giant military machine. A minstrel show is only a small part of racism, but in a racist area, it does much damage. Academically, ROTC does damage because it extends and further entrenches the power and prestige of the military in a country already over-militarized.

Morally, the military on a Christian campus is a scandal in the deepest theological sense of the word. It teaches the youth to accept the evil of killing as a necessary good. This is done by teachers who profess to be disciples of Jesus and His truth and love. By accepting the military on a Christian campus, Christian leaders cloak the military in the aura of moral value and dignity that they desperately need. The argument that it will humanize the military is often used. It will also give the aura of religion to militarism. It strengthens militarism in the nation, and weakens the influence of the Gospel.

There should be no academic recognition of ROTC because the military will reach out like an octopus into all corners of university life to debase it with the acceptance of militarism as a way of life. A course in military history, taken in isolation, prescinding from the fact that it becomes the front behind which the military hides, might have academic value. But granting credit to such courses means that a person from the Pentagon, paid by an outside power and dedicated to the militarism of youth, will be honored with the dignity of being a department head, capable of sitting on all boards and committees. As a result, the money and power of the Pentagon will infiltrate every corner of our campus [Georgetown], including the school newspaper.

We have betrayed our students by letting ROTC in. A few years ago a friendly major in charge of ROTC told me, "You will be happy to know I am not against theology. I have just come from a meeting of the academic council of the college and I just voted in favor of allowing the theology department to have a major." I told him that I had never dreamed the day would come when a military man would vote on the merits of theology and expect me to be grateful for it.

No other department is paid from the outside, takes orders from outside, pays the students for participating, or punishes its dropouts with military conscription. No other department has an aim—the militarism of youth—opposed to the ideals of the university.

The military invades the campuses to psychologize the young into accepting militarism. Training officers is of secondary importance. That could be better done at some military base in the summer time. The marines believe this and are opposed to ROTC. Admiral Eugene LaRoque argues against

ROTC on campus. He says the training would be better and more up to date if it were given for a four-month period in a camp, after college. "If the military wants to subsidize college education, let them give scholarships; but leave the students alone until after college," says LaRoque.

The military buys its way into the university. It demands that teachers be from the military, and be paid by the military. It sets up its own program and controls it. It requires students to pay back in years of service for the instruction they have been given.

I believe that if we were simply looking for what is academically best for a university, the military would not be included. The argument that a university can help humanize the military has some merit: the same merit found in the argument used by the Jesuit priests who owned slaves in the early days of Maryland. Their argument was that priests owning slaves would treat the slaves better, as in fact they did. But by owning slaves they gave massive support for the institution of slavery, doing great harm to our country and the capacity of the Jesuits to act as witnesses to the Gospel of love.

I believe that the presence of the military on campus does the same thing. It further strengthens an already overwhelming military establishment in our country and makes it less possible for the university to witness to the Gospel of love. It diverts the university from the academic goal of seeking truth and teaching the truth. The military is an intruder into the fields of academia with a different aim and a different method.

Once when I was opposing the reaccreditation of ROTC, a twenty-year-old woman student came to me and asked very sincerely, "Why can't you agree that ROTC should be open to whoever wants it?" She went on to say that no one is forced to take it; it is freely chosen.

"Let me explain my reason with a parable," I said. "Before the student chooses, the faculty members of the university have to choose among the very limited offerings that can be made available, what is best for the curriculum. What would you think of me as a sixty-one-year-old educator if I told you the following: An international prostitution ring has offered me $500,000 provided I would help get a Department of Prostitution into the university. All teachers would be chosen from the International Prostitution ring; the course would be controlled by the ring. Courses of academic excellence would be taught such as 'The Psychology of Solicitation,' 'The Process of Prostitution,' 'Comparative Prostitution and Its Cultural Components,' and 'The Leadership in Prostitution.' These courses would be taught by only recognized and certified national or international pimps. What would you think of me, if I chose that as a course offering for students on the grounds that the university needed the money, and after all, no one was forced to take it?"

The student replied, "Oh, you consider it a moral question, don't you?"

I do consider it a moral question, and if anyone thinks it is unfair to the military to compare it to prostitutes, I reply that it may be unfair to the prostitutes. Prostitution does not threaten the survival of the world. Prostitution is not supported by taxpayers' money and the power of the Pentagon.

Does ROTC belong on college campuses? No. I believe that it proposes the very opposite ideals, both morally and academically, to what a university should offer.

From the moral point of view, I believe that the Gospel commands us to love God and all human beings. This love must be universal and include enemies. I do not accept the argument that in the act of killing a person I can express love for that person, nor do I believe that the Gospel allows us to kill certain persons or groups of people in order to show love for certain other persons or groups.

I understand this imperative of love is derived from the truth that there is only one God who is the parent of all human beings. Because of this, we are all brothers and sisters and should act accordingly. I believe that no complexity of foreign policy does away with this truth. I see all war as a type of fratricide and atheism that denies the brother-sister relation of human beings under the parentage of God.

I believe the Gospel requires us to return good for evil, to do good to those who hate us, and to love those who persecute us. This is incompatible with military operations and preparations for them.

Just as war is opposed to all these Gospel commands and invitations, so is ROTC on a Christian campus. ROTC makes it very difficult for Christians to hear the Gospel message of peace. How can war be wrong if we have military training on Christian campuses? How can the buildup of nuclear weapons and our intent to use them be wrong when our Christian universities prepare our youth to join the nuclear army? No matter that Vatican II forbids us to be part of nuclear war. Universities tell us we need not bother about that by training soldiers to fight it. How can ordinary Christians see the evil of the arms race? How can they see how it deprives the poor of bread? No matter that the popes call the arms race a "crime"—aggression against the poor—a "theft," a "machine-gone-mad." "Christian" universities prepare soldiers who will use those weapons, so it must be all right: That is the lie taught by ROTC on campus.

The worst moral evil of ROTC may be that in this age of nuclear danger it blocks Christians from seeing the evil of our intent to use nuclear weapons and the evil of the arms race. Where in this nuclear age do we find in Christian universities the peace message of the Gospel? ROTC is the war message, uttered so loud and clear that the peace message is lost.

Both George Washington and Dwight Eisenhower warned our country of the danger of an overgrown military. Their worst fears have been realized. We are now a nation that spends fifty-four cents of every tax dollar on military-related expenses. We are a nation that has a peacetime Selective Service Law in force; the president is pushing for registration. I see the penetration by the military of the educational community as just one more step in the process of the overmilitarization of America. I think it should be opposed.

Equivalently, the Pentagon says to us, "Let us use your facilities for our purposes. Let us have all the personnel from the military who teach. In return we will give scholarships; we will pay the salaries; we will see to it that you get grants for all your science departments." Is this the best we can do for the students?

One test of this is to ask this question: "Would we do it if there were no money advantage?" Another test is to ask, "Is it the proper function of the Department of Defense to educate civilians?" Finally, we should ask, "How does education centered on the function of 'kill and destroy' serve God and the human family?"

# Chapter 9

## The University as Policeman

A law was passed on September 8, 1982, which escaped the notice of most people. It is a law which punishes those who refuse to register, or more precisely, some of those who refuse to register. It is a discriminatory law, because it punishes only certain classes of the million or so young men who refuse to register for a nuclear war.

This law requires that a university deny federal grants of money to college students who will not show evidence that they have registered for the draft. This law transfers the police action that normally would go to the Justice Department of the federal government onto the campuses of the universities. The federal government does not want to become unpopular by prosecuting a million young men for refusing to go along with registration, refusing to become political footballs and to allow their lives to be tossed about by presidents who are playing politics with war.

What I mean by this is that the law requires the university to be the policeman and to check up on a group of people, so it is an unfair, discriminatory law. Why discriminatory? First of all, it discriminates against only private colleges, those that don't get their funds paid by the state. It is these universities that depend most on federal grants to individual students. Second, it does not ask a university to report on everybody who is avoiding the draft but only the poor, because the wealthy do not need financial aid, so they can be ignored. Third, it does not deal with women, because they are not included in the law. Fourth, it falls heaviest on blacks and Hispanics, the minority groups who are notably in the poorest income classes. So it is discriminatory in four ways.

This kind of an unjust, punitive, discriminatory law comes out of a situation where a president, Jimmy Carter, was trying to show that he was just as macho in threatening the Russians as was his opponent, Ronald Reagan. He called for a registration without a draft. Mr. Reagan, the candidate, said he disagreed with that and that if he were president, he would not have a registration without a draft. Then he changed his mind, probably for the same macho reasons, after he became president.

The legislators were told this was just a paper transaction and the young men were just defying the government. They were told this was one way of saving the Justice Department a lot of money by having the universities do it: scare the young men into registering. But that is not true! It is not simply any sort of paper that they are signing. It is not simply going to the post office and giving in their name that is the reason why a million are objecting. It is the nuclear age in which we are living, and it is registration for nuclear war which is implicitly being asked of these young men.

They are being asked to go along with the political insanity that leads to a nuclear war, playing with the lives not only of the young men themselves but of all the people in the world. A nuclear war is mass suicide for both sides. Any young man who respects his country or anybody else's country would have a very good reason for refusing to be part of this madness, to register for it.

So it is no small issue, and it confronts the universities with a serious moral problem. Should they go along with this insanity? But if they do not, they are violating the law.

This kind of insane situation, in which young men are being policed by their universities to try to force them into something the university itself may not agree with, is one of the spin-offs of the insanity of our nuclear age. Once we have agreed, as we do, to use nuclear weapons, to kill millions of people under circumstances which we decide, then lesser insanities are going to be included in it; and this law (P.L. 97-252) is one of them.

I think there is very good reason for the million young men to say, "No, we will not be part of the insanity. We may die in a nuclear war, but we are not going to help promote one by saying 'Yes' to registration when there is no sign that this registration is in any way for the defense of our country, or in any way for the peace of the world." Rather, it is a danger to peace.

*Chapter 10*

*Tell It to the Russians*

"How do you feel now?" asked a reporter after I was arrested at the June 14 blockade of the Russian Mission at the United Nations in New York. She was standing near the door of the city bus into which the police were herding us.

"I feel that I am representing the human family in its desire to survive," I said.

She had talked with me while I sat on the sidewalk with twenty-five others blocking the back gate of the Russian Mission.

"Why are you doing this?"

"To dramatize the fact that after thirty years of petitions and promises, nothing has been done for disarmament. Martin

Luther King, Jr., said that civil disobedience 'creates a tension between the opposing sides that makes it impossible for the issue to be ignored.' "

We were only a small part of the 2,000 who blockaded the embassy doors of the five major nuclear nations (England, France, China, the United States, and the USSR).

As I prepared myself for the arrest, I had a sure sense that God was guiding and assisting me. At midnight the night before, I noticed as I went to sleep that it was cold and raining in New York. I had brought neither a raincoat nor a hat, only a suit jacket and a light sweater. When I awoke at 5:30 A.M., the rain had stopped and the sky was clearing. In the New York subway, I found a hat lying on the ground in the middle of the platform. I put it on and it fit me.

Once off the subway, I hurried in the wrong direction to our rendezvous. Coming in the opposite direction, Mike Bucci of our group met me. He led me to our meeting place on the corner of 59th and Lexington, a few blocks from the Soviet Mission. From there we walked to the mission and sat down on the sidewalk in front of a line of police standing shoulder to shoulder. Slowly and without violence the police arrested us one by one. They carried on stretchers those who would not walk to the bus.

As the city bus rolled along uptown, the dozen police standing in the aisle were questioned by us. There were forty of us: priests, ministers, nuns, laity, young and old, from all over the United States.

Father George Kuhn asked the officer nearest him, "Do you believe we are all in danger of nuclear destruction?"

"Yes, but I don't want to talk about it," replied the policeman.

"Why not? You are arresting us because we want the danger removed."

"I don't want to talk about it," he said, turning his back on George.

Another policeman beside him spoke up. "I will talk about it."

"Do you ever think that you are being used to promote nuclear death?" asked George.

"What do you mean?" asked the officer.

"You are sent here to help keep the nuclear program going."

"I just turn my mind away from it. I just block it out and do my job. Just like a priest does when he hears confession."

"No," spoke up Rev. Joe Dirr, S.J., a seat farther up. "We don't block anything out."

"Don't you ever hear peacemakers advised, 'Tell it to the Russians?' Why do you arrest us when we try to tell it to the Russians?" continued George Kuhn.

"Say, Father, is your name Kuhn?" asked the policeman.

"Yes. Why?"

"You're my cousin! You have a church in Manhattan."

"Yeah. I recognize you now, and I'm going to tell your mother on you. What is she going to say when she finds out that you arrested your cousin?" George asked. The prisoners all booed and echoed, "Arresting your cousin? Shame!"

George Kuhn stood by in the aisle and said, "I will forgive you, if you promise not to do it again." The crowded bus cheered as the priest embraced his cousin the policeman. That little drama illustrated the general attitude of the police. We had explained to them well before what we were going to do and where and when we were going to do it. We assured them ours would be a nonviolent blockade. In our songs as we sat blocking the gate, we sang "Policemen are our brothers." They responded with, "If we weren't policemen, we would be with you!"

Toward the end of the day, another reporter asked, "Will anything be accomplished by your blockade?"

"Yes, I think so," I replied. "The taproot of violence in our society is our intent to use nuclear weapons on millions of people. We are confronting this issue that poisons the entire fiber of our normal life. Our blockade says to us, to all our friends, and to everyone, that we do not have to accept the poison and die. Neither do they. Our blockade says we don't expect the governments of the world to disarm until the people force them to do it. We are a growing part of the moral-political force. We would rather be active today than radioactive tomorrow."

# Part V:

# The Process of Peace

*I believe that unarmed truth and unconditional love will have the final word in reality.*

Martin Luther King, Jr.

*The taproot of violence in our society today is our intent to use nuclear weapons. Once we have agreed to that, all other evil is minor in comparison. Until we squarely face the question of our consent to use nuclear weapons, any hope of large scale improvement of public morality is doomed to failure.*

Richard McSorley, S.J.

*They shall beat their swords into plowshares and their spears into pruning hooks. Nation shall not lift up sword against nation. Neither shall they learn war any more.*

Isaiah 2:4

*Chapter 1*

*Promoting Peace*

"What can I do to promote peace?" This is the question people often ask as they become concerned about the drift toward disaster. Sometimes it is asked in despair, as though the job were so big and impossible that nothing can be done: "What can a single person do? The task is so overwhelming!"

The answer is, "We can begin anywhere." The fact that it is so big a job means that almost everything needs to be changed: our way of thinking, our education, our spending, our ways of relating to God, to other people, and to other nations.

The answer to "What can I do?" can be optimistic if we divide it into "What means can I take?" and "What good will result?" The result does not depend on each of us alone. The result depends on the cooperation of others and on God's help. The means are dependent on each of us and are within our reach. M.K. Gandhi said, "The creator has given us no control over the end, but has given us a limited control over the means." If we say, "The means are after all only means," he replies, "The means are after all everything. We should look ahead at the goal, but give our full attention to the means."

The goal we seek is not just disarmament. The goal is making known the truth that human life is sacred. This goal includes changing hearts and minds so completely that no one would want to use weapons of destruction and death. All measures that promote this truth, this change of mind and heart, are the means I can use.

Gandhi says, "Truth is God." In witnessing to the truth, I serve God. Gandhi is phrasing what the Christian would call "following conscience" or "doing what is right because it is pleasing to God."

Once we have formulated goals and means in this manner, all kinds of means appear ready for use. All I do or refuse to do, all I say or refuse to say, can be a means to make this truth known. Making truth known is a matter of the spirit: Gandhi calls it our "birthright." It never fails. Even if we die making the truth known, our willingness to risk death is a witness to truth. Alone, I can be a witness to the truth even if no one else is.

There is no end of things to do to promote peace.

We can pray, uniting ourselves with God, the power that moves the universe. We can ask God to give us light and strength and help in our peacemaking. We can look into our use of time, money, and property. What priority do we give to peacemaking in our use of these resources?

Peace education from grade school to university needs to be developed. Education for war needs to be stopped. Investments in corporations that support war and preparations for war should be sold. The Committee for Social Responsibility organizes to pressure corporations away from war. Boycott of consumer products from war-related corporations is another peacemaking opportunity.

It may help us as we work for peace to realize the size of our work lest we be discouraged for lack of quick results. We are trying to roll back a 400-year tradition of American violence: we started our country by killing Indians, moving them off their own land, and then taking the land. We put the Indians on reservations, and then by film and folklore continue to tell our children that they are savages.

We have a history of 300 years of black slavery, and another one hundred years of segregating blacks into second-class citizenry. This US cultural addiction to violence makes peace a difficult goal indeed.

As Richard Goodwin says in his book *Triumph or Tragedy*:

> If a large-scale war ever comes, it will not come in a burst of Strangelove madness or a Fail-Safe accident but through a long series of facts and decisions, each seemingly reasonable, that will slowly place the great powers in a situation in which they will find it impossible to back down. It will be no one's fault...but it will be the fault of many—leaders, politicians, journalists, men and women in a hundred different occupations in many lands who failed to see clearly or act wisely, or speak articulately. There will be no act of madness, no single villain on whom to discharge guilt: just the flow of history.

To stop the drift toward war, we have to erase the psychology developed by our long addiction to violence. It will be difficult to erase it rapidly enough to prevent nuclear war.

As we think about our nation's history, we should recall the words Jefferson spoke during the debate on the Constitution after his efforts to have slavery excluded had failed. He said, "I tremble for my country when I reflect that God is just, that His justice cannot sleep forever."

Nations do not repent, so they should expect that they will be punished here in this life, by defeat and downfall, perhaps even with destruction. We are now living in a country which fulfills the fears of Thomas Jefferson two centuries ago. This nation may not be saved from the course of its violent past.

Nonetheless, the individual may still do a great deal for the process of peace. In fact, the individual citizen's effort will be all the more needed as public officials fail to act.

A phrase which might guide us is from the Constitution of the United Nations Educational, Scientific, and Cultural Organization (1946): "Since wars begin in the minds of men, it is in the minds of men that the defenses of peace must be constructed."

The greater the danger of war, the greater the need to replace the process of war with the process of peace. Everything from individual information and action to organized and international action is needed. Individual actions, like the refusal to register for the armed services or the refusal to pay taxes, may not stop the war process, but they help the process of peace.

When Mussolini began to organize his Fascist Party, a notice arrived in a small Sicilian town demanding all men to join the Fascist army. That same night, the school teacher posted a notice on the town hall that he would not join, believing that what the Fascists were doing was wrong. As he was being taken out to be shot, he was asked, "Why did you place the notice on the Town Hall when you knew it would not do any good?" He answered, "I did not want it [our town's compliance] to be unanimous." His example remains after the uselessness of Fascist violence has become evident.

We remember, too, that Jesus began with twelve followers to teach his message of peace to the world, to turn people from the belief that violence is the only solution to the differences between people.

Another way of encouraging our interest in peace is to understand that we do not escape the prospect of our world blowing up simply by inaction and apathy. Our lives and the witness that we give must help light the way of peace for others.

When we work toward peace, we can light the way to peace for others. When we work for peace, we can expect God's help. God's plan is that we should overcome evil with good. And the greatest evil that threatens us today is destruction through the violence of our own hands.

*Chapter 2*

*The War Process; The Peace Process*

We can learn a great deal about the process of peace and its promotion by looking at its opposite, the war process. A war process does not begin with the declaration of hostilities and the explosion of bombs; it is a process that continues day after day; it is woven into events and shapes every aspect of our lives.

We educate toward war. The military toys, soldiers, and guns that we give our children to amuse them, the violence on television, in the movies, and in our literature and drama teach violence as a way of life. For more formal education we have four military academies and the national war colleges; we have the peacetime registration which may quickly reinstate the draft and channel the lives of the youth of the country into war and violence. We have the Army, Navy, Marines, and Air Force ready for war—even before there is war. The huge bulk of each tax dollar goes for defense spending year after year.

We have a military establishment that can win its aim with its vast budget and powerful political influence. Almost 70% of all federal employees are employed by our Department of Defense, and fifty-four cents of every freely controllable dollar spent from the presidential budget is spent for war-related materials and services. The actual figures on spending are not generally known, and therefore not easily believed.

Presidents present their budgets to the people in such a way that people are led to believe that military spending is only one-fourth of the budget or less. They use the category "Defense Budget." They do not refer to "war-related" expenses. They are correct when they put "Defense Budget" at about one-quarter of the total; they mislead when they ask the public to believe that this is the total of war-related expenses.

The total is over 53.9% in 1989. Where does this high portion come from? You add the expenses of the military budget, the expenses for the veterans, expenses for the interest on the national debt (90% war-related), expenses for space technology, and other hidden military expenses like the Coast Guard (under Commerce and Transportation) and Army Engineers (under Natural Resources and Environment). You subtract from the total $329 billion which is the total in the Social Security Trust Fund. These funds are earmarked exclusively for Social Security. The Social Security Trust is an insurance scheme, and all salaried workers are required to pay into it. They collect their money again after age sixty-five.

When military-related expenses are compared with the total controllable budget (minus Social Security funds) you see that 57% of the budget is for military-related expenses.

Here is how it worked for 1989:

The total budget for 1989 was about $889 billion. The National Defense Budget was $304 billion. These figures are rounded out to their nearest whole number for easier understanding.

Not included in the National Defense Budget are the following war-related expenses: at least $300 million on internal affairs and finance. (The military committees in Congress have the largest budgets of any committees and government supervision of Pentagon spending is expensive.) About two-thirds of the $4 billion space research and technology budget is related to military projects and is directed by the military. The Department of Energy used much of its $8.1 billion budget to make nuclear weapons and other military projects. A part of the Housing and Community Development budget goes to military housing in the United States and abroad. The Commerce and Transportation budget includes all the cost of the US Coast Guard. By far the two largest military-related expenses not in the military budget are veterans expenses of $30 billion, and interest on the national debt, $141 billion. About 58% of the debt is war incurred.

These are broad categories of military-related expenses. Much more could be added by a line-by-line analysis of the budget. For example, how much of security maintained by marines at US embassies around the world is paid by the Pentagon?

Add to this the $304 billion National Defense Budget and you get a total of about $479.6 billion in defense and war-related expenses.

When you subtract the Social Security payments which swell the budget you get:

| | | |
|---|---|---|
| $1 trillion | $142.6 billion | Total budget |
| less | $253. billion | Social Security & trusts budget |
| | $889.6 billion | Total usable budget |

In a total controllable budget of $889.6 billion you have $479 billion or about 54% that is war-related. You get this $479 billion by adding the current military budget, $308.5 billion, to the cost of past wars, $170.6 billion.

Subtracting the total military-related budget from the usable budget you get:

$889.5 billion     usable
$479.6 billion     military-related
$419.9 billion     remains for all other expenses

So $419.9 billion remains for all other expenses, or 46% of total usable money when military-related and trust-fund incomes are subtracted from the total budget.

This $419.9 billion is spent by politicians, many of whom owe their political careers to supporting defense industries and military spending in their districts. Congresspeople or even presidents who oppose military spending risk losing public support. We now have over 28 million veterans, 43% of the male population. The military machine uses public funds to propagandize the people into supporting military spending. Often, the military can effect its will despite the desires of civilian officials. The military also influences the international scene: the United States has treaties to help defend forty-eight nations if they request our aid—or we intervene.

Encouraging our society to "think war" are many influences more subtle than the above. Our history books are often stories of our wars, as though there were nothing else to tell. They speak of no mistakes for which we should repent, no enemies who were good, no wars that were bad. They describe heroes characterized by military bravery; even public monuments help us to believe that almost all our heroes were military men. In history books, the atrocities of war and the killing—which are the central acts of war—are usually overlooked. In this way our minds, filled with stories of bravery and endurance, create an image of national pride strengthened by wars, and the way for more violence is prepared.

Many of the best known army films are made at an army center on Long Island, New York. The chief of the Army's Motion Picture Section points out that to "qualify for military cooperation" a film depicting an Army subject must be a picture that will "reflect favorably on the Army." Civilian actors in Army uniform are highly paid and are assisted by real soldiers.

The war process works through religious faiths: Ministers and priests wear the uniform and receive pay from the military. Some have high rank in the military services. Their presence says to the members of their faiths that religion and the Army are compatible.

The presence of student Reserve Officer Training Corps on the campuses of prestigious schools says to the student that the military life is as normal as going to school. The presence of the American flag beside the tabernacle of worship says to the worshiper that our nation is as important as God.

These subtle indirect influences of the military over civilian life are more effective in militarizing society than they seem to be. The extent of military penetration into civilian life is illustrated by the influence of the Reserve Officer Training Corps (ROTC) once it has become established in a school. It is not content with military drill and lectures. It spreads like an octopus to every facet of the institution.

The ROTC at Georgetown University illustrates this point. During the Vietnam War ROTC invited the neighboring high-school children to come to the Georgetown campus to see captured communist weapons displayed on the ball field, though they could have easily been shown at nearby Fort McNair. On the campus of a Christian university, they seem not only to have been put there by the military, but also to be sanctioned by Christianity.

In these and many other ways the military infiltrates an educational institution and spreads the philosophy that violence and killing are the American way. This philosophy inevitably leads people to the conclusion that force and violence, instead of cooperation through some international organization, or reconciliation, or admission of fault on either or both sides, will solve the world's and the nation's problems.

War is the process that leads to lethal group conflict. Its conflicts include all that divide and separate human beings from each other, such as racism, nationalism, fear, hatred, and death. The process of war leads to physical and moral death.

Through the war process each generation learns to forget the horror experienced in every war and passes on to the next generation stories of glory and heroes. Thus most young people are prepared to shoot when the signal is given.

## The Process of Peace

The process of peace is the reverse of the process of war. It is reconciliation between me, my neighbors, and God. It includes all that unites human beings with each other and with God: cooperation, friendship, love in marriage and family, racial integration and international unity. It is based on trust and motivated by love; it leads to life. Like the war process, it is total and all-pervading, affecting every facet of human thought, action and organization.

An understanding of the war process is one of the first tasks in coming to a realization of the magnitude of the problem of reversing the path to total war, and eventual annihilation of the human race. An aid to comprehending the present situation of war-ideology domination is a book by Sidney Lens, *The Military Industrial Complex*. It is important and not difficult for any person who reads to gain a basic knowledge of the main themes. Getting the knowledge is a first step towards peacemaking.

Later on in this section there is a listing of organizations which are working toward peace.

*Chapter 3*

*Action for Peace*

**Draft Resistance**

"Conscription is for slaves, not free men. These words do not come easily, but they are true and the truth needs saying. The truth, as clearly as one sees it, also needs acting upon." With these words Robert Eaton began his statement before the federal court in Philadelphia on August 27, 1969. He was being tried for refusing induction into the army. He had worked with the Quakers in North and South Vietnam and also with many of the underprivileged in American society. "We have learned that the beginning of construction has to be a clear 'No' to destruction," he continued:

> We find ourselves administering to an increasingly fossilized and violent society...established religion blesses nuclear submarines, legislatures outlaw flag burning in this country and finance child burning in Vietnam, courts back down on a solemn pledge at the Nuremberg and Tokyo war crimes trials to apply to our country the same standard of justice involving war crimes that we applied to World War II enemies.

A group of friends accompanied Bob Eaton to the courthouse. I was one of them. By his act of refusing induction and all cooperation with the Selective Service System, Bob Eaton was saying the most effective "No" to killing that can be said. Leo Tolstoy in his book *The Kingdom of God Is within You* has written that to refuse conscription is the strongest act that an individual can take against war. I agree with Tolstoy, not only because the young man who chooses prison rather than killing people sets an effective example, but also because he appeals to the most powerful force within an individual—his conscience.

Thousands of young Bob Eatons over the land who said "No" to killing in Vietnam have done much to help recall America to its ideals. From 1965 to the end of the Vietnam War, hundreds of thousands of young men applied for conscientious objector status. There were 100,000 in the single year of 1970. So influential was their impact on the war and on America that Clark Clifford, secretary of defense, told the Joint Chiefs of Staff that they could not have an increase in men that they asked. He said that 36,000 C.O.'s that year showed that the government could not go on drafting men without limits. The Joint Chiefs said they needed one million more men to win and 200,000 to continue the war. Clifford told them that the example of the C.O.'s was evidence that they could not get a million men. At that point the increase in troops stopped. The military did not get 200,000. The influence of the C.O.'s was substantial.

Resistance to induction during the war in Vietnam prepared the way for the current refusal of many to register for the draft. About one million have refused up to 1982. In order to scare the others, the government prosecuted a dozen who had publicly proclaimed their refusal. But the courts refused to convict unless the government would give good reasons for discriminatory prosecution of only a handful. The government refused, so few were convicted. Ben Sasway was one of the few convicted. His conviction inspired a dozen groups to come the aid of all resisters.

Those who resist follow a long tradition of refusal to kill that goes back to the early Christians. One example of our times was an Austrian farmer, Franz Jaegerstaetter. He refused conscription into Hitler's army in 1943. After his parish priest advised him to think of his wife and three children, he walked fifteen miles to consult with his bishop. The bishop told him it was up to higher authority to decide, and not up to a farmer. Just before he was beheaded in Tegel prison, Berlin, he wrote in a letter to his wife that "It is better that I speak the truth, even if I die. If I must write with my hands in chains, I find that much better than if my will were in chains."

Some who were refused their requests to be conscientious objectors found other ways to stay out of the Army. During the Vietnam War a friendly college professor advised a young man who had been refused C.O. status to steal his Volkswagen: that way he would be rejected by the Army as a criminal. The young man drove the Volkswagen around the block and waited while the professor called the police to report the theft. It worked. The Army refused to accept him. It didn't don't want criminals, just those ready to kill legally.

Many anti-war actions centered on the destruction of draft records. They began in the late 1960s when a nineteen-year-old Minnesotan, Barry Bondhaus, broke into his local draftboard office and dumped two large buckets of human organic waste into a filing cabinet, thereby spoiling several hundred 1-A draft records.

By 1969, over sixty Americans awaited prison after destroying draft records. The Baltimore Four—Philip Berrigan, James Mengal, David Eberhardt and Thomas Lewis—poured blood on six hundred draft records in October 1967. In May 1968, Philip Berrigan, his brother Dan, a Jesuit priest, and seven others, including a Catholic brother, a nurse, an artist, and two missionaries, destroyed draft files with homemade napalm at Catonsville, Maryland.

These groups and others made statements to explain their actions. They prayed and performed liturgical ceremonies while they waited to be arrested. They voluntarily accepted imprisonment, hoping to reach the conscience of America.

This was part of the Catonsville Nine statement:

> We throw napalm on these draft records because napalm has burned people to death in Vietnam, Guatemala, and Peru; and because it may be used on America's ghettos.... We believe some property has no right to exist: Hitler's gas ovens, Stalin's concentration camps, atomic, bacteriological, and chemical weaponry, files of conscription.... We are Catholic Christians who take the Gospel of our faith seriously.

The Camden Twenty-eight were persuaded to enter and destroy draft files by an FBI agent who infiltrated their group after they decided against such an action. Their long trial, during which the provocateur clearly admitted his spy role for the FBI, helped many to understand how the government tried to entrap those who opposed it. On that basis the jury returned a "not guilty" verdict. The trial even converted the informer.

Raids on draft boards like the Berrigans' action will not affect centralized computers. But the spirit of these actions will be carried on. New ways will be found to refuse the orders to kill when the computerized draft starts. The men and women who put the names into the computers and the young at whom the computer is directed are the modern prototypes of other men who killed and refused to kill in other wars. The "joker" of war in the future is the nuclear bomb whose terrors will cancel any advantage computers can give to the military.

Unknown numbers of soldiers went to military prisons during the Vietnam war because they were morally unable to accept the war and follow orders. They found no other way to express their convictions than to violate a minor rule, like going AWOL. Many were put out of the military with dishonorable discharges that appear on some records for the rest of their lives. From July 1961 to June 1973, there were 637,357 discharges of this kind. These figures do not include about 80,000 Americans who left the country to take up residence in Canada, 400 more in Sweden, and in other hospitable nations, rather than consent to kill in Vietnam. These men took effective and direct action against the war; their actions touched the consciences of millions of other Americans.

## Tax Resistance

"Why pay for a war you do not believe in?" is one of the slogans advocating tax refusal. In 1964 Joan Baez, the folk singer, wrote to the Internal Revenue Service saying that she was not going to pay sixty percent of her 1963 income tax.

She gave two reasons: "It is enough to say that no man has the right to take another's life. Now we plan and build weapons that can take thousands of lives in one second, millions of lives in a day, billions in a week. My other reason is that modern war is impractical and is stupid. We spend billions of dollars a year on weapons which scientists, politicians, military men and even presidents agree must never be used...[yet] people are starving to death in some places in the world. They look to this country with all its wealth and power. They look at our national budget. They are supposed to respect us. They despise us."

Archbishop Raymond Hunthausen of Seattle considers refusal to pay taxes for nuclear bombs an excellent means of non-violent resistance to the arms race. "We must take special responsibility for what is in our own back yard," he said. (Deadly Trident submarines are docked in his diocese in Puget Sound.) "When crimes are being prepared in our name, we must speak plainly. I say with a deep consciousness of the meaning of these words: *The Trident submarine is the Auschwitz of Puget Sound.*" In 1982 he refused to pay fifty percent of his income tax. He says, "The arms race is one of the greatest curses on the human race and the harm it inflicts on the poor is more than can be endured."

Hunthausen's example will affect many others. If the government arrests him, the arrest will call immense public attention to his moral view that it is wrong to pay for nuclear deaths.

The government can attach your bank account and force collection, but it cannot erase the witness of your opposition to the killing in war. Today 53.8 percent of the federal tax dollar goes to war-related expenses.

To my knowledge, no one has ever been jailed for refusing to pay war taxes. There have been jail sentences on charges of falsification of exemption claims; for example, when peace organizations or poor people are claimed as exemptions. The government wisely tries to avoid making tax martyrs. They could become heroes and their witness could become well publicized, endangering the present tax system. The government does not want that. What the government does want is money, and this can be taken from bank accounts or confiscated property.

It is quite clear, therefore, that if large numbers refused to pay because of their opposition to war, there would be a strong political effect on the government.

## Other Individual Actions

Dr. Benjamin Spock, the well-known baby doctor, showed what one man can do. He tried every legal way to stop the war. Finally he urged young people to resist the draft. He was arrested and tried for conspiracy to obstruct the Selective Service.

Over the year of Dr. Spock's trial and appeal, the news of his resistance helped many Americans think critically about the war. Dr. Spock gave them the example of a man who put his prestige, his profession, and his future on the line to express his conviction that he is just as interested in the eighteen- to twenty-year-old as he is in infants. Along with Dr. Spock the Rev. William Sloan Coffin, then a chaplain at Yale University, was indicted on the same charge. During the period of his prosecution, Reverend Coffin was strongly supported at Yale.

In the 1969 Yale graduation ceremony, a young student spoke against the war. Both Yale and Harvard and other schools began to re-evaluate ROTC on campus in the spring of 1969. The example of men like the Reverend Coffin had a strong effect on organizing this kind of response from the youth of Ivy League colleges. The indictment of these men and women and their companions also made thinking Americans wonder about our freedom of expression and about justice in our courts. Americans saw the courts refuse again and again to examine the war itself for the unconstitutional waging of an undeclared war.

A Catholic priest from Duluth, Minnesota, Philip Solem, wrote a letter to high-school graduates of a Catholic high school in Duluth urging them to resist induction. He gave reasons why he found the Vietnam war immoral when judged by the just/unjust-war theory. At the end of the letter he wrote, "I ask you to read this letter carefully and consider what I say. By writing it I violate the Selective Service Act and risk a five-year sentence." He was verbally attacked by a large number of parents and students in the school, but twenty percent of the student body, which was looking for religious leadership on the moral issue of the war, turned to him with joy and enthusiasm. He spurred the Catholic community and the neighborhood in which he lived to think more deeply about the moral issues of the war. His witness had an effect beyond Duluth on Catholics all over the United States and in the rest of the world. Had he escalated his letter writing and joined with other clergymen to reach the youth in many parts of the country, he might have been arrested for doing precisely what a clergyman should do: speak the truth on a moral issue. Had he been arrested for this, he would have received wide backing from the American public. His witness in jail would have been most effective in waking up the conscience of America to what we were doing in Vietnam.

Puerto Rican Bishop Antulio Parilla-Bonilla, speaking to thousands of students at The University of Puerto Rico in May 1969, urged the students and all others to refuse the draft. He said, "Refusal to serve in the Army or the armed forces of the United States, regardless of consequences of humiliation, jail or persecution, is a very efficacious form of protest."

A medical doctor, Captain Howard Levy, was court-martialed because he refused to continue teaching soldiers going to Vietnam. He contended that they were misusing the techniques he taught them to harm people instead of to help them. He was accused by the Army of disloyalty because he said if he were black, he would never fight in Vietnam. His refusal to use his medical knowledge to destroy people reached millions of Americans who read about his trial and his punishment.

Captain Dale Noyd, professor of psychology at the United States Air Force Academy, is another shining example of a man whose conscience helped all of us. For eighteen months he maintained that the war in Vietnam was unjust and that he would not be part of it. When he was ordered on December 4, 1968, to train a pilot to fly jets, he refused, since all those trained were sent to Vietnam. Before that he had applied for and was denied conscientious objector status. He had requested and was denied reassignment or an opportunity to resign. In the course of his court-martial, Major Smith, the prosecutor, argued that "there must be a reasonable subordination of religious faith to military service." Captain Noyd, a religious humanist, believed that there were limits to what his conscience would allow him to do. He also contended that the Nuremberg principles bound the United States to respect his conscience. The court refused to listen and sentenced him for failing to obey an order. Captain Noyd's story gave courage to officers and other men everywhere.

On April 12, 1968, a Marine court-martial sentenced Corporal Mary Elizabeth Burns for refusing to wear the Marine uniform. Back in her home town, her twenty-four-year-old twin brother, Tim, had already refused to take the step that would lead to his induction into the United States Army.

After eighteen months of service, Mary, who forwarded radio messages from men in Vietnam to their families, realized the Marine Corps' activities were inhumane and indefensible. She took her uniform to her Marine captain, saying she could no longer, in conscience, be a part of the Marines.

Despite pleas of her lawyer that she be given an administrative discharge, the military machine tried to grind her down with a court-martial. It soon found that the presence of a woman opposing its methods did more harm to Marine prestige than it did to Mary. Finally, after the court-martial condemned her to confinement to barracks and a twenty-dollar fine, the Marine Corps dismissed her with a general discharge.

John Fucillo of New York was drafted into the Army after his unsuccessful appeal for conscientious-objector status. He devised his own personal system of confronting the Army. He learned all the rules and observed them, but he fearlessly pointed out in a letter to his sergeant and to all his superior officers that the sergeant had violated Army rules in the way he treated the men. When the lieutenant attacked him for his action, John wrote more letters complaining that the lieutenant did not wish Army rules to be observed.

In the barracks, in public and in private, John spoke against the Vietnam war. He carefully observed all the rules, however. In nine months the Army discharged him for not having the proper attitude.

*The Process of Peace*

He had confronted Army officials with their own failures to live up to their own rules. It was a lonely and difficult ordeal, but he believed that he brought to the attention of many Army officials their own failures to follow the ideals that they preached. His additional expressions of his freedom to speak against US foreign policy to all those around him made him undesirable company for other Army personnel.

Daniel Ellsberg, M.I.T. professor and Defense Department expert, risked a life in jail by giving the public the secret government appraisal of the Vietnam war called the Pentagon Papers. To block their continued printing, the Nixon administration appealed to the US Supreme Court. The news of government deception of its own people rocked the nation and did much to turn the tide of opinion against the war.

I asked Daniel Elllsberg how he had the courage to do it. He replied, "I saw what others were forced to do to support the war. I saw what Vietnamese and Americans were suffering because of the war. I believed the people should know the truth, so I did it to make the truth known."

Don Dawson, a B-52 pilot during the Christmas bombing of Cambodia, refused to fly a bombing mission. He had to stand almost alone against the military in which he was an officer. At the time, Congress and most of the country were opposed to the invasion of Cambodia, but Mr. Nixon as commander-in-chief was ordering it. Don Dawson's refusal to fly strengthened those opposing Nixon. Dawson was discharged because the military feared the political effects of a public court-martial. But Dawson had to risk court-martial to give his good example.

Similar courage was shown by Major Hal Knight, Jr., of the US Air Force, who revealed the secret bombing of Cambodia to the Senate Armed Services Committee in July 1973. The bombing was illegal and the Nixon administration and the US Air Force lied to Congress to cover up their actions. Major Knight had been a key supervisor to the bombing. His stand helped others who were trying to build up their resolve to make a stand against the war.

Kathleen Guest-Smith, an Army lieutenant and a nurse, applied for dismissal from the Army on grounds of conscientious objection. When the Army tried to prepare her to give nursing care to victims of nuclear war, she asked "Is it right to have a nuclear war?" The Army held up approval of her request for six months, hoping that she would change her mind. She refused to wear the Army uniform and refused to take her Army paycheck before the Army understood she was serious and let her out.

Captain Carolyn Blaisdel, a nurse with a degree in psychiatric nursing and a teacher at Walter Reed Army Medical Hospital in Washington, D.C., applied for conscientious-objector release from the Army after she read about Kathleen Guest-Smith. She had been confronted by a psychotic soldier who screamed at her that she was a hypocrite when she advised him to turn away from thoughts of killing while she wore a uniform. His accusation plus the example of Kathleen Guest-Smith helped her recall her year of bad experience in the Army in Korea. This brought her to the conviction that by continuing in the military she was prostituting her nursing profession. She was helping the military use her for its policy of "kill and destroy" when her profession was to heal and help. "The Army can call us 'ladies in white,' " she told me, "yet we are used to make killing more acceptable."

The Army resisted her request. But it didn't want to imprison her. An officer, a nurse, and a woman in the stockade would call attention to her views of the immorality of Army activity. After six months it let her leave.

## Action by Catholics

In Cleveland on January 26, 1969, two Roman Catholic priests were carried and dragged from the altar of St. John's Roman Catholic Cathedral. The newspapers showed the priests held by police on the sidewalk. The priests were taken to jail still in their liturgical vestments even though they had asked the police to allow them to change clothes. After they were released, still in vestments, they appeared in a television interview at the prison gates.

Robert T. Begin and Bernard L. Meyer, both priests of the Cleveland area, had gone into the Cathedral to offer mass as a protest against the Catholic Church because it "coexists self-righteously and apathetically with immoral and inhumane wars, intolerable and divisive racism, and extreme and dire poverty." Both the violence of the police and the disruption of the sacred ceremonies gave Catholics of that area and of the entire United States reason to reflect.

They were arrested at the request of the pastor of the church on the basis of interrupting a religious service. The pastor declined to press charges, probably because he did not relish publicity over division among priests. The priests were released without charges.

A witness to the silence of organized religion about the war in Vietnam took place in front of the Shrine of the Immaculate Conception in Washington, D.C. As worshipers came out from their Holy Saturday ceremonies, an eight-foot crucifix was burned with napalm on the front steps in an anti-war protest. On the crucifix was a black figure of Christ.

The Catholic Peace Fellowship led by John Swinglish organized the demonstration. "By the burning of the paper Christ figure we want to signify how Christ in man is being crucified in Vietnam."

During the last forty-five days of the bombing of Cambodia, 162 people were arrested for holding pray-ins at the White House.

They entered day after day with tour groups and remained to pray.

Their willingness to suffer jail encouraged others and gave newsmen a focus for news opposing the bombing.

As the US withdrew troops and began using the electronic battlefield technique in Vietnam, Jim Douglas, a professor at the University of Hawaii, went with his friends into Air Force Headquarters at Hawaii and poured his own blood on the files. Jim was severely beaten and dragged down the stairs by an Air Force officer. At the trial the Air Force refused to show the records, so the charge was dropped.

In 1980 Jim Siemer of Columbus, Ohio, refused to register for the draft "Because I believe that Jesus Christ would not register, I refuse," he said in the public speeches. The FBI visited his father and threatened dire consequences and prosecution, but Jim was not prosecuted. Instead he spent 1981- 82 going from one Catholic high school to another in Washington, D.C., and Baltimore, explaining to students the contradiction between nuclear war and the Gospel.

In September 1980, the Plowshares Eight entered the General Electric plant near Norristown, Pennsylvania. In early morning, at 6:30 a.m., three of the group talked to a guard while the other five walked into the plant. They found the metal nose cone for the Mark 12 nuclear missile. No bomb was in it. They dented the cone with two hammers, arousing security guards who arrested them while they proclaimed they were "beating nuclear weapons into plowshares." In June 1982, their appeal was continued to hold up imprisonment. For ten years their appeals went through the courts and ended in 1990 when the Supreme Court refused to hear the case. In April 1990, they were sentenced to "time served", a sentence so reduced that it reflected the changing climate of public opinion initiated in part by their actions. The eight consisted of three priests, a nun, a Jesuit seminary student, the mother of six children, a college professor, and a lawyer.

A characteristic of all these acts is that the utmost care was taken that no injury was done to anyone.

Many of the participants were older Americans, some representing stable positions in society: teachers, clergymen, and nuns. They have confronted America with court cases to force reflection on what we were doing and why. At the Catonsville trial, Judge Thomsen said, "You may be found right by history or philosophy."

The tactic of destroying property is unacceptable to many who wish to work for peace. However, according to traditional Christian morality, a law can and should be disobeyed:

1. When the law conflicts with a higher law, for example, a law that orders a person to kill another.
2. When the disobedience to law comes as a last resort after petitions and all other legal and organized efforts have failed.
3. When those who commit the act of civil disobedience are able to show in their lives a pattern of deep respect for law, making it clear through their act that it is not an attack on law in general, but on the immorality or injustice of a particular law.
4. When those who commit such civil disobedience in order to show their deep respect for law willingly accept the punishment for what they consider to be an innocent act and appeal to society to judge the immorality of the law for which they are punished.
5. When in disobeying the law, they harm no person.

I think that all of these principles apply to anti-draft acts of property destruction better than they apply to the American colonists who dressed themselves up as Indians and poured tea into Boston harbor. Those "heroes" did not stay to take the punishment; they dressed as Indians; they helped start a bloody revolution.

Some ask, "Is not destruction of property wrong?" Dan Berrigan answers, "If I lived in Germany during the time Hitler was making ovens to kill the Jews, and if I went into the oven factory and beat on the ovens with a hammer, would it be wrong?" Most Americans would answer, "No." Dan continues with "General Electric Company is making portable ovens, each five times more powerful than the bomb that incinerated Hiroshima. These ovens, ten of them, are mounted under the nose cone of the Mark 12 missiles. If they are used, we will all die in retaliation."

The Berrigans and others do not claim that theirs was the best action. They do claim that they said "No" to war at a very high price to themselves and with no personal harm to others. They wanted their act to move others to act against the war in whatever way suited their own consciences.

Like the Plowshares Eight, the Pacific Life Community takes direct non-violent action against the nuclear death danger. Some have formed a community called "Ground Zero." Next to the fence of the Trident submarine base on Puget Sound near Bangor, Washington, they have built a peace pagoda. Thousands have been arrested for entering the base to pray or to plant a tree as a symbol of life. Jim Douglas, author and former theology professor, says, "We can stop the Trident." How? By changing hearts and minds until there is no one willing to kill with the Trident. He and the Ground Zero Community are making friends with workers and educating them about what they are doing. Ground Zero people accept the pain of going to jail regularly to testify to the truth that life is sacred. Jim and others are moving hearts and minds toward the way of peace.

## More Conventional Group Action

### *The Quakers*

The Quakers belong to a peace church which has made its mark on American history. William Penn, a Quaker, gave his name to the state founded by a group of Quakers. From the earliest days in their dealings with the Indians, the Quakers refused to take part in killing. Among the Christian communities they are one of the "peace churches."

Through the American Friends Service Committee, Quakers have worked in Vietnam, Nigeria, Biafra to meet the needs of civilian war sufferers. Their activities include medical and rehabilitation services for amputees. They collect funds for victims of war. They visit those held in federal prisons for acts of conscience. Members of the Quaker Action Group read the names of the war dead on the steps of the Capitol in June 1969. Throughout the summer months, groups of people, including congresspeople, challenged the country to remember these dead. The Quakers were briefly arrested for this activity and then released.

The Quakers, also known as Friends, have camps for training in non-violence. They hold discussion groups on war and peace, and print and distribute information. The American Friends Service Committee believes that each human life is sacred and that each person is a child of God. Quakers believe that love, expressed through creative action, can overcome hatred, prejudice, and fear. Seeking non-violent ways of solving conflict, they welcome help from all interested people.

## The Church of the Brethren

The Church of the Brethren is another peace church and has a volunteer service program serving the needy in the US and overseas. In the past, Brethren volunteers have been permitted by Selective Service to count their two-year work terms as alternative service. Military administration of Selective Service jeopardizes this arrangement. The Church of the Brethren headquarters are in New Windsor, Maryland 21776.

## War Resisters League

The War Resisters League is part of international resistance against all types of wars. The League's offices are at 339 Lafayette Street, New York, New York 10012. This group strives for close cooperation with all peace organizations in hopes of encouraging individuals and groups to renounce war once and for all, to find non-violent solutions for conflict, to withdraw from the political power struggle, and to work for a social order based on non-violence. The League holds conferences, seminars, and study-work camps, and it campaigns against militarism, conscription, violence, and injustice.

*Fellowship of Reconciliation*

This organization of 14,000 members began in 1914. It describes itself as a fellowship of individuals who recognize the essential unity of mankind and who have come together to explore the power of love and truth to resolve human conflict. It identifies with those of every nation, race, and religion who are victims of injustice and exploitation, and seeks to develop resources of active, non-violent intervention with which to help rescue them. It strives to build a social order that will utilize the resources of human ingenuity and wisdom to the benefit of all men.

Some widely known organizations which include the American Civil Liberties Union, the Congress of Racial Equality, and the American Committee on Africa came into existence through the efforts of the Fellowship of Reconciliation.

The Catholic Peace Fellowship and the Episcopal and Jewish peace fellowships all work closely with the Fellowship of Reconciliation. Their religious fellowships work to move their own religious groups towards peacemaking. The Fellowship of Reconciliation's address is P.O. Box 271, Nyack, New York. It runs an extensive mail-order service of books and pamphlets related to its work.

## The Catholic Worker Movement

This group has opposed war for almost fifty years, while it feeds the poor through hospitality houses, and engages in myriad activities to promote peace. Through communal living, the practice of voluntary poverty, and its monthly publication, *The Catholic Worker,* which still sells for one cent a copy, it tries to humanize life.

Catholic Worker founder Dorothy Day probably did more in her lifetime to move the Roman Catholic Church to action for peace than has any other person. Thousands of priests, bishops, nuns, and seminarians have visited the Catholic Worker hospitality house in New York. Through this house and others like it throughout this country, its activities have exerted influence nationwide. There are now a total of forty-four Catholic Worker houses across the United States. Catholic Worker people oppose the war machine as they care for its victims, the outcasts of US society who are the result of a misdirected economy and culture. *The Catholic Worker* newspaper is published from the Catholic Worker house at 36 East First Street, New York, New York 10003.

## Pax Christi, USA

Pax Christi is part of the International Pax Christi. The international president is Cardinal Koenig of Austria. Thomas Gumbleton, auxiliary bishop of Detroit, is president of the US branch. Among its 5,000 members are fifty-five Catholic bishops, who have a strong peace influence on the Catholic Church in the US. Pax Christi publishes a newsletter from its headquarters at 3000 N. Mango Street, Chicago, Illinois 60634.

## Sojourners

This is an evangelical Christian community that publishes a monthly magazine focusing on peace and justice. Its address is 1309 L Street, N.W., Washington, D.C.

## CCCO

The Central Committee for Conscientious Objectors, founded in 1948, is independent, non-profit, and non-sectarian. CCCO looks forward to a time when our society will adopt other means than militarism to deal with conflict. Currently it is helping those confronted by registration. It also assists men and women in the military who can no longer in good conscience carry arms. It publishes the CCCO newsletter, *The Handbook for Conscientious Objectors* and other self-help books. Its main office is at 2016 Walnut Street, Philadelphia, Pennsylvania 19103.

## Physicians for Social Responsibility

This group of physicians holds national and international conferences on the health effects of nuclear war. "Don't call your doctor," it concludes, "if there is a nuclear war. Doctors will be eighty percent dead, hospitals destroyed, transport impossible, recovery contra-indicated."

As preventative medicine, since no remedy for nuclear destruction is possible, members believe it is their job as physicians to tell their patients, government leaders, and their professional peers that they must avoid nuclear war. They promote a powerful half-hour film titled "The Last Epidemic" that shows the horrors of nuclear war. There are local chapters all over the United States.

*Clergy and Laity Concerned*

This is a national committee, formed in the emergency time of the Vietnam war, to express the moral concern of the clergy and others to the war. It is interdenominational and has a broad following of clergy and laity throughout the country. It works with many national peace groups and promotes programs of amnesty, reconciliation with Vietnam, and recently has formed a lawyers' support group to help young men who have problems with registration. The address is: 475 Riverside Drive, New York, New York 10027.

*UNA-USA*

The United Nations Association is a cooperative alliance of more than one hundred national voluntary organizations whose purpose is to provide information and education about the United Nations. The group's purpose is dedicated to strengthening our country's capacity for advancing peace, freedom, and justice in the world through the development of the United Nations and other international organizations. Working in research, information, and educational fields, it cooperates with foundations and universities supported entirely by contributions from individuals and organizations. It is independent and non-partisan. Its headquarters are at 345 East 46th Street, New York, New York 10017.

*The World Federalists*

The World Federalists organization believes in a world federal government. It seeks to convince people that such a government is essential to human survival and would preserve our basic freedoms. It feels that world government can be attained by orderly constitutional means. It has a program *World Peace through World Law* with headquarters at The Hague. It also has an office at 1346 Connecticut Avenue N.W., Washington, D.C. 20036.

The World Federalists organization is a voluntary, nonpartisan group supported by dues from many thousands of members throughout the country and works through discussion groups and talks to build wider support for its ideals.

*Nuclear Freeze Campaign*

This group recommends a US-USSR freeze on all nuclear weapons as a first step toward disarmament. It was founded by Randall Forsberg in 1981 and grew into sudden national strength as Europeans reacted to President Reagan's plans to rearm Europe.

It works at the local and national level, with headquarters at 324 Fourth Street, N.E., Washington, D.C. 20002.

*Ground Zero*

This is an educational campaign with a message expressed in the title of the book, *Nuclear War—What's in It for You?* edited by Earl Molander. The editor was assistant to a national security advisor under Nixon and Kissinger. In that position he learned that neither Nixon nor Kissinger paid much attention to arms negotiations or knew much about nuclear weapons. Although he knew very little about them himself, he was considered an expert. Appalled by the ignorance within the US government, he decided to begin an educational campaign directed towards the public. With demonstrations, media coverage, and publications, the Ground Zero organization has reached many people. Its national headquarters are at Suite 421, 806 15th Street, N.W., Washington, D.C. 20005.

*SANE*

The Sane Nuclear Policy Committee concentrates on matters of nuclear-weapons development. It has branch offices in many cities and publishes *SANE World,* a monthly. Its main office is at 711 G Street S.W., Washington, D.C. 20003.

*The Center For Defense Information*

The Center for Defense Information is a civilian watchdog group that monitors Pentagon spending and policies. Many members of the staff are retired military people. It publishes a monthly bulletin, *The Defense Monitor,* that contains excellent information. Its offices are at 1500 Massachusetts Avenue, N.W., Washington, D.C. 20005.

*Women's International League for Peace and Freedom*

This group carries on a long tradition of the women's movement which has often worked for nonviolent social change. It is an international organization which emphasizes nonviolent solutions to domestic and international problems. It has many branches with a national center at 1213 Race Street, Philadelphia, Pennsylvania 19107.

*Women's Strike for Peace*

This group organized in protest to atmospheric testing by the USSR and the US in the early 1960s. It is a network with contacts throughout the US. It holds demonstrations, conducts public information programs, and issues a monthly legislative newsletter. The Washington office is at Suite 102, 201 Massachusetts Avenue, N.E., Washington, D.C. 20002.

Many communities already have peace centers like the Washington Peace Center and the Philadelphia Peace Center.

More are forming all the time. They all welcome volunteers, and the existing ones can be contacted to get some information about starting one in your community if there isn't one at this time. One person writing letters to the editor of a local paper is enough activity to form a base for starting a peace center.

*Government or Public Action*

All of the above groups and others work to urge Congress to take more positive positions in support of peace. Peace-conversion bills which would divert military spending to social programs are continually introduced into Congress, but ignored there by leading factions and the majority of Congress.

*The World Peace Tax Fund Bill*

This bill is sponsored by Congressman Ron Dellums and over twenty-three other congresspersons. It would allow conscientious objectors and those opposed to war for reasons of faith and conscience to put the war portion of their taxes in a special peace fund. More information is available from the Council for a World Peace Tax Fund at 2111 Florida Avenue, N.W., Washington, D.C. 20008.

## Evaluating our Foreign Policy

There is no doubt that we need a big change in foreign policy. We have been destructive in our role as "policemen of the world." We have sided too often with those protecting only vested interests rather than human interest. As a people we should promote world security on an international basis.

Such a role would mean an end to negative anti-communism, to anti-revolutionary interventionism, and to support of militarism, all qualities of our present foreign policy. It means that we understand that peace must be based on justice. This peace must be on the economic, political, and social levels and must reach to the individual. It must assure human rights.

The achievement of peace involves, as Tom Stonier says, "the evolution of a constellation of attitudes and institutions, each reinforcing the other so as to construct an ever-enlarging community of international law, justice, and therefore, world order."

To make this vision clear to those in the church, in the classroom, and on the street corner is a job for everyone. It is a job involving a re-evaluation of our present institutions and the evolution of new institutions. Among these is the new US Institute of Peace. It could also involve a Department of Peace, a course on peace in every college and university, reversal of the glorification of war in secondary and elementary textbooks and practices, and in film and entertainment.

To accomplish this on the political front will require the election of candidates who have an international outlook. This would follow the creation of that international outlook among all our people. One way to further the acceptance of an international outlook is to strengthen the prestige and the power of the United Nations. Instead of criticizing the UN, we might better study it and see the limitations we impose when we bypass it as we did in the Vietnam war, in the Falkland Islands war, and in the Arab-Israeli war. As the world's major economic and military power, we could make the UN stronger by insisting that the UN deal with such conflicts instead of taking over ourselves and thus weakening the UN. How can we complain about the ineffectiveness of the UN when we ignore it in times of crisis?

Improvements in the UN are easy to suggest: an end to the "veto"—how can the UN function when a single power can block it?—representation proportionate to the population represented; Article 43 revised to provide a more capable standby force. A larger number of nations should contribute peace-keeping forces and funds for peace-keeping action. Closer bonds between the UN and regional groups like NATO could be established.

The United States could vastly increase its financial help to the UN. It could train some of its forces for transportation, communication, and support for UN duty. Seven countries now have designated units of their armed forces for emergency duty with the UN. We could train for UN duty in our colleges or in a Peace Academy, and replace ROTC with this activity. We could work for the cession of all deep-water rights to the UN. The same UN control could apply to outer space.

We could help develop an international outlook by abolition of all travel restrictions, by the recognition that we live in "a global village." We need to remember daily the astronauts' photo of our frail planet spinning in space. This is one Earth, not 161 sovereign states.

# Part VI:

# Peacemakers

*One person who can express nonviolence in life exercises a force superior to all the forces of brutality.... Nonviolence is the greatest and most active force in the world. One cannot be passively nonviolent.... A soldier of peace, unlike the one of the sword, has to give all his or her spare time to the promotion of peace, alike in wartime as in peacetime. His or her work in peacetime is both a measure of prevention of, as also that of preparation for, wartime.*

Mahatma Gandhi

*Chapter 1*

*A Sad Day in Atlanta:
The Funeral of Martin Luther King, Jr.*

As I walked in the crowd of 250,000 people, behind the body that moved ahead of us in a donkey-drawn wagon, I saw a sign printed in red, above the front door of a church, which read, "Our slain leader, Martin Luther King, Jr." That sign told of the sorrow and inspiration that blended together during the funeral of Dr. King.

I arrived in Atlanta on Sunday night. It seemed to me a city of luxury and death. Among the new, beautiful buildings downtown, there was one with a revolving dome in which a restaurant rotates to give changing views of the city. It symbolized America—its wealth and its violence.

Cars marked with the sign, "S.C.L.C. [Southern Christian Leadership Conference] Courtesy Cars" cruised the city. They offered service to the visitors; they were necessary. I found that the ordinary city cab would not take me to the "colored" section of the town, where King's body lay. Here, even on the night in which he lay dead in his struggle for justice, the cab stopped at the bridge which marked the entrance to the "colored" section of town and radioed for a "colored" cab to carry us the remaining distance.

On Sunday night King's body lay in the chapel of Spelman College, about four miles from the center of Atlanta. We reached there a half-hour after midnight. For two hours we moved slowly through the long line about a half-mile long and two or three deep. We moved across the peaceful campus to the pillared chapel. Trees above us reflected window lights on the dogwood blossoms. Above us hung a hazy moon. Slow organ tones, amplified across the campus, played the hymn identified with his struggle, "We Shall Overcome." In the darkness I reflected. Springtime and death. Death and new life. King's death meant new life for America. Black America and white America now had a new martyr; a martyr for social justice. His life and death connected the ethic of Jesus with the social and economic life of America. Here was a life and death based on belief in the brotherhood of humanity.

As I moved slowly with the silent, grieving people, I recalled marches I had made with King. I recalled the Selma-to-Montgomery March. There at the front of the line, he gave unity and confidence to all who followed. Now he does this for America.

I remember him walking up a dusty hill in Philadelphia, Mississippi. He had taken time out from the Meredith march to return to Philadelphia, Mississippi. He had been attacked and driven out of town two days before. He had returned to overcome fear. I walked by his side, as we moved up the hill, when suddenly a car with some white people in it roared down the hill, straight at Dr. King. He yelled a warning. The line opened and the car sped through. As it did, the National Guard along the road turned their guns on us. Dr. King yelled to them, "You turn your guns on us, but do not stop the car that would kill us."

That day Martin Luther King, Jr., seemed to me like the true Christian leader. He walked in the dust; he faced danger. He charted the path and led the way. He tried to protect, even with his own life, those who followed him. Now he lay here silent just ahead of us.

I asked a young black girl, in a line near me, "Did you know Dr. King?" "No, not personally," she said, "But I know what he did. I know him."

Inside the door of the church, a glass covered casket held his body. The glass cover was opaque around the edges. You could look in directly and see the length of his body. He looked small in stature but very big in meaning.

On Monday morning, Mrs. King left Atlanta to take up the unfinished march of her husband, in Memphis. In Memphis, he had been killed as he joined in the efforts of 1,300 garbage workers to gain humane working conditions.

Despite her grief, Coretta Scott King led 30,000 marchers to the city hall where she joined her plea to theirs that the city government recognize their just demands for a salary of more than $2,100 per year. She explained that throughout her life, she had supported her husband's struggle for justice, that occasionally he had asked her to substitute when he could not be in a certain place. She said she felt that he would want her to be in this march.

With her were three of her four children. How well they must have learned the lessons of courage and interest in the poor, from parents like theirs!

Back in Atlanta that evening, I visited the home of Dr. King. It was on Sunset Street in the "colored" section. It was not the slum section of the city, but a segregated section. Inside the front door, some woodcuts showed the faces of Negro men in struggle and strain. In the parlor, members of the

Southern Christian Leadership Conference invited visitors to sign the guest book and partake of a buffet supper.

Everything about the house spoke of his commitment to justice. In the parlor was a painting of Mahatma Gandhi. Decorations clearly identified his interest in Negro art and culture. In the kitchen I saw a large plaque carved in wood with the words of Mahatma Gandhi, a resolution for each day:

"Let our first act every morning be to make the following resolve for the day: I shall not fear anyone on earth; I shall fear only God. I shall not bear ill will towards anyone. I shall not submit to injustice from anyone. I shall conquer untruth by truth. And in resisting untruth, I shall put up with all suffering. —*Mahatma Gandhi, 1869-1948*."

Along one wall in the kitchen was a series of pictures: happy scenes with his wife and children. Mixed with them were some front covers of magazines showing pictures such as Dr. King and his wife at the head of the march in Washington in 1963.

What a home environment for the instruction of children! The symbols and ideals so clearly put before them, both in the example of their parents and in atmosphere of the home, recalled what Mrs. King said in her speech the day before in Memphis. She said that because her husband was so active in the service of others, he was often away from home. But although he did not have much time with the children, it was the quality of the time that counted. And the quality was good. This, it seemed to me, applied to his short life of thirty-nine years. It is not so much the number of years we live that counts, but the quality of the life in those years. The quality of his life was very good.

On Wednesday morning, the day of the funeral, I went to the Ebenezer Baptist Church.

An hour before the scheduled time of starting, thousands crowded outside the church. Only 1,300 could go in. The thousands outside made it next to impossible to see what was going on. I stopped in at the house nearest the church and asked if it were possible to watch the funeral on TV. The lady of the house invited me in and offered me coffee. Throughout the morning many others came in for a glass of water. I wonder, if the case had been reversed, and a "colored" man had shot a white leader, would the ordinary white person welcome in an unknown Negro who wished to see the funeral on TV? Yet I felt at home and welcomed in this household. Perhaps the constant endurance of suffering and oppression makes people friendlier, more human.

As I listened to the funeral ceremonies, the conviction deepened in me how perfectly King had lived out in his own life what he had taught. As with Christ, there was no separation between theory and practice in his life. Like Christ, he showed personal identification with the poor and the oppressed. What a record he had put before the world. Thirty-two times in jail to suffer for the injustice of others. Bombed in his own home, threatened with death constantly for thirteen years. He had been beaten, stoned, and stabbed. He was accused of being a communist and betrayed by those he loved and trusted. How like Jesus and St. Paul!

The high point of the funeral ceremony was the taped record with his voice telling the meaning of his own life. Other voices had been very eloquent, but when his voice, with its dynamic range and its rolling tones, came through the TV, the people in the poor home where I listened were magnetized. They responded to his remarks after almost every paragraph.

In his own prophetic way, he foresaw his own funeral and he asked that no one mention that he had received the Nobel Peace Prize or where he went to college. They should say here was a man who tried to love others, to serve others. Here was a man who visited the prisoner, who tried to clothe the naked, who tried to feed the hungry, and who left behind him a committed life. This was his own summary of the Christian life. These are also the norms for action laid out by Jesus. By these norms, Dr. King was a great Christian. By any Christian norm, he was a close imitator of Jesus.

Inside the church, the vice president, governors, mayors, and nationally known people listened to the assistant minister at Ebenezer Church say, "Martin spoke to the pharaohs of this land and said, 'Let my people go.'" The congregation and the one hundred and twenty million people who listened on television heard him call for the end of violence in Vietnam, as Martin had done.

They heard this call repeated by the Reverend Harold De Wolfe, a friend and disciple of Dr. King for the last thirteen years. They heard Ralph Abernathy, the new president of the Southern Christian Leadership Conference, say that he had been to jail seventeen times with Martin and that each time the two of them spent the first day in prayer and fasting, so that they would bear no bitterness in their hearts towards their jailers. They heard the Rev. Abernathy say that he had been fasting ever since his last meal which he shared five days before with Martin Luther King, Jr. His fasting was a plea and a prayer that God would direct him as he took over where Martin left off.

The body was carried out into the noonday sunlight and placed in the back of a farm wagon drawn by two mules. The wagon symbolized Martin's identification with the poor. It symbolized his identification with the farmer who develops life, as opposed to the destruction of life through violence.

A great march of two hundred thousand people followed Martin's body. No police and no military marched as part of their official duty. But many walked in sorrow among their friends and without their guns.

Four miles out from the city, the quarter-million followed Martin's body for the last time. As they marched, they sang the songs that many had sung marching with Martin. The words told their story: "Black and white together, we'll walk hand in hand. Deep in our hearts, we do believe that we shall overcome someday." The words were made up as the verses continued, "God is on our side; deep in our hearts we do believe that God is on our side today." Freedom songs were the order of the day; one repeated the word over and over again. It was like all funeral processions: sad. It was unlike all others that I had ever seen, because the people sang as Martin used to sing to keep his spirits up, because it looked to the future, the fulfillment of Martin's dream of brotherhood.

It was sad to walk by the State Capitol of Georgia where Governor Lester Maddox still blindly refused to see the opportunities that were passing him by. He refused to come to the funeral. Inside he was guarded by 160 men. In power and in loneliness, he sat in fear, a fear that Martin never shared, though he never had 100 armed men around him. It was sad that Martin's love which went out to him had never been accepted.

By two o'clock in the afternoon, the giant crowd was marching into Morehouse College, where Martin King had been a student. A plane from Washington brought twenty-four more senators and more than fifty congressmen. Most of the congressmen and senators stood unrecognized in the vast crowd.

On the lawn, near the back of the large crowd, I sat with Senator Phil Hart of Michigan. Many senators, no doubt, had been together at other funerals, but how often had they just been lost in the crowd? How different was this funeral, where the lowly and the humble were exalted, and the great ones of the earth were humbled by the example before them!

When Mahalia Jackson began to sing, "Take Me By the Hand," an old "colored" woman near me began having convulsions, screaming and crying. Three or four people tried to hold her, to quiet her down. In between screams she called for Jesus to hold her hand.

I took her hand and said, "Jesus takes you by the hand." She repeated what I said and began to quiet down a little. Those holding her seated her on the chair. I knelt beside her. "Martin Luther King walked hand in hand with Jesus," I said to her. "We must do the same." "Yes," she responded. Her convulsions began to subside. "Martin Luther King believed that God was his Father," I continued. "He walked, as a child, hand in hand with God. He has taught us how to walk. We must follow now that Martin has marched on with God. We must place our hand in the hand of God our Father for time and eternity. Martin has showed us the way, as Christ did. We must follow." She was quiet now; she thanked me and blessed me. She symbolized to me both the sorrow and the love of Martin Luther King, Jr. She personified the agony and the inspiration his life and death brought to all of us.

*Chapter 2*

*The Berrigans Teach Truth*

When the two Berrigan brothers, Daniel and Philip, and their six companions entered the G.E. plant outside of Philadelphia on September 9 and poured blood on the blueprints of the nuclear Mark 12 weapons and dented nuclear weapons, they were trying to get us to see what I try to get my students to see: the threat to our very survival by nuclear weapons.

"Why violate the law? Why destroy government property?" I've heard it said.

We are asked by our faith to obey God rather than men. Not all laws are good. Many Catholics in good conscience dis obey laws which protect abortion. There used to be laws supporting slavery, but they were not good laws.

Jesus disobeyed the Sabbath law by healing on the Sabbath. St. Paul disobeyed Roman law which forbade the preaching of the Gospel. St. Peter taught that we must obey God before men.

In Daniel Berrigan's view, the state goes against God's law when it acts, or prepares to act, to take millions of lives with nuclear weapons. Vatican II has condemned the use of nuclear weapons on large populations. The weapons that Daniel Berrigan dented are just those kinds of weapons.

We Catholics have listened to all that Daniel Berrigan, a Jesuit priest, and others have said and still we don't hear the message that we are offending God by paying for these nuclear weapons and by intending to use them. The US Bishops have said that even the intent to use nuclear weapons is wrong.

Statements pour out from the Vatican and from our bishops but they don't reach the people. How many people are surprised to find that a Jesuit priest will risk sixty-four years in prison to make the message known? This message should already be known. It should have been heard in our Catholic schools. It should have been heard in our parishes.

I'm sure Dan Berrigan does not want to go to prison. He does want to write, and he does want to serve the poor every week. He sees a moral responsibility to humanity. I think he is a Christ-figure of our church and a voice that is badly needed.

But I've heard it asked, "Why don't they [the Berrigans] just teach about it?" They believe they are teaching by their actions. They expect they will be in jail for their actions. They hope to rouse us from our lethargy by their suffering. They want to show us that we can do something about it, if we are willing to pay the price.

"Well, why can't they just say that?" it's been asked. They have said it, over and over again. Daniel Berrigan has written over thirty-five books—almost all of them bearing on this point. He has lectured in over one hundred colleges and universities on many continents. This is his message: We must turn away from the false worship of the god of war and return to the worship of the living God. Philip Berrigan has written five books and has lectured all over this country hundreds of times in fifteen years.

Despite all this, they see the danger growing worse, not less. The Mark 12A warhead, which they dented with hammers, has the destructive capacity to devastate three cities of 100,000 people each. They are part of the 33,000 nuclear warheads in our stockpile. These warheads carry 350 kilotons of explosive power, which is about thirty times the size of the Hiroshima bomb, which killed 100,000 people. Mark 12A warheads, when mounted on a Minuteman III missile, can devastate a ninety-square-mile area. If they are mounted on the MX missile, as is planned, they will be able to wipe out a 250-square-mile area.

The Berrigans see us preparing to spend $157 billion on our war budget next year. Dan says, "How far will we be willing to go in giving our money to the military? We give sixty-six percent of our budget now for military-related expenses. Are we ready to go to ninety-five percent? Are we willing to see more millions starve around the world to do this?"

They attacked the missiles at General Electric to wake us up, to help us to see the truth.

And the truth is: No one can win a nuclear war. The truth is: We are as naked to the nuclear weapons of our enemy as they are to ours. The truth is: Politicians lie to us when they say we are more secure with more nuclear weapons. The truth is: General Electric prepares "good things for death," contrary to their boast, "We bring good things to life."

General Electric wants us to see it as the makers of electric fans, not the builders of ovens worse than Hitler's—ovens that can cross the ocean and cremate a city full of people.

The Berrigans want us to be responsible for what we do when we give our government money to spend on nuclear weapons. The Berrigans want us to live, not to be radiated to death in an insane war.

"But couldn't they do it some other way than by breaking the law?" it is asked. The law they broke is not God's law. Turn the case around and ask, "Would it have been wrong for a German priest to go into the factory where Hitler's workers were making gas chambers and pour blood on the blueprints and damage the metal with hammers?" Was it wrong for the early Americans to dump tea into Boston harbor? Was it wrong for Martin Luther King, Jr., to violate racist laws? The answer to each case is, "No, it was not wrong." In this case, they have violated a law which puts property above human life, which protects the possibility of nuclear annihilation.

Everything that Hitler did was legal once he became head of state. He made the law, but he made many evil laws. When our government shields the preparations for deaths, all our deaths, under the name of law, we desecrate law as Hitler did.

The US government doesn't do it openly because we are still a free people. It hides from the people its preparations for their death. It makes us pay for the nuclear cyanide that we will breathe in after a nuclear exchange.

The Berrigans and their friends want to stop this process. They want us to choose life, instead of death. They show us dramatically that such a choice may cost much. They give us the good example of being ready to pay with their freedom to warn us of the danger.

*Chapter 3*

## *A Farewell to Dorothy Day*

Two years ago, three of us went to visit Dorothy Day in New York. We knew she was getting old and had had several heart attacks. She refused to go to the hospital for convalescent treatment, but was living with the poor in Mary House, the Catholic Worker house on 3rd Street in lower Manhattan.

The night before when we telephoned, we were told that Dorothy is never sure that she will have a good day, so we couldn't be sure of seeing her. She wasn't going out very much, just across the street to church and even in the house was not always able to meet visitors. Nonetheless, we decided to go.

She was able to come downstairs and have tea with us. She knew me because she knew my father. He had brought her to our house in Philadelphia where our family of fifteen children gave her a warm welcome. She remembered my father as a faithful supporter of the Catholic Worker in its earliest days.

As we sat around the table and talked, she radiated an air of serenity and peace. We talked for two or three hours and stopped only because we did not want to strain her. Throughout the conversation there was not one word of criticism of anybody. For fifty years she led the way identifying the Catholic Church on the right side of controversial issues—racism, unions, peace, and poverty. Yet she had no trace of bitterness or cynicism. All she remembered was good.

When she was asked about her disagreements with Cardinal Spellman, she had something kindly to report. At one point she said, "I was called into the chancery office. I remember going past desks all lined up, everything neat, so different from the Catholic Worker, and I came to the monsignor. He was very nice to me. I sat down by the desk, and he said, 'Now, Miss Day, I have seen you and everything has been accomplished.' He told me that he had received several complaints about what I was doing and he just wanted to inform the people that 'I have seen her, and I have talked with her, but I know what you are doing and I don't need to ask you anything. Everything is accomplished by your simply coming here, and I thank you for that!'" She gave this as a sample of the kind way in which she had been treated by the Archdiocese of New York.

The point was pressed about the strike of the cemetery workers and how the Catholic Worker people had disagreed with the cardinal on it. She replied with the story of how Cardinal Cooke had come personally in his limousine to the Catholic Worker with a medal and a citation from the pope to honor her for her work for the poor. She laughed about it. "Certainly the pope had better things to do than to be sending medals to me." But she said that the cardinal was very nice, and very friendly, and she appreciated very much how he went out of his way to deliver the medal.

Sister Evelyn Mattern asked her about women priests. She said, "Perhaps there will be women priests one day, but it will come only after there are other changes in the Church. Right now it would be much too contrary to the culture of American Catholicism to have women priests. Women now are two steps removed from the altar. The first step might be to have married priests; then after the Catholic community in America had gotten used to women being closer to the priests through marriage they might be ready to think about accepting women priests. But it will be a slow process and not abrupt."

I asked her if she thought it was essential that Catholic Worker groups identify themselves publicly and intimately with their Catholic faith. She said, "Of course, and the evidence speaks for itself. There are forty-four Catholic Workers in the country now, and not one of them has survived without this linkage of their work to their faith."

I also asked her what she thought about Catholic Worker people who lived outside the Catholic Worker but were part of the staff. She said, "Well, we have the most wonderful group of young people at the Catholic Worker in New York now. But some of them live in their own apartments and I suppose that's the way they have to do it, but I am concerned about not sharing with the poor. Still, I am not criticizing them; I just worry a bit that the identification with the poor is not as complete as it might be. But there have to be different forms of service to God, even in the Catholic Worker, and perhaps this new day requires varying ways of serving the poor. Certainly they are wonderful, dedicated young people, all of them."

As she talked, I recalled what I had heard about her. Almost singlehandedly out of loyalty to the Church she had made the Catholic Worker movement Catholic. There was no legal or organizational linkage of the Catholic Worker movement to the faith. The link was in the person of the people themselves.

Dorothy Day had exemplified how that was done by living out the Catholic faith and all of its teachings, and by publicly following those teachings. She kept the Catholic Worker movement from being just another social club, drifting along in various ways on its own. There was no missing her devotion to daily Mass, to the rosary, to the authority of the Church. Church officials, on their part, recognized in her that identification with the poor is the mark of Christ. It's to their credit that they never interfered with her.

I once heard her say, "There are two constant miracles going on in the Catholic Worker. One is that for forty-five years the poor are fed without any funding and they are fed in forty-four places across the country. The other miracle is that in all these years no chancery office has ever prohibited our work." She had no fear that would ever happen. She said once, "If Cardinal Spellman ever told me to stop doing the work of the Catholic Worker, I would stop immediately." She said it and she meant it. It was her understanding of obedience. She believed, of course, as she said, that if she stopped, others would take up the work.

Now she has stopped. On November 29, 1980, the Lord called her to the eternal banquet table, where together with the poor that she helped, she can share the joy of the poor Christ forever. We will see now who will follow her and take up the work.

*Chapter 4*

*How a Mother Teaches Peace*

A group of us listened intently as thirty-eight-year-old Barbara Roth told how she taught the Peace Pastoral to her ten children. "I had read about how God had shaken up Moses and got him to free the people from Pharaoh. Then God shook the Egyptians with plagues, and told Moses how to lead the people out to the Promised Land. That's what the bishops seemed to do in the Peace Pastoral. They told us about the moment of crisis that has reached the human family and then put before us Christ's way to peace. That's what I tried to do with my children. I told them about the horrors of nuclear war, what it would do and then I put before them the way that

Christ wants us to go. So I put *hope* before them. I didn't just leave them with the bad news of nuclear war.

"I have nine boys and one girl," she continued. "The older ones [ages fifteen to eighteen] didn't pay much attention. The boys had taken on the macho spirit of the country; they've listened to the violent culture around us, and they don't want to hear this Peace Message. So they pretty much put it aside.

"The younger group [ages eight to fourteen] listened a bit, and thought maybe I was right. A lot of their friends wouldn't agree with it.

"But the youngest group [from eight down to five] listened. They believed what I said and they wanted to hear more about it. 'Mommy, would we not see you anymore, if there was a nuclear war? Will all the houses be gone? Will we see the family anymore?' they asked.

"They wanted to hear as much about it as I would have time to tell them. And they wanted to know what to do about it. And they listened when I told them that Jesus' way was not a way of war, not a way of killing. But that his way was one of love. And they understood it. They wanted to know what to do about it.

"They were so receptive that they wanted to bring up the topic whenever they could. And the older ones listened to what I was saying to them. As time went by, they began to accept some of it too. The one exception to this pattern was my sixteen-year-old daughter, Michelle. She understood and accepted immediately.

"The family is a microcosm of the whole of society. And I think that what happened in my family is what might happen in the wider society. There are some who are ready for the message, and accept it immediately. And they try to do immediately what they can. Then, as the talk goes on and the work goes on, those others who initially refuse to listen, hear some parts of it and begin to respond. And as time goes on, they may respond more."

This seemed to me to be a modern version of the Parable of the Sower and the Seed. It is also a marvelous example of how a parent can work for peace.

Barbara Roth's presentation was amazing enough, but when I learned more about her, my amazement grew. Besides being the mother of ten children, ages four months to eighteen years, she is also the owner and operator of a day care center, which takes care of sixty-five children a day. Her husband, Ron, is a dry-wall plasterer. She also does research on social issues at West Palm Beach College, three or four days a week in the afternoons. Two or three evenings a week, she takes care of two cancer patients, one eighty-nine years old and one ninety-six years old, who need someone in the house with them in the evening.

That sounds like a full program. But in addition, she is the co-founder and organizer of a soup kitchen, which is open every day. And after she gets all her children off to school, beginning with the first one who leaves at 6:30 A.M., she drives to the soup kitchen. On the way she picks up soup, which has been prepared at various homes. She stops at a Dunkin' Doughnuts and picks up yesterday's doughnuts. She delivers the soup and doughnuts to the soup kitchen, where she stays a while to see how things are going. Then she moves on to the day care center, where she picks up twelve children in her van; she takes them out to the park for lunch. There, they are joined by another van, making a total of twenty-four children in the park for lunch.

Her three youngest children go with her, along with her sister's youngest child, because her sister has no one to care for the child while she is at work. She says that the four children in the van are her bodyguards.

At the park, the children have lunch and run around and play. About two o'clock, they are returned to the day care center. Mrs. Roth checks up on the day care center and then goes on to her research.

This sounds like a full day, but there is more. She finds time to attend the five-fifteen Mass every day at Holy Name Church, where she is an active member of the Justice and Peace Committee.

When I asked her how she became involved working for peace, she said, "Well, it's all part of the package. If you see the poor in need, and try to help them, you begin to see that something is wrong with society and, if you wonder why they don't have food, you soon see the reason. You begin to see that so much government money is being spent on weapons for death. You see the old people neglected, cast off by society. You see more of the need of compassion for each other, which is contradicted by the military program. So you go from the small to the large, and then back again to the small. Up and down, you see it is all part of the one thing. We have to be interested in each other, and help each other. I try to share with others what God has given me. Our family is not rich, but we have more than the others. So we try to share."

Barbara took in a sixteen-year-old girl who was mentally ill. The girl needed a home. Rather than see her placed in an institution, Barbara took her in.

She took in a teenaged boy from Spain, who wished to be here with an American family.

Instead of using the excuse that she has ten children, she says that it is precisely because she has ten children that she is concerned about peace, and about helping the needy in the world. "I try to show them by example how to do something about it."

Barbara Roth is an extraordinary teacher, both by word and by example.

## Chapter 5

## The Poor, the Brave, and the Archbishop Who Believed

Dorothy Day chose to live in voluntary poverty with the poor whom she served. She wrote that poverty frees one. "A readiness for poverty and a disposition to accept it is enough to begin with. We will always get what we need." She liked the Gospel passage that said, "Take no thought to what you are to eat or drink, the Lord knows you have need of these things."

It's true enough that poverty frees. The reason why most of us don't have that freedom is that we are unwilling to pay the price of that identification that is the cost of that solidarity with the poor. We fear we may not be able to pay the price.

Another person who overcame that fear and paid the price was Archbishop Oscar Romero. He said, "Christ invites us not to fear persecution, because, believe me brothers and sisters, one who is committed to the fate of the poor must run the same fate as the poor, and we know what the fate of the poor signifies: to disappear, be tortured, be captive, and to be found dead." What Archbishop Romero said applies to himself because he was found dead at the altar where the body of Christ was being broken and His blood shed. He gave us an example of how to identify our lives with the God who came on earth as a poor human being and was tortured, imprisoned, and crucified.

Maybe that's the reason why we don't want to be identified with the poor: because there's too much of a cross in it.

In El Salvador, where Archbishop Romero died, those who are poor are those who will die. If you look for the poor in El Salvador who fulfilled this definition in 1980, you would find, besides Archbishop Romero, many others who were listed in a report by the Legal Aid Office of the Archdiocese of San Salvador. The report lists 384 people killed by right-wing security forces in El Salvador between August and December 1980. Why mention such tragedies when they're so far away from us? We have enough of the poor here to take care of in imitation of Dorothy Day; people who are Americans here in our own country. Do we have to get mixed up in the conflicts of Central America? Questions like that make it appear that we need not be involved in stopping the murder of the poor in Central America.

A paper prepared by the Department of State of the United States November 6, 1980, regarding El Salvador, tells a different story. It says that the Carter administration has gradually increased US political, diplomatic, economic, and military involvement in support of the civilian/military coalition government in El Salvador. The resources invested in this effort exceed those allocated to any other hemispheric crisis since 1965. The United States is making extensive use of its military facilities in Panama in the expanded training programs for Salvadoran personnel.

From 1950 to 1979, the United States gave $16.7 million in military assistance. In 1980 and 1981 alone, we gave $11.5 million plus an undisclosed number of military advisors. In 1980, US aid has allocated $30 million for agrarian reform knowing that some 6,000 to 8,000 peasants were killed as a part of this reform. They were killed because they were considered Marxist guerrillas or guerrilla sympathizers.

From this it appears that we are far from staying out of the conflict and far from being identified with the poor of the country. We are paying through our taxes for the murder and assassination of the poor. The Reagan administration gives signs of moving even further in that direction.

As a country we are far from being in solidarity with the poor, a solidarity which has been spoken of and exemplified in the lives of Dorothy Day, Archbishop Romero, and Jesus Christ. We may say that we are simply helping the government that is in place. When that help is used in the way that it is used in El Salvador, the excuse should not pacify our conscience. We give the government our money to use on our behalf and they use it this way. Are we not responsible? Are we willing to pay even a little of the price necessary to reverse the process which now identifies us with the murder of the poor?

## Chapter 6

## *Four Bishops Stand up against Nuclear War*

Four Catholic bishops took time out of their national meeting in Washington, D.C., last November to explain to an audience at Catholic University why they had taken a stand against nuclear weapons.

Bishop Thomas Gumbleton, auxiliary of Detroit, said his peace journey began when he was asked to talk to Catholic peace activists of Detroit during the Vietnam war. The priests and sisters involved were embarrassing the archdiocese.

"The bishop asked me to talk to them, find out what they were doing and why. We got into some good discussions and before you knew it, I was on some of those marches. I then began to think and pray about it. I went back over the writings of Thomas Merton, Dorothy Day, and Gordon Zahn. I got involved in helping with the 1971 Bishops' Conference resolution against the Vietnam war, which made me think things through very carefully. I made a prayerful attempt to search out the Scriptures and I came to a deeply held conviction that I can put in the words of Father John McKenzie: 'If Jesus does not reject violence for any reason, we do not know anything about Jesus. Jesus taught us not how to kill but how to die.'

"Jesus rejected violence for any reason. To come to this conclusion was a slow process. I had opposed the Vietnam war on the basis of just-war theology, but gradually as I searched more deeply and prayed, I came to the conclusion that a faithful follower of Jesus has to be a proponent of nonviolence.

"So it is easy to evaluate nuclear bombs as inconsistent with nonviolence. To reach this point, a conversion is needed; a change of heart, not just study."

Bishop Leroy Mathiesen of Amarillo, Texas, said he was approached by one of his deacons who worked at the local Pantex plant and asked for a moral opinion on whether it was wrong to work where nuclear weapons are made.

"I didn't have a clear answer ready," the bishop told us. "I took time to find out more. Up till that time I had said nothing, yet I knew what was going on. I had read a statement by Chaplain George Zabelka, who was military chaplain on Tinian Island when the American plane, Enola Gay, took off from there to destroy Hiroshima. Father Zabelka said, 'I told the men what they were doing was necessary. I knew they were bombing civilians, but I kept quiet. Afterward, I learned that two entire convents of nuns in Hiroshima had been vaporized. I realized that I failed as a priest and as a chaplain.'

"About the time I read that," Bishop Mathiesen continued, "news came out that a seventy-six-year-old nun was raped and murdered in the house just next to where I live. The city of Amarillo was in a rage over the rape-death of one nun. So was

I. But how come two entire convents, full of nuns, were burned to death in Hiroshima and no one spoke against it?

"I decided I must speak. I told the deacon it was immoral to work at making nuclear weapons. I made a public statement asking workers on nuclear weapons to consider leaving. I said that this type of bomb destroys any concept of just warfare. They are totally immoral. So it is immoral for us to build them, assemble them, deploy them, and threaten to use them.

"I asked those involved in these kinds of things—I did not single out Pantex—to reflect on what they are doing and consider the possibility of resigning."

Archbishop Raymond Hunthausen of Seattle, Washington, said he was moved by the faith and courage of Jim Douglass of his archdiocese.

"Jim is a quiet, gentle man, author of several books and a former professor of theology at Notre Dame and the University of Hawaii. He asked to see me. He was going to begin a thirty-day fast related to the nuclear first-strike intent of our government and wanted my support.

"At that time I wrote to my priests that we have to be much more serious about the nuclear danger in our own lives and in our preaching and praying. It is a reality that isn't going to go away. We must treat it seriously.

"After that, I was a bit more public. I was invited to a parish council meeting in a military area and found the hall filled. That forced me to think through the matter more keenly. It helped me understand the impact of the nuclear issue on the people I was trying to serve through the Gospel.

"I was invited by a Lutheran bishop to speak on war and peace at the Lutheran Synod. I planned to say something about unilateral disarmament. But a day or two before the speech, I met a young man working for the Seattle Church Council. He had been withholding taxes for some time and is really very conscientious and prayerful about it.

"It seemed to me that if he is willing to do that, it is a feasible strategy. And people are looking for a way of doing something about this horrendous danger, but seem unable to oppose it. It seemed to me that war-tax resistance was a way of doing something about it.

"That example, plus the presence of the Trident submarine base in Seattle, and agreeing with the statement that 'The taproot of violence in our society is our intent to build nuclear weapons,' all of this moved me to speak out."

Bishop Walter Sullivan of Richmond, Virginia, said his journey to peacemaking began during the Vietnam war. "I became very involved with one of our priests who refused to pay war taxes. The tax collectors met with me and asked to garnish his wages. I tore the papers up in front of them and put them out of the office.

"Another event that moved me was my decision to give a talk on peace to a group of Knights of Columbus during the Vietnam war. By the middle of the speech, as I spoke about Jesus being our peace, I realized I was giving people indigestion. The hostility got stronger and stronger.

"After the meal, a crowd surrounded me for forty-five minutes. Very hostile. At the end of this a man walked up to me and said, 'Bishop, I am a Marine sergeant.' I said to myself, 'Oh, cripes, what is going to happen now?'

"He was the only person in that audience of 500 who said I want to thank you, 'because you saved my son for me.' I had mentioned conscientious objection in my talk. The Marine said, 'My son wants to be a conscientious objector. Now I know what I have to do.' That started me on my journey of peacemaking.

"After that, I visited conscientious objectors in jails. I visited the Berrigans and others. I experienced hostility to my visiting jails, yet I thought it was a corporal work of mercy.

"This hostility made me look into my stand. I joined Pax Christi. Bishop Gumbleton has been an inspiration to me. I don't call myself a pacifist, but I could not be a part of a nuclear war or any war."

These four bishops were not moved by superior holiness or knowledge of technology. They were moved by the faith of their people, as the lives of those people touched theirs. Their own faith was kindled by the Holy Spirit working in the lives of those around them. This shows how the Church is moved—by the living faith of the people of God.

*Chapter 7*

*Peacemaking As a Vocation*

One reason why we don't have enough peacemakers is that we try to make peace with half a heart and half a will. We easily ignore the Gospel saying, "No one can serve two masters; he will either love the one and hate the other or hate the one and love the other."

The arms plant worker doesn't want to kill or make war. He or she just wants a job. The big corporations like General Dynamics that make Trident submarines don't want to kill; they just want profits. The priest or minister who is silent about the immorality of intending to use nuclear weapons doesn't want war; he or she just wants to be well thought of.

The politician who votes money for weapons doesn't want to kill; he or she just wants to get elected. The ordinary citizen who pays for weapons with taxes doesn't want to kill; he or she just wants to avoid trouble.

The ROTC member doesn't want to kill; he or she just wants a paid education. The soldier who kills doesn't want to do it; he or she just wants to serve the country.

We all slip into war by forgetting that we cannot serve peace and war. We cannot serve life and death. We cannot serve both God and money.

Another way of saying it is that we cannot make peace through war. Violent means bring violent results. The means must be compatible with the end.

Another reason that there are not enough peacemakers is that peacemaking is difficult. Gandhi and Martin Luther King, peacemakers of our age, paid with their lives; their lives were the very price of peacemaking. Jesus, the model of all peacemakers, died a condemned criminal for his peacemaking. Many unsung heroes of the Vietnam war resistance have suffered separation from family and homeland because of their commitment to peace. Others who spoke out against the war at home lost jobs and friends and found they had to set about the task of remaking their lives. If we are to be followers of such leaders and such people, we must expect to pay a high price. We must believe that peace is worth the price.

It is.

*Chapter 8*

*Horace McKenna: Servant of the Poor*

A few days before he went home to God, I visited Horace McKenna at Georgetown University Hospital in Washington, D.C. His eyesight was limited to a few feet so before he recognized me I began with "May the blessing of Almighty God, Father, Son and Holy Spirit descend upon you." As I continued, he blessed himself, held out his hand in welcome and asked, "How are you? How is your work for peace going?"

It was typical of Father McKenna that he would talk about me and my work. Over long years he had developed a knack of turning the conversation on the concerns of the one to whom he talked. His interest was so genuine. You scarcely noticed how he kept to that topic. Here he was still doing it at age eighty-three with only a few days to live. Though we talked only a few minutes, he said it as though it was a summary of his life, "You know, one of the most important things I have learned is that Jesus Christ is present in every human being."

This was a theme on which he often talked. "When I look in the mirror what do I see?" he once said. "A child of God. When I came down to breakfast in the morning, whom do I see? I should see a child of God, because God is present there." He really did see Christ in others. "Christ is present in each hungry man and woman. Christ is hungry and homeless in each hungry, homeless person," he said.

This was the secret of his strength and perseverance of fifty years of personal identification with the hungry poor. In each he saw Christ poor, Christ hungry. I count the years 1948-1952 that I lived in the same house with him at Ridge, Maryland, as special blessing. By the way white people talked about Father McKenna, I got my first glimmer of the evil of racism. "He is a good, holy man, but he wastes his time with those do-nothing blacks," they said. "He just throws money away on those black people."

Why did they talk that way about so good a man? True, Father McKenna was pastor of an all-black parish; dean, teacher, and fund raiser for an all-black high school and grade school; director of an all-black credit union and adult education program. Yet the white people said, "He is just as nice to the whites as he is to the blacks, but he spends all his time with them."

"They need more help," he would say when asked about it. In 1950 he said to me, "Segregation is a deep wound to the mystical body of Christ. An all-black parish is just a Band-aid on that wound. I am going to stop being a Band-aid and try to cure the wound." From that day on he worked to end segregation.

Yet his sympathy always went, preferably, to the poor, and most of them were black; so it was that these parishes—St. Peter Claver, Ridge, Maryland; at the Gesu in Philadelphia, Pennsylvania; and St. Aloysius in Washington—came to know him as a true friend.

Among his Jesuit brothers, he was highly esteemed as a learned man. (He knew Latin, Greek and Hebrew very well.) But more important, he was seen as a Christ-like servant of the needy poor. To all who knew him his outstanding characteristic was charity; love for each individual person he knew. Out of this love came his encouraging word for whatever good you were doing. A priest said to me once, "Horace will kill me with his kindness," after Father McKenna had responded with kind acts to his complaints.

Although he wanted to work with the poor, he wanted to do it as a part of the Church. "If the Church does not care for the poor, they will be neglected," he said. So he always worked with the poor as part of a parish. He yearned to see the Church ever more identified with the poor. "That is the test of our faithfulness to Christ—how we relate to the poor," he would say. Even by his own high standards he was most faithful to Christ, to the Church, and to his community, the Society of Jesus.

His departure leaves an empty space in the church of Washington, D.C., in the ranks of the Jesuits, in the hearts of thousands of friends, especially the poor. All experienced Christ's charity in the life and person of Horace McKenna.

## Chapter 9

## *The Future of the Peace Movement*

The basic strength of the peace movement is that it is linked with the power of God through faith. The second strength lies in its reasoned analysis of what the destructive force of nuclear technology can do. How these strengths may work in the future may be illustrated by comparing militarism with racism.

There is a comprehensive and intimate parallel between racism and militarism. Both are based on the same misguided theology: namely, that not all human beings are God's children, equally precious in God's eyes. Racism says whites are superior to blacks. Militarism says that we are superior to our country's enemies.

Both racism and militarism are defended by the same types of arguments. Racism asks, "Would you want your daughter to marry a black person?" Militarism asks, "What would you do if your mother was being attacked by bandits?" In like manner almost every argument supporting militarism resembles a parallel argument supporting racism.

Both militarism and racism are opposed by the same persons, for example, Mahatma Gandhi, Martin Luther King, Jr., and Jesus Christ.

Both militarism and racism are supported by the same persons, for example, Richard Nixon, Ronald Reagan, and the prime minister of South Africa.

Martin Luther King, Jr., opposed both racism and militarism on the moral grounds that both deny that we are all children of God. Stokeley Carmichael, a black-power leader in the United States, went along with Martin Luther King's campaign of active nonviolence not on moral grounds but on the strategic ground that a minority of ten percent had no chance of winning through violence.

The parallels to this in the peace movement are those who work for peace from a faith basis and those who work for peace from a humanistic or rational basis.

I think what happened in the United States on the racial issue is on its way to happening in the world on the peace issue. In 1955 King announced his Alabama bus boycott. By 1958, both the Catholic bishops and the mainline Protestant and Jewish churches had denounced racism as immoral. In May 1963, 250,000 people marched on Washington demanding the enactment of a comprehensive civil rights law. In 1964, the law was passed. A fair housing law was passed in 1965. A coalition of moral and tactical supporters so changed conditions that now, twenty years later, racism gets no public support either from churches or politicians. Racist politicians have to speak in codes.

I think that a parallel process is now under way toward militarism in the United States. In June 1982, one million people marched for peace in New York City. In May 1983 and August 1983, the Catholic Bishops and World Council of Churches denounced the use, threat to use, and the stockpiling of nuclear weapons. On August 27, 1983, 300,000 marched in D.C. for peace, jobs, and freedom. Books on the moral evil of nuclear weapons and on the facts of nuclear destructive capacity have multiplied and spread. They have spread wider than ever before. More people have taken a decision to commit acts of civil disobedience, and more have been arrested in 1988 for these acts of nonviolent civil disobedience in opposition to the nuclear buildup than in any previous year. President Reagan's nuclear buildup has raised the nuclear consciousness of many and helped them to shake off their apathy and act for peace. Professional groups—physicians, lawyers, educators, labor unions, and others—have bonded together for peace. More colleges, high schools, and even grade schools are learning about nuclear danger. The process is slow. Some say it will take another nuclear disaster to waken enough people to act. Yet never before in history have so many people in so many lands been actively opposing governments on nuclear policies.

Militarism is harder to oppose than racism because governments are ashamed of racism; and it sometimes, as in the United States, lacks the support of federal law. That extra difficulty is more than compensated for by the growing human fear of atomic disaster, and the illegality of nuclear weapons under international law. The strength of peacemaking based on shared faith is the divine strength and allies God with peacemaking. Based on faith, the progress in peacemaking is likely to be more persevering, more permanent, and more confident. That is the way it was with the civil rights struggle. The strength of those opposing war, violence, and nuclear danger based on a rational analysis of nuclear technology is as universal as science. There is a strong power in uncovering the truth of the situation, the facts of what will happen and what is happening because of this arms race. Taken together these two strengths give the peace movement more power than the civil rights struggle. To promote these two forces is to promote the future of the peace movement and the future of humanity into a world without violence, a world of reconciliation among us with God.

*Chapter 10*

*The Rosary Can Be Disarming*

Catholics in the United States who are concerned about peace and justice are generally not interested in public devotion to the rosary, or to the private apparitions of Fatima and Lourdes. Most of those interested in Fatima and Lourdes do not seem concerned about justice and active peacemaking that goes with prayer. Why? Partly history. These apparitions preceded Vatican II, which taught that justice and peace are essential to Catholic faith.

Before Vatican II, the focus of Catholic morality was on sex-related sin, which seemed to limit moral issues to personal sin. Social sins, like war, racism, greed, and economic exploitation, were seen as political, outside of morality.

In the same way, the apparitions of Fatima and Lourdes were interpreted in the light of personal sin, the focus of morality at the time. Avoiding social sins did not appear to be part of the message. A call for prayers for the conversion of Russia, which was certainly good and necessary, carried with it the implication that nothing else was needed but to pray and Russia would be converted. Nothing was mentioned about the conversion of the United States. In fact, prayer for the conversion of Russia was seen as support for US anti-communist foreign policy, which seemed also to apply to support for US military policy and military operations.

Some Catholic publications continue to illustrate this point of view. Several of them are strong in support of devotion to our Blessed Mother and the rosary and sometimes also support the anti-communist foreign and military programs of the United States. They seem to see no contradiction in promoting devotion to Mary, Queen of Peace, and building nuclear weapons to kill the Soviets. Never do these publications support war-tax resistance, refusal of draft registration and conscription, or disarmament. Nor do they call for economic justice, racial justice, or a preferred option for the poor. They illustrate how wide is the age-old division between prayer and action, for the same hand that holds the rosary helps make nuclear bombs to be aimed at Russia. Many Catholics pray for the conversion of Russia and pay taxes for nuclear weapons. Many pray for peace yet are in favor of more and more bombs. Many pray for this country while voting for a congressperson who favors more weapons. Their prayer is peace, but their work is war.

If some Catholics emphasize prayer at the expense of taking Christian action, others emphasize action at the expense of prayer. On the action side of this division, public devotion to Mary is rare or nonexistent. At one large coalition of peace activists opposing the Vietnam war a young woman once suggested "Let's have a human rosary as part of our demonstration." There was dead silence. I seconded the idea, but no one else agreed. The idea was completely ignored without discussion. Since then I have not heard of any large peace demonstration that featured or even included the rosary or any other prayer to our Blessed Mother.

Since devotion to Mary is almost exclusively a Catholic tradition, its absence might be excused at an ecumenical gathering for peace. But Catholic peace groups and publications do not have that as an excuse, and yet they do little or nothing to promote devotion to the Blessed Mother or the rosary. They emphasize action over prayer to the point that their advocacy or practice of prayer becomes invisible. They may pray in private, but their prayer is seldom social or public. Thus, actions for disarmament, peace, Nicaragua, peace in the Persian Gulf, support for blacks in South Africa, for the hungry of the world, or strengthening the United Nations rarely, if ever, are included in public prayer. One group of activists carried this furthest when they didn't even want to announce a prayer vigil for peace that was being held right beside their meeting place.

In the United States only two leaders have united public prayer with action for justice and peace: Martin Luther King, Jr., and Cesar Chavez. Both brought God into every public speech; and public prayer has been a part of all their actions. Chavez has been unique in promoting devotion to Our Lady of Guadalupe as he and the United Farm Workers struggle for economic justice. King constantly preached, "We are all children of God, black and white together." This was the basis of his struggle for peace and justice. Religious hymns of prayer accompanied all of King's demonstrations.

Why this division between prayer and action? Partly because it is easier to do one thing than to do two at the same time. Yet, the division is dangerous. Prayer without action is hypocrisy, and action without prayer to guide it can be and often is destructive.

The daily appearance of Our Blessed Mother in Yugoslavia during the last seven years heals such division. Her appearances occurred after Vatican II, in a communist country, in the nuclear age. Her message is peace—the peace of Christ. The way to peace is faith, she says, "Believe the Gospel! Believe especially the command to 'Love one another' and 'Love your enemies'." To do this one needs strength available only through prayer and fasting. Constant prayer is the atmosphere in which the love of God and neighbor can grow, and fasting is essential to help one do this.

The appearances at Medjugorje suggest a Gospel formula for integrating peacemaking with faith, conversion, prayer, including the rosary, and fasting. All the strength to follow Gandhi's search for truth through nonviolent action can and does flow from this foundation. Tax resistance, draft resistance, conscientious objection, opposition to the death penalty and abortion, marches, boycotts, strikes, and all forms of nonviolent resistance can and should be based on faith, love, conversion, prayer, and fasting.

A Christian doesn't have to believe that the Blessed Mother is appearing daily in Medjugorje to know this. It is a Gospel teaching. It is also the teaching of Gandhi, King, and Chavez. All three have taught what the Blessed Mother is reported teaching daily through six young adults in Yugoslavia. Her message indicates that there should be no division between prayer and action, between faith and practice.

Medjugorje illustrates what happens when prayer and action come together. All one has to do is look at the fruits that come from following this teaching. Before the apparitions, Medjugorje was in a valley with five separate villages ethnically divided, fighting each other, even killing each other. Today there is harmony, unity, cooperation among them. Where before there was an ordinary parish where the Gospel was preached but apathetically followed, there is now a parish vibrant with energy in which every family is represented at Mass every day, half the village fasts twice a week on bread and water, almost all families join in daily prayer, the sacrament of reconciliation is received by hundreds every day, young people pray hours each day and fast twice a week or more, and a communist government still talking atheism runs a store that sells rosaries and medals of the Blessed Mother. The police of Medjugorje say, "Before we arrested people who believed in the apparition. Today we arrest anyone who doesn't."

As one of the local parish priests, Father Pervan, says, "Here it is a question of 'before' and 'after'. Before, there was a parish no different from any other. After, you have a parish energized to live the Gospel. It is like the apostles before the resurrection and after. Now there is some energizing force that moves the people to live the Gospel today. We are not waiting for tomorrow. Today we live and leave tomorrow in God's hands."

After my visit to Yugoslavia in September 1986, I started again to say the daily rosary that I had neglected for many years. I consider it a powerful instrument for peace and recommend it to all peace groups. If all that change has happened in Yugoslavia, a communist country, it can happen anywhere, provided there is enough faith.

*Chapter 11*

*The Peace Message at Medjugorje*

The Blessed Mother is giving a peace message in communist Yugoslavia. That sounded interesting. I went twice to find out.

After eight days there I was convinced that Our Lady is really appearing there every day. My reasons for believing, put as briefly as possible, are : first, I consider it morally, physically, and psychologically impossible for five young adults and one eighteen-year-old to live the kind of daily life they do and at the same time promote a group lie. All of them spend two or three or more hours every day at prayer and Mass. They fast two or three days each week on bread and water.

They are opposed by their government and their bishop. Initially they were also opposed by their parents and parish priests. They receive no money and have ruined prospects for future careers. They bear all of this plus the endless questions of millions of pilgrims because they say the Blessed Mother appears to them each evening.

They all come from different families. They live normal lives at home, at school, at work in the fields. I believe they could not do this every day for six years and, at the same time, lie about the Blessed Mother's appearances.

Second, the messages they give are beyond their capacity. They are theologically uneducated but the messages they give are Gospel messages far too developed and too wise to be thought up by young people untrained in theology. They say that the Blessed Mother appears as the Queen of Peace, teaching that the way to peace, the peace of Christ, is to believe, "What my son says, especially the command to love one another and one's enemies." This can be done by total conversion to God, and total conversion away from sin. All of this is difficult but the energy to do these difficult tasks can be supplied by constant prayer and regular fasting.

I do not believe that teenagers could put together such a message and respond day after day to thousands of questions about them unless they had continuing guidance from someone. They say they receive that continuing guidance from the Blessed Mother. The only way it could be from some other source would be that they were lying and conspiring to deceive. Even if they tried to do that, I think it would have been impossible to continue it for six years without being discovered.

I questioned two of the visionaries, Ivan, age twenty-two, and Marija, age twenty-two. My questions to Ivan were in an outdoor public meeting with sixty American pilgrims. I questioned Marija in her own home and spoke with her through an interpreter while she prepared the family meals. I asked both of them the same questions and got about the same answers from both of them:

*Question:* "Since Our Lady says we should love our enemies, does that mean we should love communists?"
*Answer:* "Yes."
*Question:* "Since the Blessed Mother says that we should love communists, does she mean not to kill them?" (This question provoked one American in our group to yell out, "Next question!" Others murmured their disapproval of my question. I insisted on my question.)
*Answer:* "All the messages agree with that."
*Question:* "Since it is wrong to kill, is it also wrong to pay taxes for killing?"
*Answer:* "The Blessed Mother didn't say anything about taxes. It would be better to use the money to help the poor."
*Question:* "Could a person in good conscience deduce my conclusion about not paying taxes for killing from what the Blessed Mother said?"
*Answer:* "Yes."
*Question:* "Did the Blessed Mother say we should do anything for peace beyond prayer?"
*Answer:* "Yes, she said we should help others."

Later one of the Americans in the group asked, "Why did you ask those questions? You knew the answers." "I asked because I wanted you and the others to hear the answers from the visionaries. You saw how I was being accused of being un-American and going contrary to church teaching for even asking the questions." I asked them also because they are at the heart of the messages of Medjugorje and the Gospel. Their answers satisfied me that the message of Medjugorje fully agrees with the Gospel. It is the Gospel of peace. I am glad I went.

# Part VII:

# Answers to Arguments against Pacifism

*Chapter 1*

*Argument: The Lesser Evil*

Some of the strongest objections against Christian pacifism come from Reinhold Niebuhr, who was a pacifist before Hitler came to power. His books, *Why the Christian Church Is Not Pacifist* and *Moral Man and Immoral Society,* made him the most influential Protestant theologian opposed to pacifism. He writes with the understanding developed in his years of pacifism. His arguments are the best, so I take them first.

He prefaces his arguments with important concessions to pacifism. He agrees that Jesus is a pacifist. "It is very foolish to deny that the ethic of Jesus is an absolute and uncompromising ethic...the injunction 'resist not evil,' 'love your enemies,' 'be not anxious for your life,' are all of one piece, and they are all uncompromising and absolute." Niebuhr supports the pacifist position when he says that when Christians take up arms, there is nothing in either the teaching or example of Jesus that would justify their saying they are imitating Jesus. "Nothing is more futile and pathetic than the effort of some Christian theologians, who find it necessary to become involved in the relativities of politics...to justify themselves by seeking to prove that Christ was also involved in some of these relativities; that He used whips to drive the money changers out of the temple, or that He came 'not to bring peace but the sword.' " He says that the debate between the pacifist and the non-pacifist is not about Jesus' pacifism, but only about the extent Jesus intended it to be used in an imperfect world. The question is not "Does Jesus command this?" (Does Jesus require pacifism?) Rather, the question is: "Does He mean us to obey what appears to be a plain command?"

Niebuhr argues that the Gospel cannot be applied directly to politics, and cannot be lived out. It was written for a rural community two thousand years ago, not for the present industrial state. It cannot be applied directly. National states cannot live according to the beatitudes. The Gospel can be a norm to discriminate between the lesser of two evils: a guide to show us how far off we are from the ideal. This is the function of the Gospel. It is not a direct guide for us in deciding for or against war. The strength of this argument is that the Gospel is used; it is not put aside, but it is used as a "discriminate" norm.

What does "discriminate norm" mean? It means that the Gospel helps us decide, among the alternatives open to us, which one is more in accord with the ideal of absolute love taught in the Gospel. For example, writing in 1969, I look at South Vietnam. It is being overrun by the North. I don't want to kill. I don't want South Vietnam to suffer. I look at the Gospel ideal of universal love. I see that it is more in accord with that ideal that I go to war against North Vietnam, rather than do nothing and let communism overwhelm South Vietnam. The Gospel has become my "discriminate" norm. I choose the lesser of two evils.

I give extra attention to this argument about the "lesser evil" because it is often used. To begin with, a clarification is needed between "physical" evils like sickness or surgery, and a "moral" evil like murder.

All of us face situations where alternative choices include two evils. For example, we may suffer in accepting surgery, or suffer without it. Mostly, they are choices of physical evil or suffering. This is not the same as "choosing the lesser evil" in Niebuhr's sense. He talks about choosing between a moral evil, such as killing the tyrant, and a physical evil, such as accepting his tyranny. When I choose a moral evil in order to accomplish some good, I am acting far differently than when I am choosing between two physical evils.

## First Reply to "The Lesser Evil"

God never requires us to sin. To believe that God ever puts us in a situation where we are compelled to commit sin by deliberate choice makes nonsense of the Gospel message that God's grace is sufficient for us; that God will help us in every need, in every temptation, to do what is right, not what is evil. "You can trust God not to let you be tried beyond your strength, and with any trial He will give you a way out of it, and the strength to bear it." (1 Corinthians 10:13.)

If God required us to sin, then God would be the cause of sin. This is blasphemy. It makes God the source of evil. God does not require us to do moral evil (sin), in order that good may come of it. God does not ask us to use a morally evil means to achieve a good goal.

### Second Reply to "The Lesser Evil"

Between the two ways of sinning, that is, accepting either war or tyranny, there is always a third alternative: nonviolent resistance. It may be very difficult, yet it is the way of the cross exemplified by Jesus. In fact, Jesus was faced with the dilemma of the "lesser evil." In His cause, the founding of the Kingdom, He was endangered by enemies. If He was killed, His disciples would be scattered and leaderless. If He wished, He could have asked His Father "Who would promptly send more than twelve legions of angels to My defense." (Matthew 26:53.)

He could have put aside His ethic of absolute love. He did not. He believed that sacrificial love could completely change a situation and create most unexpected consequences. He chose the cross, and the result was not defeat, but resurrection and victory over death and suffering.

### Third Reply to "The Lesser Evil"

Is war ever the lesser evil? Once the passions of war and nationalism are aroused, is it ever possible to make a relatively unbiased judgment, which is clear and compelling enough to justify action—an action which would otherwise be condemned by the same ethic on which we base our "lesser evil" objection?

Consider the Vietnam war. We know now from the Pentagon Papers that we were lied to about the facts of the war, about the casualties of the war. We know from Senate testimony that we were lied to about the facts that led to the Tonkin Gulf Resolution on which the first actions of the war were based. Was it possible for anyone to look ahead and see what this war would cost us, and on the basis of that decision decide that it was clearly the lesser of two evils?

Consider World War II. Could the ordinary person or anyone foresee how the defeat of Hitler with the help of Stalin would make the Soviets and the USA world powers, poised at each other's throats and ready to destroy themselves and the world with nuclear weapons? If they could foresee it and all the other evil consequences, could they judge it to be clearly the lesser of two evils?

The burden of proof is on the government or individual who chooses war. The making of war is a great evil. It is not clear what good comes of it. It demands loyalty to a national state, in place of loyalty to the way of love or universal brotherhood that forbids war. War brings with it many evils: murder, rape, starvation, lying, hunger, nakedness, plague, cruelty, hatred, loss of faith, despair, and all the other related evils.

When all the consequences of war are balanced against the consequences of "not-killing," war surely begins to appear the worse evil, not the lesser. Only when we blind ourselves to the moral evils that are an essential part of war, only when we judge killing to be morally good, can we find war a lesser evil.

## Fourth Reply to "The Lesser Evil"

The first question a Christian should ask should not be "Which is the lesser evil?" but, "What does God want me to do? What would Christ have done? Is war Christ's way?" If the answer is that Christ's way is not war, but the cross, then by choosing that way, we invite the inrush of God's help that can transform us and change the situation. The cross, the way of nonviolent revolution, is always an alternative beyond war and surrender, for both individuals and nations. The Christian never needs to choose only from evils.

## Fifth Reply to "The Lesser Evil"

A weakness of the argument for the "lesser evil" can be illustrated by an example. Suppose I consider the bombing of a nuclear power plant under construction a lesser evil than allowing it to operate. Would it be morally right for me to bomb the plant to destroy it? All governments would say, "No." Yet these same governments use the "lesser evil" argument in their own favor when they make war. This limiting of the application to circumstances favoring oneself exposes the double standard underlying its use.

*Chapter 2*

## *Argument: People Are Sinful*

People are so sinful that they are incapable of practicing the unselfish love ethic of Jesus. There is a gulf between a perfect God and sinful humans so great that no love-ethic can bridge it. War is justified because people are sinners and must be coerced. International order is always dependent on a balance of power. This condition is due to human sinfulness.

**Reply to "People Are Sinful"**

This argument springs from an unscriptural view of human nature. On purely rational grounds—assuming that humans are naturally aggressive—the argument would do better.

Do the Gospels present humans as sinners who must be driven by force? The Gospels give a different picture. Jesus saw the world as God's world, not "wholly other" than God's world. He drew His lessons from birds and flowers; from the growth and work of people. He saw God in men like John the Baptist. He saw good in an ex-sinner, Mary Magdalene. When a sinner comes "to himself," the sinner arises and goes to his father (the prodigal son). The mustard seed grows secretly—the nature of the world fosters the growth of God's purposes. Nature is on God's side. He taught us to pray, "Thy will be done on earth."

Paul's Epistles corroborate this Gospel view of human nature. Because creation is redeemed, continuance in sin is intolerable. There is a loving personal relationship between God and His creation. This excludes a theology like Niebuhr's that separates the natural from the redeemed and regards nature as depraved.

Niebuhr's pessimistic view of human nature contradicts the joy and hope of the Gospel. It sees the Incarnation as a Divine intrusion, instead of the appearance of a Brother.

In this view of human depravity there is no room for the indwelling of the Holy Spirit, and for "enabling" grace. God dwells in us and we call God "our Father." Niebuhr sees grace as "pardon" rather than "power."

Yet grace is "power." It is an essential part of Paul's faith.

Paul speaks of being "helped only by His power driving me irresistibly." (Colossians 1:9) Paul boasts, "There is nothing I cannot master with the help of the One who gives me strength." (Philippians 4:13) According to Paul, the servant of Christ is capable of perfect obedience because he is transformed in the make-up of his being: no longer a servant, but a child of God.

*Chapter 3*

## *Argument: Personal, Not Group Morality*

Morality is concerned with my personal relationships. I do not rob, rape, or murder my neighbor. Morality does not apply to war. The state is not bound by personal morality. It is amoral and follows military necessity. It may be guided by some type of ethics, but not by morality. Morality is personal.

**Reply to "Personal, Not Group Morality"**

This is Niebuhr's argument on "moral man and immoral society." It assumes the separation of private and public morality. This is false when applied to the state as Pope John XXIII writes in his letter *Peace On Earth*. "The same rights and obligations that apply to the individual, apply to groups." It is even more false when applied to the church. The church is a group. Should the church be considered an amoral group?

The church, with Divine help, has the mission of making known the truth and leading people to the truth. Its example is meant to help individual morality. According to God's plan, the Church can lead the way to Divine truth. It is not meant to be less moral than the individual. It can lead and help the individual. This is one group—the very one Niebuhr talks about—that disapproves of his argument. The same is true of all other groups. They are made up of humans, all subject to God's laws. Whatever the group does as a group—a state or an army—is either in accord with morality or opposed to morality.

*Chapter 4*

*Argument: Self-Defense*

What about self-defense? Doesn't a nation have a right to defend itself?

**First Reply To "Self-Defense"**

Self-defense is not a Gospel principle. It is a principle of reason, used by Cicero and Aristotle, long before Christ's time. Christ did not defend Himself when the soldiers came to arrest Him. He taught that redemption comes from self-suffering, not from inflicting suffering on others. Whoever would save his life must lose it.

## Second Reply to "Self-Defense"

Self-defense by immoral means is contrary to the Gospel. For example, when a medical doctor wants to help a woman who has an unwanted pregnancy, the doctor may not kill the fetus to relieve the woman. Neither may a government kill because it wants to defend. A good end does not justify the use of an evil means.

## Third Reply to "Self-Defense"

There is no known or foreseeable defense against nuclear missiles. Even a fully working anti-ballistic missile system (and no one has such a system) would *at best* stop only one missile out of five. Weapons have evolved to the point where national states can no longer defend themselves. Just as the development of long-range cannons marked a point in evolution that ended the era of the city-states with their fortified walls, so the era of ballistic nuclear weapons ends the era of the nation-state. We are already in an international world; a world of transnational corporations, world-wide communication and transportation. Preparing nuclear weapons today may be deterrence or offense, but not defense.

Even deterrence gives no security when you consider the spread of nuclear weapons. Experts judged that in 1985, thirty-five nations would have nuclear weapons. The deterrence program of today is leading the way to more nations with more nuclear weapons. History is full of weapons build-ups that were meant to deter but ended with explosions. This is even more certain in the nuclear age.

A book by the British General Stephen King-Hall, *Defense in the Nuclear Age*, argues that the military betrays England if it plans any strategy that includes nuclear weapons. Any nuclear exchange would reduce England to a radioactive ash heap. On a straight military-strategy base, he argues how step by step the British should: renounce use of nuclear weapons, form a political alliance with non-nuclear powers, step up the war of ideas—psychological, political and economic, reduce conventional forces to a token border control group, and begin to think of war as resistance to occupation after it occurs.

At the same time the people might begin to think about how to stand up for or die for what they really believe in, under occupation. General King-Hall sees the risk that this might not work, that all would be killed; but he also sees some possibility that it might succeed. He sees no possibility at all in the use of nuclear weapons succeeding. To him military experts who recommend nuclear strategy for England are guilty of treason.

The question presupposes that there is some method of defense in the nuclear age. One way to answer it is to retort, "How would you do it?" Obviously, it can't be done. Even with space technology, the majority of missiles would simply pass each other in the air.

## Fourth Reply to "Self-Defense"

Self-defense may be the argument of a tyrant, or of a state that deserves punishment, rather than continued existence. God asked Isaiah and Jeremiah to warn the chosen people not to defend themselves against threatening enemies, since God was using these enemies to punish Israel for her sins. Does God want a defense of each and every state?

## Fifth Reply to "Self-Defense"

Self-defense is falsely used to cover all sorts of aggression. What is self-defense or "living space" for Hitler is aggression in the eyes of many others. South Africa today argues its right to self-defense; but what it defends is the right of a minority government of whites to exclude blacks from a decent life in their own homeland. The United States could not honestly argue self-defense in its wars against the US Indians. The United States used the "domino" theory to argue that our war in Vietnam was self-defense.

The word "self-defense" has many broad meanings. If it is to have any validity at all, it must be clearly defined. A usable definition might be a defense which uses moral means (not killing) against an unjust aggression. "Moral means" might be the strategy of nonviolent action, organized by Mahatma Gandhi in the defense of India against British domination, and organized by Martin Luther King, Jr., against racism in the USA. "Self-defense" of this kind is very much in line with the Gospel.

## Sixth Reply to "Self-Defense"

Mary, the mother of Jesus, stood by her Son's cross as He was crucified. She did not try to organize some defense for her Son who she knew to be innocent. She is held up as a model for all Christians. She accepted her Son's teaching that suffering and death embraced are redemptive. "Unless the grain of wheat falls into the ground and dies, it will not bear fruit." "He that would save his life must lose it." "I must suffer and be put to death by evil men and on the third day, rise again."

*Chapter 5*

## Argument: Protecting Your Loved Ones

If you were walking down the street with your mother and she were attacked by a robber who intended to rob and rape her, would you just stand by and do nothing, or would you defend her?

If you would defend her, even by killing the robber if necessary, then you should also accept a use of defense of the innocent.

**First Reply to "Protecting Your Loved Ones"**

This is not war, but a person-to-person conflict. I do not use weapons of mass destruction and kill all the relatives and innocent fellow citizens of the robber in order to stop his attack on a loved one. Even if I killed the robber (and I don't agree that such killing is moral), the parallel to war is false. War means killing people. I can't rely on the word of a government that may be deceiving me about the guilt of the enemy, the reasons for asking me to kill, and the amount of killing done on both sides. In this case I see and know what is going on without any intermediary.

### Second Reply to "Protecting Your Loved Ones"

Even St. Augustine, who first formulated the just/unjust-war theory, says that I may never kill on private authority, even to save life.

### Third Reply to "Protecting Your Loved Ones"

Killing the robber is never the only means I have of defending a loved one. I could always do something short of killing. I could put my body between the robber and my loved one, scream for help, try ways of physically thwarting the robber, or even simply give him the money, if that's what he's after.

What I do will depend a great deal on the attitude I have before the robber appears. If I believe that, as a last resort, I must be ready to kill robbers, then I will carry a gun. If I do carry a gun, my gun may be the reason the robber uses his gun. (The British police do not use guns; killing of police and of bandits is much less there than here.) If I do not believe in killing, even as a last resort, then I will not have a gun when the robber appears.

In summary, I would not kill. I cannot imagine circumstances where the only alternative I have is killing and I do foresee that even my known intent to kill may endanger my loved one. Neither do I consider taking a human life on a par with losing money or enduring rape, though these are also terrible happenings.

## Fourth Reply to "Protecting Your Loved Ones"

This is a hypothetical situation, which is used to justify real-life mass murder. My mother is long dead (God be good to her), yet every day the military of the world prepares young men and women to kill, and orders them to kill. This horrible mess is not justified by an appeal to my love for my long dead mother.

This is like one of the hypothetical questions used by abortionists: "Would you like to help curb the levels of misery, poverty, and child abuse that families in our country suffer through?" The answer from anyone with a social conscience is always "of course I would." But this doesn't justify abortion as being part of alleviating misery. A person involved with abortions, though, takes this good question and turns it into a hypothetical justification for his innumerable crimes with the unborn in the same way that the military takes good questions, such as what our level of love for our family is, and twists them around to make them justify its countless crimes.

On the hypothesis that I would defend my mother's life, I am asked to go along with nuclear warfare that would kill hundreds of millions of people in any major exchange between nuclear powers. If my mother were alive, she would most likely be killed also. I would not be defending her; it's all a lie. The military's hypothetical question of protecting my mother has two answers, one purely hypothetical and the other based in reality. The hypothetical answer, that of the military, is that my mother will be protected by it. The other answer, based in reality, is that she will not be.

I am certain, though, that if my mother were alive today, she would not want to be "protected" at the expense of millions of other mothers, their husbands, children, friends, and homes. In her life, she seemed always to have put greater emphasis on the real than on the hypothetical.

## Fifth Reply to "Protecting Your Loved Ones"

A robber who is intent on killing would not be ready to enter into the presence of God. I believe as a Christian that I would, myself, be better ready to meet God if I gave my life for my loved one and spared the robber so he might have time to repent before death.

*Chapter 6*

*Argument: What About the Russians?*

**W**hat about the Russians? It would be very nice if we could put aside our arms because of belief in the Gospel, but the Russians don't believe in the Gospel. If we lay down our arms, the Russians will walk all over us, so we need to keep the upper hand (or at least equal power).

**First Reply to "What About the Russians?"**

We like to imagine our military policy as more moral than the USSR's, because we tend to categorize ourselves as a "Christian" country, possessing some sort of morals, and them as an atheist one. But is there really much difference? Are we a "light to the world," pressing peace, or are we an aggressive participant, pushing competition higher?

We are invited directly by God to follow the Gospel. Our response is not conditioned by what the Russians do. We are not asked to go just as far as others go. We are asked to follow God, to take up our cross, to be lights to the world, whether others do it or not. Jesus did not say, "Love others, if they love you." His commands are not reciprocal, dependent on the response of others.

### Second Reply to "What About the Russians?"

The Russians have been second in every initiative of the nuclear age. We first developed the atom bomb. We first used it on Hiroshima and Nagasaki. We first developed the H-bomb, submarine missiles, MIRV (multiple targeted, independent re-entry vehicles), the ABM (anti-ballistic missiles), the cruise missiles, the Trident submarine with long-range maneuverable, mirved missiles, and the neutron bomb.

We have constantly shown a "win" syndrome. Never have we been content with preparing for defense, or deterrence. For this reason in the early days when we alone had the bomb, we refused to put it under some kind of international control or to renounce further development of it. Many of our experts, generals and secretaries of defense, have asserted that we need no more than fifty or 100, or 200 to 400 megatons delivered on target to deter any of our enemies. Yet we have gone on making more and more nuclear weapons until we have over 35,000 nuclear weapons in our arsenal, and are currently spending about $12 billion for research and development of more and newer nuclear weapons. This is evidence of our seeking to "win" instead of "defend." We cannot honestly blame the Russians for all this.

Development of weaponry with potential for greater and greater accuracy, like the cruise missile and Trident missiles, are also evidence of our "win" syndrome. These weapons are capable of hitting very accurately the Russian missile silos. These silos would presumably be empty in a war of defense. Less accurate bombs would suffice if we were merely thinking of defense or even retaliation.

What about the Russians? They are always hastening to follow what we do. They, too, are burdened, politically and economically, by the arms race. Their survival, like ours, is at stake. Maybe they would respond to a ten-percent reduction of the arms race. The risk in trying this is nothing compared with the risk of continuing the race.

We do have a good example of a peaceful initiative by the US that was responded to in kind by the USSR. In 1963, President Kennedy ordered a halt to US nuclear testing in the atmosphere without requiring a signed agreement before he took this important step. The presidentially-ordered nuclear testing halt was to continue so long as the Soviets and other countries did not test. The Soviets responded favorably and a Soviet-American deadlock was broken. The result was the signing of the Limited Test Ban Treaty by the US and the USSR. This treaty has been the most important achievement in the long history of arms control negotiations between the US and the USSR.

With regard to our belief in the Gospel, how does our belief show itself as different from that of the Russians when we ring them with bases, and continue to develop more and more weapons? We threaten to kill them massively. How can they see any light of the Gospel in our plans or actions? How are we any better than the Russians in our attitude towards war, towards the taking of human lives? If we were Russians, would we see the US as Gospel oriented, and Gospel directed? We publicly assert our separation of church and state. Does the church have any separate military policy from the state? The answer should be "yes." The church is opposed to the use of nuclear weapons for any reason.

*Chapter 7*

*Argument: Pacificism Is Not Practical*

Pacifism is not practical. It is a naive solution to a complex problem.

**Reply to "Pacifism Is Not Practical"**

Nothing is more impractical than making more nuclear weapons, and hoping for peace through them. Whether pacifism is practical or not depends on what you think of the cross of Christ. Obviously Christ thought it was the way to establish His Kingdom and to bring peace on earth. In this sense He considered it practical. But in order to work, it has to be practiced. There is no evidence that it does not work where it is tried.

There is abundant evidence that wars do not bring peace. They set the conditions for the next war. In the nuclear age even our technology tells a person without faith that nuclear weapons will not bring peace. Is it practical to try for peace without any reference to God? The Gospel tells us that the way to peace is through the paradox of the cross; the program for peace is detailed in the beatitudes. In the sense that peace is God's work and humans are God's instruments, peace is never just the result of human effort, and never practical in the sense of being done by human power alone.

# Chapter 8

*Argument: What Alternative Is There?*

If you oppose war, you must offer some alternative. What is your alternative to war?

**First Reply to "What Alternative Is There?"**

An alternative is another way of achieving the same result. War is so evil, with such evil results, that no substitute way of achieving the same evils is likely to be found. The presupposition of this argument is that war brings peace, or protects peace. The Christian belief is that God and humans, working together according to the pattern set out in the Gospel, bring peace. War is not part of this program. War brings more war. The reason Christians have had such little peace and have such small hopes for peace is that they have deserted the Gospel in the seeking of peace and sought it through war.

I see no obligation in pointing out an evil like war to offer an alternative. The mere pointing out of the evil is a good work in itself and stands by itself. So if I point out that lying, robbery, rape and oppression of the poor are evils, I do something good. Perhaps I will be listened to more closely if I suggest some alternative. Something better can be suggested, even though it is not an alternative in the sense that it achieves the same results as the evil.

In the way of suggesting something better than war, I suggest imitating Christ, following the pattern of Gospel living according to the beatitudes, and organizing that pattern along the lines followed by Mahatma Gandhi in India and by Martin Luther King, Jr., in the USA. If only a small part of the time, talent, and treasure spent on preparing for and supporting war were put into training for nonviolent actions for peace, much could be accomplished.

On the individual level I think we should begin with refusing to pay taxes for nuclear weapons and for other war preparations. We pay for war while we pray for peace. If Christians on the basis of conscience organized resistance to war taxes, there would be changes in our national policy of war spending and war making. The trust that we thus put in following God, speaking to us through conscience, would become our alternative, our "better way" than war.

## Second Reply to "What Alternative Is There?"

This question presupposes what isn't true. It presupposes that at the present time our arms give us security. It presupposes that the more arms we have, the more security we will have. Neither of these statements is true in the nuclear age. We have no security now.

We cannot defend ourselves, and so as an alternative to the insecurity that we already have, an inability to defend ourselves from the nuclear weapons of our enemies, there are various alternatives. One is laid out in the book by General Stephen A. King-Hall, *Defense in the Nuclear Age,* in which he, from a professional military strategy point of view, shows that the use of nuclear weapons will result in reducing Great Britain to a radioactive ash heap. So the realistic military strategy should begin with overcoming the mental block which says that we can overcome force only with more force, and with studying nonviolent ways of organizing against an invasion, once the invasion has taken place. In his book he shows how there is some hope that this will succeed, but no hope at all of going on with the arms race. And that is true of the United States also.

There is no hope militarily of the arms race bringing peace or security to the United States. The more the US advances its nuclear technology and nuclear stockpiling, the less hope for peace there is. So from a straight technological argument, from the strength of our weapons and the direction in which we are going, three alternatives are possible: either some sort of a national organizing toward nonviolence and trying to bring the rest of the world in with us as King-Hall does; or some sort of a federation of the nations of the world to work as the world federalists do; or building up a world government with a federation of states that support it with a prohibition of national armies that would interfere with it.

*Chapter 9*

*Argument: Unilateral Disarmament*

Unilateral nuclear disarmament is insane. For instance, if you are out on the desert and a wild tribesman is bearing down on you, do you go out and kneel down and ask for mercy? He would run you right through with his sword. The least you can do, if you have to die, is to die fighting (and killing), to take as many of the enemy with you as you can. The same is true of nuclear weapons.

**First Reply to "Unilateral Disarmament"**

The first question that a Christian should ask about unilateral disarmament is, "What are the circumstances, and what should a Christian do in those circumstances?" The circumstances of nuclear deterrence are that both sides are fully able and ready to destroy each other, no matter who starts the war. This is not the case of the wild desert swordsman—so the analogy does not apply.

### Second Reply to "Unilateral Disarmament"

Why was the tribesman attacking? If you had weapons and were coming to his home, and had previously threatened to destroy him, the attack might be due to your conduct. In that case, you would be the aggressor. But if you changed your mind, put aside your weapons, went out and asked "mercy," there would be some possibility that your change would change him. Even if it didn't, your death in such a case would be far more an imitation of Christ than going ahead with your aggression.

### Third Reply to "Unilateral Disarmament"

If the case is that of two armed tribesmen, both constantly threatening to kill each other, and it ends in a confrontation in which both are killed, neither has acted as a Christian should—with love for each other because of faith in God. Both die uselessly and in defiance of God's law. This case makes clear the relationship between our faith, our thought processes, and our action. If we have faith in God and live according to it, our actions are different than they would be without that faith.

### Fourth Reply to "Unilateral Disarmament"

Even from a military point of view, unilateral nuclear disarmament makes more sense than going on with the arms race. The military view is presented in a book by British General

Stephen King-Hall, *Defense in the Nuclear Age,* discussed earlier.

### Fifth Reply to "Unilateral Disarmament"

Nuclear weapons have become a military monster beyond the control of the military. They have changed the nature of warfare so much that the name "war" should no longer be used, but rather something like "mutual suicide" or "death trigger." Any and all cuts in their nuclear-weapon preparation, possession, or use make more sense and give more hope than depending on them.

## Chapter 10

## *Argument: Saint Thomas Aquinas*

Thomas Aquinas agreed that war is morally permissible in certain circumstances, and he is a great theologian. What about that? (Aquinas is highly esteemed among Catholic theologians because he was the first theologian to write a synthesis of Aristotelian philosophy and Christian theology. His 12th-century compendium of theology is influential even today.)

**Reply to "Saint Thomas Aquinas"**

Yes. St. Thomas Aquinas agreed with the just/unjust-war theory theory of Augustine. If he were alive today and considered what nuclear weapons have done and can do, what technology has done to unite the world, what modern popes and Church Councils have said about all this, he might have led the way in discarding the just/unjust-war theory (making *all* war and military action wrong).

In his own day Thomas didn't do much more than affirm the 4th-century opinions of Augustine. In his arguments he uses the same texts, the same interpretations as Augustine; he adds little or nothing of his own. It seems to me that he did not investigate the question himself. The arguments showing the weaknesses of Augustine's theory are in Chapter Two above.

Here are some points from Aquinas' arguments. In answering his own question, "Is fighting war always a sin?" (*Summa Theologica* II-II, prologue and part of Art. 1), Thomas never cited the pacifist statements of the early Church Fathers. He also interpreted pacifist texts from the New Testament in a very narrow sense. For example, Jesus' command to His would-be defender Peter, "Put up your sword...all those who take the sword shall perish by the sword." (Matthew 26:52) Thomas limits the application of this text to those who "take the sword without official authorization." Thus, Jesus' statement is forced against the context, to harmonize with Thomas' requirement that proper authority is needed to initiate warfare. The Gospel says that Jesus prohibits the act of using the sword. There is no reference to permission from authority. (*Summa Theologica*, II-II, 40, 1 Obj. 1)

Two texts that forbid resistance to evil are taken in a meaning not only not warranted by their Gospel context, but are taken so as to limit and turn them around so that they fit into the just/unjust-war theory, and come to mean almost the opposite of what they say.

This is Jesus' counsel in the Sermon on the Mount: "But I say to you, offer the wicked man no resistance." (Matthew 5:39) And Paul's, "Never repay evil with evil.... Never try to get revenge. Leave that to God's anger...." (Romans 12:17-

19) Thomas limits the application of these texts only to cases of self-defense, involving no more than two private citizens. He denies that they apply to soldiers, or even to a civilian defending others. How does he arrive at this? Where is his evidence?

He goes further and says the texts do not apply to external acts, but only to the dispositions in the mind. (*Summa Theologica,* II-II, 40, 1 Art. 2: 64-67, & Art. 5)

Does this mean that I may kill a person as long as I don't intend to kill? May I drop an atom bomb that kills, and intend only defense, not killing? This is what Thomas seems to say. But he says it only about war. It should follow that I can commit adultery, as long as I intend love and affection; idolatry, provided I intend only to please the devotees of a false god; and so on with all sins. I cannot agree with Thomas on this, if this is his meaning. The commands of Jesus and Paul are turned around to allow the very violence that they forbid. When this has to be done to uphold a theory, it doesn't say much for the agreement of the theory with Scripture.

Thomas found direct support for warfare in judicial precepts of the Old Testament. In applying these to Christians in the New Testament, he ignored God's special use of warfare in the Old Testament and how that ceased to apply with the coming of the New Testament.

It is not surprising that Thomas repeated the just/unjust-war tradition of Augustine. Thomas lived in the age of the crusades, when popes were urging war.

Thomas' teacher, Albertus Magnus, was commissioned to preach a crusade. Three of Thomas' blood brothers were soldiers. When Thomas is considered not only for his work, but in the context in which he lived, there is a wide divergence from the example of Jesus. The influence of fighting and conquest was strong. Culture and circumstance had much to do with shaping his acceptance of the war theory of Augustine. What he wrote showed little thought of his own. He uses no original texts, and merely copies Augustine.

Just as he accepted slavery, an almost unquestioned tradition in his day, so he accepted war. Had he lived in our age of nuclear weapons and machine labor, in which slavery is no longer accepted, he might be the lead voice in explaining the evil of both slavery and war.

Why? Because he was an innovator and synthesizer in his day. He brought the works of Aristotle into harmony with Christian thought. Maybe if he lived today he would have synthesized technology and theology. We know only the Thomas of his age.

Both Augustine and Thomas lived at a time when the state religion of the Holy Roman Empire was Christianity. Aquinas taught that the state could burn heretics, for they constituted a grave danger to the highest good of its citizens, which was their Christian faith. Today we reject that teaching as wrong and unjust; a clear sign that Aquinas, too, in this, as well as in his treatment of the just/unjust-war theory, was a product of his age.

# Chapter 11

## Argument: Obedience to Authority

Pacifists respect authority, but they recognize a hierarchy of authority. When a civil command or law is not in conflict with divine law, it is to be obeyed. But when a civil command is in conflict with the divine law, it is not to be followed. Divine law takes precedence.

**Reply to "Obedience to Authority"**

The pacifist does not oppose legitimate authority, but questions the legitimacy of the authority of the state to kill or to order the citizens to kill. No Christian can say to the state, "I will do anything you tell me to do, no matter what." The

Christian's first duty is "Seek first the Kingdom of God," as Jesus told us, or in the words of Peter, "We must obey God rather than man."

Every modern state, except India, was born in homicide, and continues in existence by threatening death to all who oppose it. The Christian attitude towards such an institution should be a suspicious questioning of all that is commanded, until the commands can be weighed in the light of conscience. When the orders are in accord with conscience, the Christian finds God's authority in legitimate authority. Where conscience objects to the order, the Christian obeys God, rather than man. In this sense the Christian is the "loving adversary" or "witness to truth" that helps the state become what it ought to be: the promoter of the common good for all.

## Chapter 12

## *Argument: Spiritual Values Need Defense*

There are worse things than war. The destruction of spiritual values is one of them. These values must be defended. Pacifists lose sight of this.

**First Reply to "Spiritual Values Need Defense"**

Of course, spiritual values need to be defended. But if spiritual values are to be defended, the means used must be such that they do not *destroy* spiritual values. Defense must be by moral means. Pacifists argue that "killing people is not a moral means." The end does not justify the means. Defending spiritual values (a good end) does not justify using evil means (killing).

## Second Reply to "Spiritual Values Need Defense"

Revolutionaries often argue that unjust tyrants need to be overthrown, so they organize and kill the tyrant. In order to seize power they become unjust murderers. In the process of seeking justice, they act unjustly. One unjust tyrant has been substituted for another. Something similar happens when spiritual values are defended by killing. In the process of seeking justice, some revolutionaries act unjustly. One unjust tyrant has been substituted for another. Something similar happens, when spiritual values are defended by killing. In the process of seeking to defend them, spiritual values are lost. Most Christian leaders under Hitler sought to protect spiritual values by going along with Hitler's wars. They would have defended spiritual values better by refusing to follow Hitler.

## Third Reply to "Spiritual Values Need Defense"

The way to defend spiritual values is the way of Christ, of Gandhi, of Martin Luther King—nonviolent resistance to evil. Christ did not kill or advise killing to spread His Kingdom. The reason is that killing does not spread His Kingdom: rather the opposite. He taught us how to die for what we believe and not to kill for it. Gandhi applied the love-ethic of Jesus to national and international conflicts. He organized nonviolent resistance on a national scale to free two hundred million Indians from the domination of the British Empire. In the course of it, he defended and even strengthened spiritual values. Martin Luther King freed millions of American blacks from the worst features of legalized racism. In the course of his nonviolent national defense of blacks, he strengthened spiritual values of both whites and blacks.

Jesus taught us that by losing our lives, we save them. He gave us the example of the way to do that through his life and death. He defended spiritual values. Those who say that this is not an efficient way of doing things, that there is no chance of success without military defense, ought to ask themselves what they think of the cross. Was that efficient? Was that a successful defense of spiritual values?

## Chapter 13

## *Argument: Vatican Council II Allows for a War of Self-Defense*

Vatican Council says that military who engage in wars of self-defense are instruments of peace.

**Reply to "Vatican Council II Allows for a War of Self-Defense"**

Vatican II never mentions the words "war" or "self-defense" in the context quoted. It speaks of "legitimate" defense as long as there is no world authority capable of maintaining peace. The entire section of Vatican II (Church in the Modern

World) is introduced by a call for an entirely fresh and new evaluation of war, because of the massive destructive power of new weapons. It condemns the use of these weapons on whole areas and their peoples as crimes against God and man. Such a condemnation says that no theory that includes use of nuclear weapons be allowed. No self-defense that uses nuclear weapons is allowed.

Vatican II appeals to conscience. It calls on all military to disobey in conscience any orders that ask them to use weapons of mass destruction. It calls on all governments to respect in their laws those whose conscience forbids them to bear arms.

Vatican II calls on all nations to consider nonviolent means of defense as more in line with the Gospel and more available to all nations, especially the weaker nations.

These are the elements of the new vision of peacemaking Vatican II presents: condemnation of use of nuclear weapons, conscience, and nonviolence. It is in this context, and under severe pressure from a small number of bishops, that it speaks of the "right to legitimate defense." No mention of the just/unjust-war theory is made, not even in a footnote. "War" is not mentioned either. In this context "legitimate" cannot mean use of nuclear defense. This is condemned. It seems also that any defense that risks nuclear war is not "legitimate." This would include any war by a nation that possesses nuclear weapons. It is not clear what defense could be legitimate. Nonviolent defense would be legitimate. In India, Gandhi used it successfully. In the United States, workers formed unions to secure their rights. Martin Luther King organized boycotts. Our government uses economic sanctions. All of this is legitimate.

The word "legitimate" here is a balancing statement in a document that is otherwise a clear call to peacemaking along the lines indicated. This wavering note of "legitimate defense" illustrates the failure of the Fathers of the Council to rise to the vision of peace put before them in the letter of John XXIII, *Peace On Earth*.

Nonviolent defense certainly could and I think should be considered as a type of legitimate defense, and may have been what was in the minds of the drafters of the document. Nonviolent defense means resistance that is short of using violent force, and such actions include a wealth of opportunities that tend not to be considered by most national governments today. However, they are not unknown and include economic sanctions such as those the US has used with the Soviet Union in our grain trade with Russia.

But even with this failure or waffling, the Council does not approve of the just/unjust-war theory, or of wars of self-defense. It talks about "legitimate" defense in a context that leaves up in the air what kind of defense it considers legitimate and a context that makes some kinds of defense clearly illegitimate.

To admit that no use of nuclear weapons is allowed and also maintain that it is morally allowed to manufacture and possess nuclear weapons without intent to use them, is the modern version of weighing how many angels can dance on the head of a pin. It is also a good illustration of how the just/unjust-war theory does not apply in the nuclear age.

## Chapter 14

### Argument:
### Conscientious Objectors Are Cowards

Pacifists are cowards, afraid to die. But there are worse evils than death: slavery, denial of freedom to worship God, and denial of other freedoms.

**Reply to "Conscientious Objectors Are Cowards"**

Conscientious objectors are no more afraid of death than anyone else. As one American soldier in Vietnam wrote to me, "I do not fear death. What I do fear is to die in the act of killing in a war that I believe is immoral." That states the difference between a pacifist and a soldier. The difference consists in a willingness to kill, or a refusal to kill.

To the argument "There are worse things than death," the conscientious objector replies, "Yes, I agree. Killing another, when I believe God forbids it, is worse." Death, slavery, and other physical evils cannot destroy my soul. Sin can and does. If the Communists bomb us with nuclear weapons, they destroy our bodies. If we plan to use nuclear weapons on them, we destroy our souls even before we press the button.

## Chapter 15

## Argument: Deterrence Works

Deterrence has worked for thirty-seven years. Why abandon it? It has kept the peace and has prevented nuclear war. What alternative do you offer?

**Reply to "Deterrence Works"**

The argument presumes what is not true. Is it true that the major powers have been stopped from anything they would otherwise have done because of the nuclear threat? Would the Soviets have destroyed us with nuclear weapons if we had no deterrence? That is only speculation. No one knows for sure.

The Cuban missile crisis, despite the threats in the beginning, was finally resolved by negotiations, not by deterrence.

Three fallacies presumed true by the question are: Deterrence is a response to, rather than a cause of, our hostile world climate. Second, we have no other choice, even if we wanted to use one. Third, deterrence is a stable, static condition. Our acceptance of these and similar fallacies blocks us from a serious look at what deterrence is and what it does; and it leads us to a false trust in deterrence.

After thirty-seven years of deterrence, we are closer to nuclear war than we were before. There are 35,000 nuclear bombs today. At Hiroshima, we had two and the Soviets had none. Now, seven nations have nuclear bombs, and twenty more are rushing to possess them.

"In twenty years," asserts the Committee for Economic Development, a prestigious group of business leaders, "one hundred countries will possess the raw material and the knowledge necessary to produce nuclear bombs." By the year 2000, it says, "the total plutonium expected to have been produced as a by-product of nuclear power would be equivalent in explosive potential to one million bombs of the size that destroyed Nagasaki."(Sidney Lens, *Day Before Doomsday*, p.218.)

While the industrial nations spend $6 billion a year on arms, the poor starve even as they grow in numbers. Instead of responding to this by stopping the mad race, we speed it up. In this way, both from the military point of view and from the economic point of view, deterrence fuels the arms race, and works against the very peace it claims to produce.

Deterrence depends on a balance of terror between the US and the USSR. Our push to get new and better weapons is a push to get superiority over the USSR. That push imbalances deterrence and threatens war. We race the USSR as though we were the whole world. But in a few years, twenty nations will have nuclear bombs. Then the balance between the US and the

USSR will not stop nuclear war. Deterrence is what moves the world toward unparalleled disaster.

To admit that no use of nuclear weapons is allowed and also maintain that it is morally permissible to manufacture and possess nuclear weapons without intent to use them, is the modern version of weighing how many angels can dance on the point of a needle. Deterrence is the taproot of violence in our society: our intent to use nuclear weapons on people. This intent has corrupted the fiber of our moral life to such an extent that in the US alone we have one and a fourth million abortions each year; violence and killing have become staple entertainment on our television screens; our prison population has doubled, and our military budget has more than tripled. All of this is linked to our acceptance of a deterrence policy which has at its heart our intent to use nuclear bombs on people.

It can be argued that the US does use nuclear weapons, although it has not exploded any on a civilian population since the bombs dropped on Hiroshima and Nagasaki. During the fifties and the early sixties, we used many bombs in nuclear-weapon tests and exposed US soldiers to radiation effects. These tests were coordinated with foreign-policy objectives in Korea, and cold-war diplomacy with the Soviet Union. Also, threats to use nuclear bombs have been made in times of crisis, as in the beginning of the Cuban missile crisis in 1962. Is this really use of nuclear weapons? Is it use of a gun when I hold the gun to another man's head and ask him for money? Such threats have been used openly and secretly by all US presidents since 1945, with the possible exception of President Ford.

The logic of deterrence would have us believe that there is no other choice, so therefore, there is no moral question about it, and no sin in following it. Why? Because following it is the only option. This silences the moral challenge, so that deterrence has become accepted militarily and morally by some. If we accept this "only option" position, we define peace as an ever increasing speeding to disaster during which we starve the poor, corrupt our moral lives, and leave God out of our plans. In accepting deterrence, we cut ourselves off from the moral roots in the Scriptures and make a mockery of the Gospel. We trade our worship of the true God for a worship of gods of metal. Instead of living reconciled to each other, we make life a mutually hostage relationship.

## Chapter 16

*Argument:*
*We Are Not All Children of God*

We are not all children of God, and brothers and sisters to each other. We become children of God by Baptism. The unbaptized are not children of God. Pacifists say we are all children of God.

**Reply to "We Are Not All Children of God"**

Baptism of desire also makes one a child of God. Baptism of desire is the desire to do all that God wants you to do. It includes the implicit desire for baptism where water baptism is impossible. This is the way Catholic theologians answer the question "What happens to good people who live a good life and die a good death but never heard about Jesus or about baptism?" Without this answer God would not be seen as just, because God would be keeping good people out of heaven without any fault on their part.

This does away with the exclusionist viewpoint that can be found in the Old and New Testaments. No one is excluded from salvation.

We are all children of God also by creation, conservation, and by redemption. We are all created by God, and all that God made is good. (Genesis 1.) Jesus tells us (all of us) to say to God, "Our Father." Jesus said, "Whatsoever you do to the least of my little ones, you do unto Me." How could that be true if we were not all God's children?

We are all God's children by conservation. God keeps us in existence. We are all God's children by redemption. Jesus promised paradise to the thief. Jesus came to redeem all. He is the universal savior. He didn't come just for one people. Just as in creation, God is prolific, magnanimous, in the multiplication of seeds, of animals, and of other life forms, so in the world of grace. God's gift of sonship and daughtership is unlimited.

Do you have to be baptized to go to heaven? What is Jesus' view of this from the cross? To the repentant thief, Jesus promised paradise.

This idea of the inherent goodness in each person is the theme of Pope John XXIII's great encyclical letter, *Peace On Earth*. Humans are not evil. The idea, that people are evil and are rescued from that evil by Jesus coming down on earth, is not the Catholic view. The Catholic view is not that we are evil, but are saved by Christ's blood that is thrown over us as a cloak to protect our evil from the just judgment of the Father. Evil, in the Catholic view, is the absence of a perfection that should be there. Evil is not something in itself but the absence of a good which should be present. What should be present is the integrity of our nature so that all our senses and desires be under the control of, subordinate to, our reason. But that subordination was broken by original sin. In that sense we have fallen from God's grace and need baptism to regain it. In this sense baptism restores us fallen humans to the state of grace lost by our first parents. We became Children of God by a visible sign of God's grace, baptism. Thus we become God's children by baptism although by creation we already were God's children. How can this be? It is mysterious! Vatican Council II calls the Church "the mystery of the people of God." God is mysterious. It follows that all our relations to God, if we search deeply enough, are mysterious. For example, how can I be both a child of God and a sinner? Yet I am. How can a person be a child of God and an atheist?

A human analogy may help. An atheist is like a child who is separated from his father at an early age so that he never knows his father. We still say that he is a child of his father, even if he does not know or recognize his father. We would consider his statement wrong if he said, "I have no father." Likewise a sinner is like a child who refuses to obey his father and leaves home to live in sin. He is disobedient, sinful, rebellious, but still a child of his father. His return to the father through repentance is like being born again. In a good sense he is "born again" because he recognizes who he is and has a new life of closer unity with God.

But are not the righteous separated from the unrighteous along the lines of Matthew 25 and not simply Christian in name only? (Cf. Matthew 7:21) Yes, God separates the sheep and the goats at the last judgment, but that judgment is done by God. We don't have the wisdom to make that judgment; moreover, we are told, "Judge not." So the fact that we believe that God will judge in the future doesn't help us much here and now to decide who is responding to God's call and who is not.

*Answers to Arguments against Pacifism*

Thus in many ways we can be and are God's children because we are related to God in many ways; creation, redemption, baptism, obedience, faith, repentance.

The Society of Friends seems to recognize this when it says, "There is that of God in every person." The importance for Christians of accepting as universal as possible a definition of "Children of God" is illustrated by how the failure to recognize it has led to wars among religious sects. Even in the Old Testament, God complained to the Jewish people that their offerings were unwanted. "Do you think I want these sacrifices? I have more than enough of the sheep you burn." (Isaiah 1:11) God asked for true sacrifices: for the care of the widowed and the care of the weak and the oppressed. Let justice and mercy flow like rivers; that is the true worship of the Lord. (Isaiah 1:10-20) This shows God as caring for all of us as the Parent of us all. This idea of God's universal fatherhood/motherhood connects and systematizes the theology of creation, redemption, sacraments, original sin, and love.

Seen in this light, the peace issue is central to Christian theology, not peripheral or marginal. Peace defined as "reconciliation with God my Parent and my human brothers and sisters" is so close to love itself, that it is almost the same as the doctrine of love.

All Christian theology is so affected by what we say about peace because peace is the prelude and companion to love. It follows that the theology of peace must be taught, believed, and practiced or we risk distorting every aspect of faith.

How can we believe all the ramifications of the Incarnation: God with us in human form; all of us related to Jesus as brothers and sisters; God dwelling in us through grace; all of us loved personally by God shown in Jesus? How can we believe all this, and then use weapons of mass destruction to kill? How can we believe that we are all one body, united in Christ, and also believe we can kill each other on government orders? How can we believe that each one of us is precious in God's sight and be ready or even preparing to kill each other on government orders?

If we cannot believe that killing is wrong because of our faith, a common-sense look at the lethal technology of our nuclear age will teach us that same lesson. The realistic alternative of our times is that we must cooperate together, or perish together in the flames of our planet.

Our hope cannot be in weapons, gods of metal. In that way lies death. God offers us the choice of life or death. Both faith and technology make it clear that we must choose life for others too, as well as for ourselves. If we choose to kill, we will certainly write our own death sentence for this world; and unless we repent, for the next.

With God's help we do not need to choose death, or killing. We can depend on God to help us if we trust in God, not in weapons of death. Pope John XXIII in his final letter, *Peace On Earth*, asks every believer to be a small light. "Every believer in this world of ours must be a spark of light; a center of love; a vivifying leaven. This is the peace, which we implore of Him with the ardent yearning of our every prayer."

www.ingramcontent.com/pod-product-compliance
Lightning Source LLC
Chambersburg PA
CBHW050616300426
44112CB00012B/1536